M000118162

A NEW Desire

A DAILY DEVOTIONAL

Brenda J. Robinson

WINEPRESS WP PUBLISHING

© 2001, 2002 by Brenda J. Robinson. All rights reserved.

Printed in Korea.

Packaged by WinePress Publishing, PO Box 428, Enumclaw, WA 98022. The views expressed or implied in this work do not necessarily reflect those of WinePress Publishing. Ultimate design, content, and editorial accuracy of this work is the responsibility of the author(s).

No part of this publication may be reproduced, stored in a retrieval system or transmitted in any way by any means, electronic, mechanical, photocopy, recording or otherwise, without the prior permission of the copyright holder except as provided by USA copyright law.

Unless otherwise noted, all Scriptures are taken from the King James Version of the Bible.

PostScript is a registered trademark of Adobe Systems, Inc.

ISBN 1-57921-380-4
Library of Congress Catalog Card Number: 2001088906

Acknowledgments

The greatest blessing ever bestowed upon me was that of eternal life, but God's blessings in my life extend far beyond the gift of salvation. These additional blessings are manifested through each staff member of New Desire Christian Ministries. A special thanks to each one for their hard work and commitment in God's kingdom work. You all are truly vessels of honor, and you are my special blessings from God.

There are three very special staff members that I must give great thanks and appreciation to for their enduring efforts to see this work completed:

Karen Tinsley, my personal assistant—Thanks for all the hours you have put in and the sacrifices you have made to see this work accomplished. You have surely been the eagle's eye upon every phase of this publication, from formatting to finality.

Brooke Cason, my daughter-in-law and baby girl—Thanks for your faithfulness to type, proof and re-proof. Thanks so much for your words of encouragement when I felt like this work would never come to pass. Thank you for believing in my work and for being my greatest Bible student. Brooke, you bring such joy to my life.

Jessica Helms, assistant and my greatest admirer, a position of which I am unworthy. Thanks, Jessie, for loving me and for all the hard work you have put into this book. Thanks for not giving up on typing when the devil tried to discourage and defeat you. You are my inspiration.

Thanks for being teachable and for applying what you've heard me teach. You're my special blessing.

Thanks also to my husband, Dan. I love you with my whole heart. Thank you for your patience and understanding as this project has robbed much of our time together. Your support in my life is overwhelming. You are my gift from God.

This book is dedicated to Karen Tinsley. Karen was the inspiration for the completion of this 10 year endeavor. Thanks, Karen, for all your hard work and dedication. I could not have finished this book without your help and steadfastness. You are the greatest personal assistant of all time.

Contents

Introduction

I invite you to join me in the spiritual transformation of *"A New Desire."* We will walk where Jesus walked, and we will see His reflection of love and instruction in every page.

The Word of God holds vast amounts of wisdom. Therefore, as we study and consume the Scriptures we must prepare our hearts for a transformation. I have experienced this transformation; I have been transformed from darkness to light. "For many years, I lived a life so pleasing to myself. What I thought was accomplishment was sin that leads to death. Then early one morning in the midst of my fire, God placed within my heart a burning desire. From that day on, my whole life changed; from death to life, I was never the same. Jesus gave me *A New Desire.*"

A New Desire is waiting for all who long to experience God's righteousness. Throughout the pages of this devotional there are experiences that will relate to your situation and Scriptures that will comfort your heart. The new desire will then swell within you. You, too, will grow from an experience with God into a personal relationship with Him.

Some of the private experiences that changed my life as a child of God have been included in this book. Those changes took place as I heeded to God's instruction. They will come for you, too, if you purpose in your heart to obtain this spiritual transformation.

Join me in developing *"A New Desire."*

A New Year's Resolution

SCRIPTURE READING: 2 Peter 3:8

As we face a new year, many of us have made New Year's resolutions. We will try to stop doing certain things, or we'll vow to start doing some things. In the beginning, we'll all be "gung ho," but as time progresses, and the commitment becomes harder and harder, we'll begin to slack off of what we had resolved to change. We use the excuse that "a year is a long time."

Our Scripture text for today says, "But, beloved, be not ignorant of this one thing, that one day is with the Lord as a thousand years, and a thousand years as one day." When making resolutions for the new year, we often feel like one week is an eternity. Few ever accomplish what they set out to do at the beginning of a new year.

We don't have the power to change anything within us. Resolutions are never accomplished if they are not made for the honor and glory of God. We must recognize God as our Deliverer. We need to see Him as our source of strength, otherwise resolution after resolution will be wasted and unfinished.

This year, make your resolution to have a personal, intimate relationship with Jesus Christ. This resolution can be achieved and will have everlasting results. If you're not saved, choose salvation as your resolution. Second Corinthians 4:18 says, "While we look not at the things which are seen, but at the things which are not seen: for the things which are seen are temporal; but the things which are not seen are eternal." Simply accept it, believe it and confess it. Romans 10:9 says, "That if thou shalt confess with thy mouth the Lord Jesus, and shalt believe in thine heart that God hath raised him from the dead, thou shalt be saved."

"Make your resolution to have a personal, intimate relationship with Jesus Christ."

Resolutions or Repentance?

SCRIPTURE READING: Philippians 4:13

We are entering another year. People everywhere are making New Year's resolutions. They are vowing to give up smoking, drinking and overeating. Maybe their vow is to work more, or to work less and spend more time as a family. The list goes on and on, and it is usually the same list they used last year. Why do you think resolutions are usually forgotten and never accomplished?

Vows are broken because they are usually made under our own power instead of God's power. We truly think that we can change these things on our own initiative, making a resolution impossible to achieve.

However, there is a way to succeed in our resolutions. It is called repentance! God can and will deliver you if you will let Him. Repentance is the sincerity of your good intentions. In other words, repentance is turning from something by depending upon God's power instead of your own for the change. Repentance is willingness; a resolution is just the thought of making the change.

God wants to see you make positive changes in your life, changes that will make you more pleasing to Him and more peaceful and holy in your whole life. It all starts by depending upon Him for the power to overcome. As you make your New Year's resolutions, why don't you let the first change start here, by making New Year's repentance? Today's Scripture text says, "I can do all things through Christ which strengtheneth me."

"God wants to see you make positive changes in your life."

New Beginnings

SCRIPTURE READING: 2 Corinthians 5:17

At the beginning of each new year, everyone is ready for a change. We want something different to take place in our lives. The past year has brought many changes and left us scarred, crippled and defeated. For most of us, just the hustle and bustle of everyday life has left us completely drained of energy and enthusiasm. The flesh feels exhausted, and our hearts and minds feel hopeless. We long for refreshing. We look for a better way, but the solution seems distant and out of reach.

Jesus Christ gave us a solution over 2000 years ago as He hung on Calvary's cross. He gave His life so we could be made free from this life of sin and sorrow. He delivered us from chains of darkness and hopelessness. He brought us into His eternal light.

Jesus gave us access to new beginnings. Today's Scripture text says, "Therefore if any man be in Christ, he is a new creature: old things are passed away; behold, all things are new." Jesus gave us a new and better way. We have a new beginning through His death, burial and resurrection.

If you have received Jesus Christ as your personal Savior, then you have the solution to all your problems. You have the provision for all your needs. You have the comfort for all your sorrows and troubles, and most of all you have forgiveness for all your sins.

New life in Christ gives you all these things. Start your life anew with Jesus today. Begin your day, your year and your moment with the only One who will never leave you or forsake you.

"Start your life anew with Jesus today."

Treasures Unseen

SCRIPTURE READING: 2 Corinthians 4:18

What is it in our lives that holds eternal value? It could be our homes, our nice cars, antique furniture or other material possessions. It could even be a day at the ball game or a night at the opera, but most definitely it is none of the above. According to our Scripture text, all of these things are temporal. It says, "While we look not at the things which are seen, but at the things which are not seen: for the things which are seen are temporal; but the things which are not seen are eternal."

The things that we cherish so dearly in this life are only ours for a little while. They have never been, nor will they ever be, eternal. They are blessings from God, yet we abuse them and use them for our own honor and glory or for the work of the devil. God wants us to be happy and to enjoy everything we have, but not to the point that we forget Who gave them to us.

The things that hold eternal value in our lives are the things which are not seen. This is our salvation and our joy. It is the ability to trust in God's Word and to live by faith. We have eternal life through the blood of Jesus Christ. These are the only things that have eternal value. They are treasures unseen.

Matthew 6:33 says, "Seek ye first the kingdom of God and His righteousness." This passage of Scripture is the key to understanding the things that are truly eternal in our lives. If comprehended through the knowledge of Jesus Christ, it will erase all thoughts of confusion about what is eternal. What holds the most value in your life, things temporal or things eternal? Are your treasures easily seen by others, or are they treasures unseen?

> *"God wants us to be happy and to enjoy everything we have, but not to the point that we forget Who gave them to us."*

Experiencing the Eternal

SCRIPTURE READING: 2 Timothy 2:15

We can only experience those things that hold eternal value when we are abiding in Christ. As we learned yesterday, it is easy to place our value on the temporal things of this world. How do we overcome this temptation to put the gift before the Giver?

The Bible is our weapon for fighting off the lusts of the world, the lust of the eyes, and the pride of life. Second Timothy 2:15 says to "Study to show thyself approved unto God, a workman that needeth not to be ashamed, rightly dividing the word of truth." If we neglect to study and trust God's Word, we set ourselves up for spiritual defeat. God's Word reveals the true desires of our hearts. Hebrews 4:12 says, "For the Word of God is quick, and powerful, and sharper than any two-edged sword, piercing even to the dividing asunder of the soul and spirit, and of the joints and marrow, and is a discerner of the thoughts and intents of the heart." If we don't allow God to show us our true desires through His Word, we will quickly set our values back on the things of this world that are only temporal.

Rest assured that nothing can ever take away the love, joy, peace, contentment, salvation, redemption, power or glory that we have in Christ Jesus. Get into God's Word and let Him reveal to you the eternal values that make our lives so free and victorious in the Lord.

> *"God's Word reveals the true desires*
> *of our hearts."*

Our Eternal Purpose

Scripture Reading: Ephesians 4:1–6

The most important of all of our eternal values is our eternal purpose. Without a purpose in life, we can only walk in a circle. We never get anywhere or accomplish anything. As born again Christians, we have a responsibility to fulfill. Fulfilling this responsibility is our eternal purpose.

Paul defines our responsibility in today's Scripture text. It says, "I therefore, the prisoner of the Lord, beseech you that ye walk worthy of the vocation wherewith ye are called, With all lowliness and meekness, with longsuffering, forbearing one another in love; Endeavouring to keep the unity of the Spirit in the bond of peace. There is one body, and one Spirit, even as ye are called in one hope of your calling; One Lord, one faith, one baptism, One God and Father of all, who is above all, and through all, and in you all."

Our purpose is to walk worthy of the love of Jesus Christ by being examples to those around us. It is our responsibility to manifest our faith and trust in our Almighty God to those we come in contact with each day. In everything that we do, our purpose is to let our lights shine for Jesus. Our responsibility is to be like Jesus at home with the children, on the phone with a friend, at the ball field, in the workplace, everywhere and in all things.

Today, I challenge you to start reaching out to others for Christ. I challenge the older to reach out to the younger and the younger to reach out to the older. Wives reach out to your husbands, and mothers reach out to your children. Friends reach out to friends, but most of all the saved should be reaching out to the lost. Make it your purpose today to share with others the unseen treasures in your life.

> *"Without a purpose in life, we can only walk in a circle. We never get anywhere or accomplish anything."*

A NEW DESIRE

Contentment

SCRIPTURE READING: Philippians 4:11

Paul says in today's Scripture, "Not that I speak in respect of want: for I have learned whatsoever state I am, therewith to be content." Can you say that about your life?

I challenge you to take a look at some of your greatest complaints about life. Where did you come up with the expectations that have not been met? Perhaps you are unhappy with yourself; you feel like you have no worth. You can't see any future direction for your life.

The truth is that you have been deceived by Satan. You are looking for a fantasy life that does not exist. Your discontentment with your husband can't be fulfilled by some formula that the happy couple on TV prescribed for a perfect marriage. Being the center of attention will not satisfy that emptiness in your life either. We have always based our happiness on our material possessions, outward appearances and our social and professional lives. This is our greatest hindrance in learning to be content with what we have.

When we long for possessions, power and prestige, we become weak in the flesh. Satan uses this weakness against us by deceiving us into temptation. First Corinthians 10:13 says, "There hath no temptation taken you but such as is common to man: but God is faithful, who will not suffer you to be tempted above that ye are able; but will with the temptation also make a way to escape, that ye may be able to bear it." Temptation can be overcome, but better still it can be avoided.

Let's learn, like Paul, to be content with what God has given us.

"When we long for possessions, power and prestige, we become weak in the flesh."

The Sins of Discontentment

SCRIPTURE READING: Hebrews 12:1–2

Contentment can only be found in Jesus Christ. He is our happiness. He is our life, for it is in Him that we have life (John 14:6). The contentment that we find in this world is only for a season.

Discontentment with God's provisions for our lives leads to sin. First we fall into idolatry because we put the things we want before God. We spend all of our time trying to get what we want rather than serving God. Discontentment always leads to strife and conflict with others. When we're not happy with ourselves, we make everyone else unhappy, too, and we usually blame others for our miserable condition. We spend all of our time trying to get what we can't have rather than serving God. Uncleanness follows, whether in thoughts or actions, because we allow ourselves to be overcome by desires that are outside of God's will. The spiral continues moving downward.

For the sake of Jesus Christ, let's get beyond all of these sinful hindrances. Today's Scripture text says, "Wherefore seeing we also are compassed about with so great a cloud of witnesses, let us lay aside every weight, and the sin which doth so easily beset us, and let us run with patience the race that is set before us, Looking unto Jesus the author and finisher of our faith; who for the joy that was set before him endured the cross, despising the shame, and is set down at the right hand of the throne of God." These verses teach us where to find contentment.

Lay aside the sins of discontentment and find life in Christ.

"Contentment can only be found in Jesus Christ."

Battling Bitterness

SCRIPTURE READING: Hebrews 12:15

Bitterness is something we all experience. Bitterness stems from feelings of failure, trials and tribulations, broken relationships or financial stress. Most often, bitterness is the result of shattered expectations. Thoughts of disappointment and failure lead to bitterness.

Bitterness defiles the heart and soul. Today's Scripture text says, "Looking diligently lest any man fail of the grace of God; lest any root of bitterness springing up trouble you, and thereby many be defiled." God's Word also says about bitterness in Job 3:20, "Wherefore is light given to him that is in misery, and life unto the bitter soul?" Proverbs 14:10 says, "The heart knoweth his own bitterness; and a stranger doth not intermeddle with his joy."

Bitterness usually takes root in our hearts as the result of hurt. Satan takes that hurt and manipulates it into thoughts and actions of bitterness. We begin to lash out at others, and we often even lash out at God. We find fault in everything and everyone around us. We blame others and harden our hearts toward them, especially if they've been successful in the area in which we've failed. Our minds soon become so full of bitterness that we can no longer see the truth. James 3:14 says, "But if ye have bitter envying and strife in your hearts, glory not, and lie not against the truth." We are faced with "confusion and every evil work (James 3:16)."

Don't dwell in your bitterness. Instead of doubting God about your circumstances, seek Him and listen to His voice as to why things have not gone the way you planned. Win the battle against bitterness by praying, serving and shining for Jesus.

"Bitterness is the result of shattered expectations."

Alleviating Anger

SCRIPTURE READING: Ephesians 4:26

The Bible says in Ephesians 4:26, "Be ye angry, and sin not: let not the sun go down upon your wrath." Being angry is not a sin. Anger only becomes sin when we allow it to overcome our thought patterns. Dwelling on the circumstances that caused our anger leads us, without our knowledge, to thoughts of revenge. We become so determined to get even that we base our actions on the desires of the flesh. When we allow our anger this much control over our actions, we take matters into our own hands, leaving God out of the situation. This is how anger leads to sin in our lives.

Anger makes hatred, and hatred brings upon us the wrath of God. Romans 1:18 tells us, "For the wrath of God is revealed from heaven against all ungodliness and unrighteousness of men, who hold the truth in unrighteousness."

Why does the Bible instruct us not to let the sun go down on our anger? When we do this, we automatically wake up the next day even more angry than we were when we went to bed. The longer we harbor our anger, the greater it becomes, leading to more and more sin in our lives.

Ephesians 4:31–32 is our key to alleviating anger. Remember these words, and meditate on them next time your find yourself angered by someone or something. It says, "Let all bitterness, and wrath, and anger, and clamour, and evil speaking, be put away from you, with all malice. And be ye kind one to another, tenderhearted, forgiving one another, even as God for Christ's sake hath forgiven you."

"Anger only becomes sin when we allow it to overcome our thought patterns."

Defeating Defeat

SCRIPTURE READING: John 16:33

For the last two days we've studied bitterness and anger. The end result of bitterness and anger is defeat in our Christian walk. We become bitter, angry and defeated because of hurt in our lives. We begin to feel that God no longer cares about our daily woes, and our prayer time becomes less frequent. We want revenge, change and satisfaction in whatever circumstances caused these feelings.

Defeat stems from being self-centered. It is caused by trying to satisfy the flesh and falling into Satan's deceptions. When we allow ourselves to become defeated, we have lost our faith and trust in Jesus Christ. The Holy Spirit's presence in our lives is quenched by our own feelings. Confusion overtakes us, and giving up seems to be our only alternative.

Satan deceives many Christians into believing the lie that he has won. We have not been defeated just because our expectations have been shattered. Feelings of defeat often come because we wanted our own self-will to be done rather than God's will, but our plans are not always best for us. When our dreams are shattered, Satan uses the opportunity to convince us of defeat and to rob us of our peace, but we have victory through Jesus. John 16:33 says, "These things I have spoken unto you, that in me ye might have peace. In the world ye shall have tribulation: but be of good cheer; I have overcome the world."

Jesus Christ has overcome the world. He is our victory. Through Him we have victory in any situation, regardless of the outcome, because He's already won.

"When we allow ourselves to become defeated, we have lost our faith and trust in Jesus Christ."

Nehemiah's Example

SCRIPTURE READING: Nehemiah 1:6–11

Today's Scripture text, which we will study for the next few days, says, "Let thine ear now be attentive, and thine eyes open, that thou mayest hear the prayer of thy servant, which I pray before thee now, day and night, for the children of Israel thy servants, and confess the sins of the children of Israel, which we have sinned against thee: both I and my father's house have sinned. We have dealt very corruptly against thee, and have not kept the commandments, nor the statutes, nor the judgments, which thou commandedst thy servant Moses. Remember, I beseech thee, the word that thou commandedst thy servant Moses, saying, If ye transgress, I will scatter you abroad among the nations: But if ye turn unto me, and keep my commandments, and do them; though there were of you cast out unto the uttermost part of the heaven, yet will I gather them from thence, and will bring them unto the place that I have chosen to set my name there. Now these are thy servants and thy people, whom thou hast redeemed by thy great power, and by thy strong hand. O Lord, I beseech thee, let now thine ear be attentive to the prayer of thy servant, and to the prayer of thy servants, who desire to fear thy name: and prosper, I pray thee, thy servant this day, and grant him mercy in the sight of this man. For I was the king's cupbearer."

This is Nehemiah's example of effective prayer. Let's study it and learn the keys to effective prayer.

"Let thine ear now be attentive."

Effective Prayer

Scripture Reading: Nehemiah 1:11

Nehemiah said in today's Scripture text, "O Lord, I beseech thee, let now thine ear be attentive to the prayer of thy servant, and to the prayer of thy servants, who desire to fear thy name: and prosper, I pray thee, thy servant this day, and grant him mercy in the sight of this man. For I was the king's cupbearer." Nehemiah needed to get in touch with heaven, and God heard and answered Nehemiah's prayer.

Nehemiah had overcome any doubts about the proper way to pray. He lived with the blessed assurance and confidence that God hears all of our prayers, whether they be systematic or spontaneous. Nehemiah had an inner security that his prayer life was both disciplined and powerful. What secrets can we learn from him?

Before we study Nehemiah's prayer life, I'd like to give you the seven elements that have proven to be victorious in my own prayer life: repentance, praying with faith, praise, thanksgiving, specific prayers, dedication to prayer, and discipline in prayer. As we study Nehemiah's prayer life, apply these principles, as well as those you'll learn, to your own prayer life. See for yourself what a difference it makes when you, like Nehemiah, have inner security about the effectiveness of your prayer life.

"God hears all of our prayers."

Types of Prayer

SCRIPTURE READING: Mark 11:24

For the next few days, I want to share with you the elements of four different types of prayers. Together, we will learn how and when to apply each type of prayer to make our lives for Christ flourish. Regardless of the type of prayer, today's Scripture text tells us what makes each effective. It says, "Therefore I say unto you, What things soever ye desire, when ye pray, believe that ye receive them, and ye shall have them."

So often, we live a defeated Christian life because of our insecurities about doing things right in the eyes of God. Do we witness, study and pray correctly? We see in our Scripture text for today that an effective prayer life is the key to overcoming and achieving all things in our Christian walk.

We need to learn to be like Nehemiah. We need to overcome our doubts and insecurities about whether or not we're praying correctly. God hears and answers every prayer of faith. He may not answer the way we want Him to, but He answers nevertheless.

There are four types of prayer. They are systematic prayer, spontaneous prayer, specific prayer and serious prayer. Neither one of these types of prayer is more effective than the others. They're all effective when they're prayed in faith. Let's learn about each type so we can have more confidence in our prayers.

"An effective prayer life is the key to overcoming and achieving all things in our Christian walk."

Systematic Prayer

SCRIPTURE READING: Matthew 6:7

The first type of prayer that I want us to look at is systematic prayer. What is systematic prayer, and is it good or bad?

Systematic prayers are those payers that we usually rush through just for the sake of saying them, like the blessing at each meal. We often say them just to be released from the guilt of forgetfulness and carelessness. Saying a systematic prayer also makes us feel good about ourselves because they make us look "holy."

Jesus said in our Scripture text, "But when ye pray, use not vain repetitions, as the heathen do: for they think that they shall be heard for their much speaking." God condemns shallow, traditional prayers that are not from the heart.

Does this mean that we would be better off to skip those meal blessings? No, it does not. We should simply be more aware of what it is we are doing. Our prayers, for any reason, should be sincere with God. Prayer should come from a sincere heart. God commends persistent prayer. God doesn't tire of hearing us say a blessing at each meal; He tires of hearing us say the same prayer at each meal that we've said everyday, for every meal just because we're supposed to say it. God doesn't even mind hearing the same words over and over again, as long as they're said with sincerity.

Systematic prayer often becomes simply a pretty prayer with no action. The same prayer, said from the heart rather than from memory or tradition, can touch heaven. Discipline your prayer life to one of sincerity, and you can see great results even from a systematic prayer.

> *"Our prayers, for any reason,
> should be sincere with God."*

Spontaneous Prayer

SCRIPTURE READING: Nehemiah 2:4

Our Scripture text today shows Nehemiah in spontaneous prayer. Nehemiah had approached the king for permission to return to Jerusalem and rebuild the city walls. Nehemiah was afraid when approaching the king. When the king asked, "For what dost thou make request?," in a spontaneous moment, Nehemiah called out to God for guidance.

As we read on in Nehemiah 2, we find that the king granted Nehemiah permission to return to Jerusalem. Obviously, spontaneous prayer can be very productive, but what we ask for must be in agreement with God's will. Whatever we ask for, and however we ask for it, must be for the uplifting of Jesus Christ.

We should also be spiritually prepared to receive whatever we ask for spontaneously. We often exercise impulsive prayers to escape an uncomfortable situation which we are not prepared to handle. In these situations, we should evaluate our purpose for prayer. Perhaps we should examine all of our spontaneous prayers to see the true intents of our hearts.

If we pray on the spur of the moment, we often expect the answer on the spur of the moment. If we are not spiritually rooted in Christ Jesus, this could lead to problems. If the answer does not come immediately, we become weak in the faith and open to Satan's deceptions. In order to practice effective spontaneous prayer, we must first learn to exercise spiritual maturity by applying faith even to our spontaneous prayers. James 1:6 says, "But let him ask in faith, nothing wavering. For he that wavereth is like a wave of the sea driven with the wind and tossed."

Don't waver in faith just because you're prayer is spontaneous. Believe that God hears it just because it's a prayer of faith.

"To practice effective spontaneous prayer, we must first learn to exercise spiritual maturity by applying faith even to our spontaneous prayers."

A NEW DESIRE

Specific Prayer

SCRIPTURE READING: Matthew 21:22

Specific prayer is often the target of Satan's attacks because this type of prayer is the one which we often get confused about. Specific prayer can cause us to believe that we are praying selfishly. Today's Scripture text is the key to defeating our foe on this. It says, "And all things, whatsoever ye shall ask in prayer, believing, ye shall receive." We can ask for "all things" in prayer without guilt. First Timothy 2:8 says, "I will therefore that men pray everywhere, lifting up holy hands, without wrath and doubting." God is big and loving enough to give us whatever our hearts desire.

However, God expects honesty and sincerity in specific prayer, just as He does with systematic and spontaneous prayer. Being able to ask God for specific things is a blessing and benefit that comes with being a born again child of God. God honors specific prayer that honors Him. God does not honor specific prayer to fulfill the lusts of our flesh. God will not answer prayer for things which will strain our relationships with Him or hinder our service for Him.

Nehemiah prayed for several specific things, and God heard and answered his prayers. Specific prayer is rewarding if we follow God's plan for prayer. Nothing pleases God more than to be able to reveal Himself to us by answering our prayers.

Specific prayer is the best way to see God in action. For the honor and glory of God, pray specifically and watch God reveal Himself to you as a God who hears and answers prayer.

> *"Specific prayer is the best way to see God in action."*

Serious Prayer

SCRIPTURE READING: Romans 8:26

As we close our study on prayer, let's look at the final type of prayer found in Nehemiah. Nehemiah's prayer was a serious prayer. All of our prayers, whether they be systematic, spontaneous or specific, should be serious. If we would only pray seriously, instead of worriedly, then we could have the same confidence in prayer that Nehemiah had.

We must put aside all of our doubts, fears and confusions about how to pray properly and focus on the positive, serious side of prayer. If we pray at all, we are praying correctly in God's eyes. It pleases God when we sacrifice our time to talk with and trust Him in prayer.

To pray seriously simply means to recognize God as the Father, Jesus as the Son, and the Holy Spirit as the Comforter. Jesus gave His life for our sins so we could have access to the Father. His Holy Spirit guides us in prayer. Romans 8:26 says, "Likewise the Spirit also helpeth our infirmities: for we know not what we should pray for as we ought: but the Spirit itself maketh intercession for us with groanings which cannot be uttered."

Serious prayer requires us to set time aside each day to steal away somewhere to pray, meditate and worship. Serious prayer consists of praying for the needs of others over our own needs and praying consistently until we've seen results. Serious prayer is at its best when we can get on our knees before God just to praise Him and thank Him for all our blessings.

Let's be like Nehemiah and get serious with God in prayer.

"Serious prayer is at its best when we can get on our knees before God just to praise Him and thank Him for all He has blessed us with."

26 ~   A NEW DESIRE

Responsibilities

SCRIPTURE READING: Matthew 10:37

We know what our daily responsibilities are for our homes, our families and our jobs. Each day we get up with the intention of fulfilling those responsibilities. Without hesitation, we go to work each day, and we rearrange schedules to accommodate spending time with our families. However, we often leave off the responsibilities we have to Jesus Christ and His Gospel.

Sometimes we tend to shrug off our irresponsibility in these matters by telling ourselves that God understands the demands on our lives and the weaknesses and temptations we face. God does understand, but He also allows us to face the consequences of our irresponsibility. Adam's irresponsibility caused him to have to toil in sweat every day of his life for what God had been providing freely. Moses' lack of responsibility caused him to miss out on entering the promised land. David was irresponsible in his duties as king, and it cost him the life of his child.

It is our responsibility to praise God every day. We also need to study His Word and share and protect the Gospel of Jesus Christ. These are as much our daily responsibilities as going to work, providing for our homes and protecting our families. Jesus commands us to love Him first with all of our heart, soul and mind. The time and place for fulfilling these responsibilities is found in today's Scripture text. "He that loveth father or mother more than me is not worthy of me: and he that loveth son or daughter more than me is not worthy of me."

Each morning, it is our responsibility to put God first above everything and everyone. What is first in your life?

"It is our responsibility to put God first
above everything and everyone."

Fulfilling Our Responsibilities

SCRIPTURE READING: 1 Peter 5:8

Knowing our responsibilities doesn't make it easy to fulfill them, but God is worthy of our love, praise and undivided attention. The joy of fulfilling our responsibilities in Christ is found in 2 Corinthians 4:16. "For which cause we faint not; but though our outward man perish, yet the inward man is renewed day by day." Each day we stand for the Gospel's sake, we will be renewed, through either suffering or excitement, with the strength of God through the Holy Spirit.

We must not allow the lust of our flesh to take precedent over our responsibilities for God. Hebrews 12:6 tells us that there is a price to pay for this. "For whom the Lord loveth he chasteneth, and scourgeth every son whom he receiveth." We must also be cautious against the snares of the devil. Our adversary will give us many alternatives to fulfilling our responsibilities. Satan takes our wants, desires and weaknesses and uses them to distract us from serving God, and he's very subtle about doing it. Second Corinthians 11:3 says, "But I fear, lest by any means, as the serpent beguiled Eve through his subtilty, so your minds should be corrupted from the simplicity that is in Christ." Today's Scripture text says, "Be sober, be vigilant; because your adversary the devil, as a roaring lion, walketh about, seeking whom he may devour." God can protect us from the enemy and show us how to overcome the desires of our flesh so that we can fulfill our responsibilities.

Jesus faithfully and willingly fulfilled His responsibility as He hung on the cross. Let's become responsible Christians, and let's honor our Lord and Savior each day by serving Him no matter what the cost.

"Let's honor our Lord and Savior each day."

Three Simple Steps to Discipleship

SCRIPTURE READING: Luke 9:22–26

In today's Scripture text, we find Jesus telling the disciples of His upcoming death and resurrection. He said, "The Son of man must suffer many things, and be rejected of the elders and chief priests and scribes, and be slain, and be raised the third day. And he said to them all, If any man will come after me, let him deny himself, and take up his cross daily, and follow me. For whosoever will save his life shall lose it: but whosoever will lose his life for my sake, the same shall save it. For what is a man advantaged, if he gain the whole world, and lose himself, or be cast away? For whosoever shall be ashamed of me and of my words, of him shall the Son of man be ashamed, when he shall come in his own glory, and in his Father's, and of the holy angels." Jesus' intentions were not to impress His disciples by boasting of what He would have to endure. His purpose was to teach them the principles of becoming dedicated disciples.

Understanding how such unpleasant methods can generate us into true discipleship is hard. Why must we suffer, be rejected and even be slain just to prove our profession of faith? This is often easy for a new convert to understand. The excitement of our new life in Christ makes it easy to endure almost anything. However, when the excitement wears off, defeat often comes. It seems that our prayers go unheard and that God has forgotten all about us. In this time of weakness, Satan seeks to devour us before we grow any closer to the Lord.

Perhaps you have faced some battles through the years in your work for the Lord. Feelings of defeat may have caused you to lose your job. Maybe you've decided you'd rather be a bench warmer rather than taking the chance of being hurt or disappointed again.

In the Garden, Jesus probably felt much the same way, but He didn't give up. Rather, He gave in, not to feelings or emotions, but to God's will. Jesus taught His disciples the secret to such dedication in the three simple steps we'll study for the next few days: following, fighting and faithfully serving.

"The excitement of our new life in Christ makes it easy to endure almost anything."

Following Jesus

SCRIPTURE READING: Luke 9:23

The first step in discipleship is following Jesus. Jesus described what it means to follow Him in today's Scripture text. "And he said to them all, If any man will come after me, let him deny himself, and take up his cross daily, and follow me."

In order to follow Jesus, we must deny ourselves. We must be willing to lay aside our own wants and needs for the sake of Jesus Christ. Jesus denied Himself for our needs. His self-denial can be seen throughout His earthly ministry. When Jesus prayed, "Not my will, but thine, be done," He laid aside even His life for our sins.

Following Jesus also requires us to sacrifice our time and pleasures to spend quality time with the Lord and in His service. Jesus spent endless days and nights teaching people to forsake all they had to follow Him. Matthew 8:19–20 says, "And a certain scribe came, and said unto him, Master, I will follow thee whithersoever thou goest. And Jesus saith unto him, The foxes have holes, and the birds of the air have nests; but the Son of man hath not where to lay his head." Our Lord gave up His heavenly abode with His Father to dwell among man without even a place to lay down for rest. Jesus explained to the scribe in this verse that he would have to sacrifice many things as a result of his decision to follow Him.

Submission is the final key to following Jesus. Submission forms a relationship between Christ and ourselves. In other words, we must submit ourselves to a state of obedience to Christ. First Corinthians 11:3 says that Christ is the head of every man.

Let's follow Christ through self-denial, sacrifice and submission.

"In order to follow Jesus, we must deny ourselves."

Fighting

SCRIPTURE READING: Luke 9:23

O nce again, we find the main principle for discipleship in Luke 9:23. "And he said to them all, If any man will come after me, let him deny himself, and take up his cross daily, and follow me." Our Lord bore a literal cross on Calvary, but He also carried a spiritual cross of rejection, persecution and mockery every day leading up to Calvary.

The battles that we must fight do not come when we are in a state of sin; our battles come when we are living in righteousness. Jesus said in Luke 12:51, "Suppose ye that I am come to give peace on earth? I tell you, Nay; but rather division." This division is righteousness against unrighteousness. The unrighteousness of the flesh, the world and Satan are constantly at warfare with the righteousness of the Spirit within us (Galatians 5:17).

Our salvation places us into an eternal position with Christ through which we have power to win any battle. The key to victory is abiding in Christ. John 14:27 says, "Peace I leave with you, my peace I give unto you: not as the world giveth, give I unto you. Let not your heart be troubled, neither let it be afraid."

Every battle won is a step toward a more intimate relationship with God. Each battle lost or given up only sets us back in our spiritual growth. God uses our battles to strengthen us for His ministry. Paul said in 2 Corinthians 12:9, "And he said unto me, My grace is sufficient for thee: for my strength is made perfect in weakness." God uses our weaknesses in the battle to prove His strength.

The battle is His, and the victory is ours. Fight the good fight of faith and become a dedicated disciple.

"God uses our battles to strengthen us for His ministry."

Faithfully Serving

SCRIPTURE READING: Luke 9:24–25

We cannot be disciples of Christ until we are willing to serve. Jesus gives us an example of a faithful servant in today's Scripture text: "But whosoever will lose his life for my sake, the same shall save it." Giving up our lives is the principle of becoming a servant.

Giving up our lives is a strong statement, but it is meant for us to take literally. In order to become a servant, we must die to the flesh, giving up our old life and desires to become separated from sin and unrighteousness. We are already dead to sin (Romans 6:6–11), but we must crucify the flesh and its lusts daily.

Our life is found in God when we become faithful servants. We walk in the Spirit, rather than the flesh, desiring to serve God and others. This is the example that Jesus set for us. He gave up His life to become a servant to sin and death, taking the penalty of sin from us so we could have eternal life. Philippians 2:7 says that He "made himself of no reputation, and took upon him the form of a servant, and was made in the likeness of men."

Paul urges us to take upon ourselves the same type of humble service as Jesus did. Philippians 2:5 says, "Let this mind be in you, which was also in Christ Jesus." In order to take on the mind of Christ and become a faithful servant, we must come humbly, willfully and ready to live an unhindered, dedicated Christian life.

A life of following, fighting and faithfully serving will be full of mountains and valleys, but God has promised that He'd never leave nor forsake us. Remember, for every battle scar there is a reward in Heaven.

> *"We cannot be disciples of Christ*
> *until we are willing to serve."*

A Cure for Spiritual Affliction

SCRIPTURE READING: James 4:6–7

When children are young, they often have a hard time understanding that someone will always have authority over them. Have your children ever told you that when they grow up they'll get to be their own boss? Most children do, and unfortunately many of us, even as adults, have this misconception.

There is always a Higher Authority. Even for those who are self-employed, we are not our own bosses. We all have to answer to God for our actions at work, at play and in life. When we recognize His authority in our lives, our responsibility is to put ourselves in subjection to Him, subordinate ourselves to His power and submit to His leadership. This is the cure for spiritual affliction, for "if God be for us, who can be against us (Romans 8:31)?"

For the next few days, let's study the principles of submission, subordination and subjection to Christ. If He can die for us, the least we can do is live for Him by putting the free will He has given us under His authority in every way. Victory over spiritual afflictions is won when we surrender. James 4:6–7 says, "But he giveth more grace. Wherefore he saith, God resisteth the proud, but giveth grace unto the humble. Submit yourselves therefore to God. Resist the devil, and he will flee from you."

Learning to surrender is the key to victory.

> "Victory over spiritual afflictions is won when we surrender."

Subjection

SCRIPTURE READING: Romans 13:1–5

What is the ultimate authority in your life? We often allow ourselves to be controlled by Satan or our own self-will. We deceive ourselves into believing that God can't see us because we can't see Him. This type of thought pattern leads to spiritual decline because it prevents us from total subjection to God.

We, like our children, don't like the thought of being controlled by someone else. We like to think that we are in control and without the need for anyone else. Eventually, this determination to rule our own lives rather than subjecting ourselves to God's authority will lead to trouble and heartache. Giving in to self-will causes us to end up in subjection to Satan.

Satan tempts our self-will through the lust of the flesh, the lust of the eyes and the pride of life (1 John 2:16). Giving in to either one is like falling into a trap. What you thought was only a small matter of self-indulgence ends up as spiritual warfare with Satan. Romans 13:1 says, "Let every soul be subject unto the higher powers. For there is no power but of God: the powers that be are ordained of God." That Scripture will protect us from those traps set by Satan if we will apply it to our lives sincerely.

Total subjection to God is the first key to spiritual victory. Total subjection means believing on Jesus unto salvation, giving yourself wholly and completely to His service, and acknowledging His power and authority in your life by confessing Him in every step, move and breath you take. Jesus is the power in your life for everything that you face. Philippians 4:13 says, "I can do all things through Christ which strengtheneth me."

> *"Total subjection to God is the first key to spiritual victory."*

Subordination

SCRIPTURE READING: Luke 7:6–8

Subordination goes hand in hand with subjection for becoming a Christ-minded Christian who can overcome spiritual afflictions. Today's Scripture text gives us a beautiful picture of subordination.

In verse eight, the centurion sends a message to Jesus saying, "For I also am a man set under authority, having under me soldiers, and I say unto one, Go, and he goeth; and to another, Come, and he cometh; and to my servant, Do this, and he doeth it." Centurions were Roman military officers. Although generally disliked because of their harshness and domination, this particular centurion's humility and faith stood out to Jesus. This man of authority sent the message to Jesus that he felt unworthy, as powerful as he was, for the Lord to personally approach him. He humbled himself saying, "Lord, trouble not thyself: for I am not worthy that thou shouldest enter under my roof: Wherefore neither thought I myself worthy to come unto thee: but say in a word, and my servant shall be healed." The centurion's recognition of Jesus' authority over things that were out of his own control was rewarded; immediately his servant was healed.

We have access to all the promises of God if we are willing to be under His authority. Jesus Himself said in John 14:13–14, "And whatsoever ye shall ask in my name, that will I do, that the Father may be glorified in the Son. If ye shall ask any thing in my name, I will do it." Psalm 10:4 says, "The wicked, through the pride of his countenance, will not seek after God: God is not in all his thoughts."

Lay aside your pride and humbly submit your authority to the Lord just as the centurion did.

"We have access to all the promises of God
if we are willing to be under His authority."

Submission

SCRIPTURE READING: James 4:6–7

Once we've learned to live in subjection and subordination to God's will, we must learn to submit to it. Recognizing His authority and placing ourselves under it are only effective when we submit to it.

To be in submission to God means surrendering our all to Him, literally giving ourselves and everything we have to Him. It also means that we are in total obedience to His will for our lives. If we surrender ourselves and become obedient to God, then being controlled by God and under His authority automatically becomes a part of our daily walk.

Salvation is the gift God freely gave to us; we should give submission in return. This will require sacrifice. God has blessed us with everything we have, but He wants us to use it all for His honor and glory. If the things in our lives hinder us from submitting to God's will, we should realize this and be willing to let them go. Revelation 3:17 says, "Because thou sayest, I am rich, and increased with goods, and have need of nothing; and knowest not that thou art wretched, and miserable, and poor, and blind, and naked." Our worldly possessions are no good unless they are used for God.

Submitting ourselves to God is often easier than submitting our possessions to Him, but God can't have control if we are not willing to give Him all. Jesus submitted Himself to God, willingly and obediently going to the cross for our sins. Don't become so entangled in possessions that you forget your need for God. He gave His only begotten Son so that you could have eternal life in Heaven. What in your life is more valuable than the price He paid for you?

"To be in submission to God means surrendering our all to Him."

Conflict

SCRIPTURE READING: Philippians 1:29

Many Christians are under the impression that life in Christ is full of blue skies, rainbows, wealth and prosperity. This concept is easily misunderstood by many because they've never been taught differently. We mistake the happiness that material possessions and worldly success give us for the true joy that is found only in God. It is hard for those with these beliefs to understand what has happened when problems arise.

We see in today's Scripture text that the Bible completely contradicts the teaching of "health, wealth and prosperity." "For unto you it is given in the behalf of Christ, not only to believe on him, but also to suffer for his sake." From Genesis to Revelation we are taught that being Christ-like means suffering and conflict. Jesus was "bruised for our iniquities." He faced many conflicts in His ministry each day. He was despised and rejected by the very people for whom He came to die.

Romans 5:3–4 gives us hope while enduring the conflicts we face. "And not only so, but we glory in tribulations also: knowing that tribulation worketh patience; And patience, experience; and experience, hope." Jesus endured conflict with the hope of seeing the world come to repentance. Our hope in conflict is both in seeing others come to repentance and in seeing our Lord come again some day soon to call us away from this world of conflict.

Conflict in our lives is a sign of one of two things. Either we are distant from God and He is trying to get our attention, or we are in the center of His will and growing and learning from our experiences. Sometimes it's hard to understand, but God will not put more on us than we can bear.

"Jesus endured conflict with the hope
of seeing the world come to repentance."

Confidence

SCRIPTURE READING: Philippians 1:6

Despite the conflict we face as Christians, we can have confidence in our victory over them through Jesus Christ. His death, burial and resurrection gives us confidence for every area of our lives because He has given us victory over even death, hell and the grave.

Our confidence can be increased through studying God's Word. His Word is our assurance of victory through all of life's trials. Hebrews 13: 5–6 says, "Let your conversation be without covetousness; and be content with such things as ye have: for he hath said, I will never leave thee, nor forsake thee. So that we may boldly say, The Lord is my helper, and I will not fear what man shall do unto me." Confidence in life requires contentment in life. That is the principle taught in these verses.

We must learn to be content with what God has given us and where He has placed us. If we try to do things outside of God's will or ahead of Him, we set ourselves up for spiritual warfare. Trying to walk independently, we place our confidence in ourselves and in our fellow man. We leave God completely out of the picture, and when our plans fail, we lose confidence in Him. However, there is no reason for lack of confidence in God. Instead, we must learn to trust in Him completely.

Jesus gave His life for us; we should learn to trust Him for all of our needs. When we learn to trust Him in all things, we will find that even our conflicts increase our confidence in Him, for even in conflict He is working His will in our lives. You can overcome conflict by "being confident of this very thing, that he which hath begun a good work in you will perform it until the day of Jesus Christ."

"Confidence in life requires contentment in life."

Continuance

SCRIPTURE READING: Philippians 1:21–25

Confidence that we can overcome the conflicts we face gives us the strength to continue on in our journey. Paul understood that conflict was necessary, that victory was guaranteed and that there was a reason to continue on in spite of it all. Paul said in Philippians 1:12, "But I would ye should understand, brethren, that the things which happened unto me have fallen out rather unto the furtherance of the Gospel." Paul knew that the conflicts and victories in his life were all for the purpose of spreading the Gospel in some way.

Are you continuing on in your work for the Lord, or have you quit on God because things became more than you thought you could bear? Paul came to a point where he, too, wanted to quit. In Philippians 1:21–24 he said, "For to me to live is Christ, and to die is gain. But if I live in the flesh, this is the fruit of my labour: yet what I shall choose I wot not. For I am in a strait betwixt two, having a desire to depart, and to be with Christ; which is far better: Nevertheless to abide in the flesh is more needful for you." Paul knew that leaving behind the troubles of this world and being in the presence of the Lord would be better for him, but for the sake of others and the furtherance of the Gospel, he chose to continue on in his work for the Lord. Paul's love for the people at Philippi was greater than his weakness of suffering in the flesh.

Our greatest example of continuance is found in Jesus Christ. Jesus died, rose the third day and then ascended into heaven where He sits at the Father's right hand making intercession for you and me. What if He had left one of these undone? Where would we be today?

Be joyful in the Lord and continue in His service!

*"Our greatest example of continuance
is found in Jesus Christ."*

Dealing with Doubt

SCRIPTURE READING: Matthew 14:31

Doubt can work in our lives in two ways. For the next few days, we will study the ways in which doubt can affect our lives and learn from the biblical examples of others who dealt with doubt.

Our Scripture text today finds the disciples in the middle of a storm. It says, "And immediately Jesus stretched forth his hand, and caught him, and said unto him, O thou of little faith, wherefore didst thou doubt?" The disciples were scared, both by the storm and by this man walking on the water. Jesus spoke to them telling them to "be not afraid." Peter asked Jesus to bid him to come to Him on the water if He was truly the Lord. When Jesus bid him to come, Peter started out on the water in faith, strong and ready to follow the Lord's command. As he walked a little farther, Peter became afraid of the circumstances around him and began to sink. Peter started out in the will of God, but he ended up in fear and doubt. God had given him the power to walk on water, but Peter allowed his insecurities to overcome God's will.

Many times we respond to God's will for our own lives just like Peter did. We are anxious to know God's will for our lives, but we are afraid to act on it. Even if we do find the faith to begin the journey, we often let those voices of doubt discourage us. "Are you sure this is really the right thing to do?" "Are you ready for all of this?" "Are you sure that was God telling you to go in this direction?" Doubt begins to set in, and you lose all hope that you will ever really know the will of God for your life.

God can restore our hope if we will learn to seek Him in our state of doubt. James 1:5 says, "If any of you lack wisdom, let him ask of God, that giveth to all men liberally, and upbraideth not; and it shall be given him." Don't give up on God's will; follow in faith!

*"God can restore our hope
if we will learn to seek Him in our state of doubt."*

A NEW DESIRE

The Principles of Doubting

SCRIPTURE READING: James 1:5–6

Two biblical examples of doubting stand out above all others. One is Zacharias; the other is Thomas. Their stories reveal to us the principles of doubting that can make a great difference in our walk with God.

Zacharias doubted the message the angel brought to him from God. God promised to give Zacharias and Elizabeth a child, but Zacharias failed to believe God's promise. Immediately, Zacharias was made unable to speak because of his doubt. Thomas, on the other hand, received no "punishment" for his failure to believe the other disciples when they told him the Savior lived. What made Thomas' doubt any different than Zacharias'?

First, Thomas' doubt was a learning experience for him; it was part of his growth. Zacharias' doubt was simply a lack of faith in God's power to do that which seemed impossible. Second, Thomas' doubt was a temporary doubt based on what he had heard from man. Zacharias had been praying for a child for many years, and he had allowed himself to become so rooted in doubt about God's ability or desire to answer his prayer that he didn't believe even though God sent an angel to give him the good news. Thomas had learned not to put his trust in man alone. Thomas' doubt was more of a need for divine reassurance than a lack of belief.

Doubting is safe as long as we allow it to be a learning process for us. When in doubt, we should go to God for assurance, just like Thomas did. Don't let yourself dwell in doubt like Zacharias did. Today's Scripture text says, "If any of you lack wisdom, let him ask of God, that giveth to all men liberally, and upbraideth not; and it shall be given him. But let him ask in faith, nothing wavering." Seek God's will and rest in it!

"Doubting is safe as long as we allow it to be a learning process for us."

Defying Doubt

SCRIPTURE READING: Philippians 1:6

Don't let doubt dwell in your life. We've already learned that God will give us the wisdom to deal with our doubts. Secure yourself in His will, and then do God's will without looking back at the doubts.

Choosing to live for God always brings doubt. Doubt is one of Satan's finest weapons. Satan knows that if he can place doubt in your mind, then you are a target for deception. However, you can overcome doubt if you know God's will for your life.

Your doubts about God's will for your life can be resolved by reading God's Word. God's Word is His voice to you, and it can be depended on to verify God's will in your life. Thomas doubted God's plan when he heard it from man, but when Thomas got the message from God he never doubted again. We should handle our doubts just as Thomas did. Seek God's Word, listen for His voice and trust Him.

We should confidently serve God and praise Him for using us. Our Scripture text for today says, "Being confident of this very thing, that he which hath begun a good work in you will perform it until the day of Jesus Christ." If God began a work in you, He will be faithful to finish it. If you are a born again child of God, you have a power inside of you that will not let you quit on God. That power is the Holy Spirit within you. He will never leave you nor forsake you; He will guide you in your work for the Lord.

When Peter walked on the water, he began to doubt, "and immediately Jesus stretched forth his hand, and caught him, and said unto him, O thou of little faith, wherefore didst thou doubt?" (Matthew 14:31). Jesus' hand is stretched out to you now. Defy the doubt and take His hand.

*"God will give us the wisdom
to deal with our doubts."*

Loving Others with God's Love

SCRIPTURE READING: Ruth 1:1–22

The story of Ruth, Naomi, and Boaz is a beautiful picture of God's love that can teach us a great lesson. Both Ruth and Naomi had lost everything they had, but Naomi had suffered the greater loss. In a ten year period, Naomi had not only lost her husband, but she had lost both of her sons as well. We read in the first chapter of Ruth that Naomi was so bitter over her losses, she changed her name to Mara which literally means bitter.

Ruth, on the other hand, had an enduring love and loyalty towards her mother-in-law. No matter how hard Naomi tried to push her away, Ruth never gave up. Ruth's love for Naomi goes far beyond our human comprehension. Ruth 1:16 says, "Intreat me not to leave thee, or to return from following after thee: for whither thou goest, I will go; and where thou lodgest, I will lodge: thy people shall be my people, and thy God my God." Could you say that to your mother-in-law? Could you even say that to your own mother or to your husband?

Loving others with God's love wouldn't cost us anything with the exception of our time. Sometimes sharing quality time with others holds far more value than anything money can buy. The difference it could make in someone's life might amaze you. Look how it changed Naomi. The woman who had changed her name to bitter ended up saying in Ruth 4:14, "Blessed be the Lord, which hath not left thee this day without a kinsman, that his name may be famous in Israel."

Whose life can you influence just by showing them God's love?

> *"Loving others with God's love wouldn't cost us anything, with the exception of our time."*

"The Lord Recompense Thy Work"

SCRIPTURE READING: Ruth 2:1—4:22

Yesterday, we saw how sharing God's love can change someone else's life. Today, we'll see how it can change our own.

Ruth's loyalty and enduring love for her mother-in-law led her to glean in the fields of Boaz, and what an impression she made on this man. Ruth 2:11–12 tells us how impressed Boaz was by Ruth's attitude toward Naomi. He said, "It hath fully been showed me, all that thou hast done unto thy mother in law since the death of thine husband: and how thou hast left thy father and thy mother, and the land of thy nativity, and art come unto a people which thou knewest not heretofore. The Lord recompense thy work, and a full reward be given thee of the Lord God of Israel, under whose wings thou art come to trust."

Boaz fell in love with this Moabite woman, and Ruth fell in love with him. Ruth's humility and obedience influenced Boaz' affections toward her. In chapter four of Ruth, the wedding day came. Ruth was rewarded for all of her goodness and the trials she had patiently endured. The Lord did recompense Ruth's work, and a full reward was given. Ruth's willingness to show Christ's love to someone else paid off even greater dividends for her than it did for Naomi. Ruth was placed into the line of Christ! Wow, what a repayment for taking the time to simply love someone else with God's love!

"Sharing God's love can change someone else's life."

True Love

SCRIPTURE READING: 1 John 4:7–8

Love has lost its meaning in this modern world. We need to remind ourselves of the definition of true love. Where did our parents and grandparents get their definition of love? The pure, sincere love that our parents and grandparents knew was learned from God's Word.

What is God's definition of love, and from where did it come? John says in today's Scripture text, "Beloved, let us love one another: for love is of God; and every one that loveth is born of God, and knoweth God. He that loveth not knoweth not God; for God is love."

Without God in our lives we have no love. Many of us know someone who is unsaved, yet they seem to have love in them. We often mistake affection, infatuation and the lusts of our flesh for true love, but, my friend, make no mistake about it, until you have received Jesus Christ as your Savior you cannot know true love.

God's love can make the most loving person you know more loving, for he will experience a new love that he has never known before. Inviting Jesus into a rocky marriage can give a marriage that had fallen apart a new love to stand on. Someone who has received God's love into their heart through Jesus Christ can love people they never thought they could.

True love is only found in Jesus. Through His true love, you can experience new heights of peace and contentment that you thought never existed. Second Corinthians 13:11 says, "Be perfect, be of good comfort, be of one mind, live in peace; and the God of love and peace shall be with you." Let's get back to the true meaning of love and learn to live in God's peace.

"True love is only found in Jesus."

Choosing to Love God

Scripture Reading: Matthew 22:37–39

Love is a decision of our will. When we want something material, we long and yearn for it until it becomes ours. When we get it we become ecstatic with love for it, and nothing else can take its place.

Have you ever seen a newlywed couple when they've decided to have a child? That was a decision of their will, and soon they became focused only on fulfilling that desire to have a baby. When the baby was born, he became the center of their lives. They chose to have him, and they loved him. God gives us the same choice in loving Him.

God will never force His love on us. We can either choose to accept His love and love Him in return, or we can choose to love this world and die in our sins. God should be the focus of our love. Our Scripture text for today reminds us that God calls us to love Him first and foremost, with all of our heart, soul and mind. We are to love God above our spouses, our children and our parents. We are to love Him more than our jobs, our homes, our cars and everything else we have.

God's blessings can hinder our love for Him. If the newlywed couple's baby becomes so much the center of their lives that they forget Who blessed them with him, then the baby has hindered their love for God. Anything that we love more than we love God becomes sin in our lives.

Jesus said in today's Scripture text, "Thou shalt love the Lord thy God with all thy heart, and with all thy soul, and with all thy mind. This is the first and great commandment." Today, lay aside all of the things you've chosen to love more than God and choose to love God first.

"God should be the focus of our love."

Falling in Love with God

SCRIPTURE READING: 1 John 2:15–17

Once we've chosen to love God, we must learn to fall in love with Him. This may sound like a difficult task, but it's not. Do you remember how you fell in love with your spouse? Falling in love with God works the same way. Couples fall in love by spending time together. The more two people are together, the more they find to love about one another. Soon, they find it hard to be away from each other. They have fallen in love with one another, and they want to be together forever.

In order to fall in love with God, we must spend as much time with Him as we do in our other relationships. We must come to know everything about Him that we can. We can only learn about God by spending time in His Word and in prayer on a daily basis. In order to do this, we must lay aside the things of this world that we put before spending time with God. The Bible teaches us that our God is a jealous God. Anything we put before Him is looked upon by Him as another god. Today's Scripture text reminds us that the things of the world will pass away, but he that does the will of God abides forever. It says, "Love not the world, neither the things that are in the world. If any man love the world, the love of the Father is not in him. For all that is in the world, the lust of the flesh, and the lust of the eyes, and the pride of life, is not of the Father, but is of the world. And the world passeth away, and the lust thereof: but he that doeth the will of God abideth for ever."

Jesus said in John 15:9, "As the Father hath loved me, so have I loved you: continue ye in my love." Verse 13 says, "Greater love hath no man than this, that a man lay down his life for his friends." Jesus laid down His life for us. Can't we love Him more than anything or anyone else?

The decision is ours to make. Choose not only to love God, but to fall in love with Him. Spend time with Him, find out all you can about Him, and soon you'll find it hard to be away from Him.

"God should be the focus of our love."

Loving One Another

SCRIPTURE READING: 1 John 4:7

God expects us not only to love Him, but to love others as well. Loving others reveals God in our lives, and God is pleased when we love others with a godly love. How can we demonstrate our love for one another?

First, we show love to others by telling them that we love them. Saying "I love you" is nothing to be afraid of. First John 4:18 says, "There is no fear in love; but perfect love casteth out fear: because fear hath torment. He that feareth is not made perfect in love." You can also show love by praying for others, by sharing your testimony with them and just by being there to listen and share God's Word with them.

God knows the true intents of our hearts. He knows every evil thought we have about the Christian brothers and sisters we profess to love. We must get beyond those thoughts in order to love them with the passionate love of God. The actual Greek form of the word "passion" means to suffer. Until we can learn to love others enough to suffer for them, we cannot truly love them with God's love. In order to have a godly love for others, we must be willing to look beyond their faults and allow God to perfect His love in and through us.

Loving others matures us in our walk with Christ, but more importantly, it is commanded by Christ as being second only to loving God. The first and great commandment is to love God. Jesus said in Matthew 22:39, "And the second is like unto it, Thou shalt love thy neighbour as thyself."

First John 4:7 says, "Beloved, let us love one another: for love is of God; and every one that loveth is born of God, and knoweth God."

"Loving others matures us in our walk with Christ."

A NEW DESIRE

"That the World May Know"

SCRIPTURE READING: John 17:23

The greatest reason for loving one another is found in today's Scripture text. Loving one another brings us together as a family of God. It is through sharing our love that the world sees Jesus and His love. Exercising our love for one another wins souls to Christ. A born again child of God is the only true love a lost person sees. Jesus prayed in our Scripture text, "I in them, and thou in me, that they may be made perfect in one; and that the world may know that thou hast sent me, and hast loved them, as thou hast loved me."

People everywhere are reaching out for a love that, unless they receive Christ as their personal Savior, they will never find. It is sad to see Christians who have grown to think that they can save the world on their own through good works. Too many Christians confuse love and good works, and they neglect opportunities to show true love to others because they are too busy getting in another "good work" for God. If people can't see or sense love in our actions, then our works are not effective for God.

Jesus did many great works during His earthly ministry, but He never neglected to love others. In every work He did, love was manifested to everyone present. When Jesus passed through a crowd, He left them with His compassionate love. We, as Christians, should be the same way. We never know who in our lives is reaching out for the love that God can only give them through us.

First John 3:18 says, "My little children, let us not love in word, neither in tongue; but in deed and in truth." Let's not just say an empty "I love you" or get caught up in "good works;" let's truly love one another with God's love that the world may know God loves them.

"Exercising our love for one another wins souls to Christ."

An Eternal Love

SCRIPTURE READING: 1 John 5:11

We know that God is love, and God is eternal. Therefore, God's love is eternal. Jesus Christ is God's eternal, passionate love extended toward us. First John 5:11 says, "And this is the record, that God hath given to us eternal life, and this life is in his Son." Without Jesus we could not have eternal life or eternal love, but in Him we have both.

We must love others eternally in order to love them with God's love. True love is not a feeling or an affection of the flesh. It is an eternal growing process that begins in salvation and is perfected in Christ. Until we learn that love is eternal, not something we can turn on and off like a light, we will struggle in our walk with God.

We should not be competing with others in our work for God. We must learn to love our fellow laborers with God's love. We've already learned that our love for one another allows the world to see Jesus in us. When the world sees Jesus in us and in our works, we are effective for God. Jesus demonstrated God's eternal love to us by giving His life for us. How can we demonstrate God's eternal love to others? First John 3:16 says, "Hereby perceive we the love of God, because he laid down his life for us: and we ought to lay down our lives for the brethren."

Do you truly love others with God's eternal love, or are you just saying empty words when you say "I love you"? Those words are more than just a saying for a Christian. "I love you" is a commitment to love another person with a godly, passionate, eternal love. First John 4:11 says, "Beloved, if God so loved us, we ought also to love one another."

> "We must love others eternally
> in order to love them with God's love."

$\mathcal{A}$ Sincere Heart

SCRIPTURE READING: Proverbs 31:11–12

In Proverbs 31, we find the perfect example of a sincere heart. What a beautiful picture of love and devotion this passage presents. The Proverbs 31 lady is devoted to God and family, and she gently cares for her home. Her affections are for her husband only, while her heart belongs to God. Procrastination is never a problem for her; her obligations are always fulfilled at their proper time. Her priorities begin and end with God, therefore her family, church and social life fall into their proper place. Her loving heart makes every gesture a sincere one.

Learning to love with a sincere heart, as this lady did, is a challenge for today's woman. We get so caught up in ourselves that we make marriage and motherhood more of a burden than a blessing. We grumble and complain at the smallest of things, and we often feel neglected or used. Our schedules are hectic, and our priorities are way out of order. We need to change our hearts from selfishness to sincerity.

We all must realize that we have been blessed with certain qualities that come only from God. We must allow those qualities to be used for the sake of Jesus Christ. The greatest quality bestowed upon us all by God is that of a loving heart. We should use that love to build closer relationships with our husbands, our children and our friends by sharing God's love with them.

The Proverbs 31 lady was not perfect, but she was pleasing to God. Why? She had a heart that loved God, and she used that love to make her walk with God effective and successful in her family and her social life. Let's learn to have a sincere heart!

> *"The greatest quality bestowed upon us all by God is that of a loving heart."*

Becoming a Proverbs 31 Lady

SCRIPTURE READING: Mark 12:30–31

What does it take to become a Proverbs 31 lady, a lady with a sincere heart? In order to become a Proverbs 31 lady, we must have a willing heart and a readiness to serve. We must be willing to sacrifice our own needs for the needs of others. Our first love must be Jesus, and He must be the center of our lives. We must seek with love, excitement and joy to please our husbands and to protect our marriages. A beautiful reflection of a Christian woman is one who can talk through marital problems instead of shouting and quarreling.

Today's Scripture text reminds us of God's command to love. "And thou shalt love the Lord thy God with all thy heart, and with all thy soul, and with all thy mind, and with all thy strength: this is the first commandment. And the second is like, namely this, Thou shalt love thy neighbour as thyself. There is none other commandment greater than these." Today's woman must fill her heart with this special love in order to develop the sincere heart of the Proverbs 31 lady.

The Proverbs 31 lady is created by God's love. She, in turn, shares that love, making her a woman of virtue and victory. We must become totally dependent on God, allowing Him to produce these characteristics in us, in order to become the Proverbs 31 lady.

God holds us responsible for reflecting these qualities in our lives. God has given us a heart that loves; let's please Him by spreading that love. The world needs to see more Proverbs 31 ladies.

"We must be willing to sacrifice our own needs for the needs of others."

A Heart That Loves

SCRIPTURE READING: Ephesians 5:19

Described in today's Scripture text is the joyous life of a Spirit-filled Christian. This is how we should appear as Christians every day, "Speaking to yourselves in psalms and hymns and spiritual songs, singing and making melody in your heart to the Lord." Notice that the Scripture tells us to do these things in our hearts. When we find our security in the Lord, we can perform these joyous acts even when times seem tough. We can even share the joy of Jesus with others by giving them a kind and sincere word or special touch that reflects Christ.

When we make melody in our hearts to the Lord, we are in a constant state of praise. We are abiding in Christ, and as a natural result of this state we spread His love abroad. Do you abide in this state enough that others can see God through your love? We, as Christians, hold that responsibility. We should allow our hearts to reach out and uplift someone each day, whether we feel like it or not.

Jesus has such a loving heart for all mankind. He is no respector of persons. We are all equal in the eyes of God, every man, woman, boy and girl. God is proud of each one of us because we are His through Jesus Christ. God knows us and loves us, and it thrills His heart when He sees us helping others along the way.

Jesus is always love, joy and peace, and we have His character living in our hearts through the Holy Spirit. Submit yourself to sharing the love of your heart with someone today and every day. You are only giving them Jesus, and everyone needs Him. Be joyful! Be happy! Sometimes that's all the love someone else needs.

"Submit yourself to sharing the love of your heart with someone today and every day."

"By Love Serve One Another"

SCRIPTURE READING: Galatians 5:13

A heart that loves is a heart full of God, for God is love. With the heart of God, we automatically have the desire to serve others. A godly heart doesn't have time for petty selfishness and jealousies. A godly heart focuses on others and strives to share its love with them. A godly heart is full of compassion and understanding, and it is always willing to distribute its last ounce of energy to comfort someone else. A heart that loves takes pride in securing the needs of others, whether they be friends or strangers. A godly heart of love overlooks other's faults by grasping to find the needs and then filling those needs by exercising love.

Perhaps there is someone in your home or neighborhood who needs to be served by your godly love. You see, a heart that loves is also a heart that serves. Today's Scripture text says, "For, brethren, ye have been called unto liberty; only use not liberty for an occasion to the flesh, but by love serve one another." We are free to please those around us by serving them with God's love.

You can serve God's love to someone in many simple ways. A pretty card, a short phone call or a sincere word of prayer is not only rewarding for that other person, but it is rewarding for you as well. First Peter 5:2, 4 says, "Feed the flock of God which is among you, taking the oversight thereof, not by constraint, but willingly; not for filthy lucre, but of a ready mind; And when the chief Shepherd shall appear, ye shall receive a crown of glory that fadeth not away."

Let's share our love with someone today. It will be a refreshing and maturing experience for us as well as for others.

> *"A heart that loves takes pride*
> *in securing the needs of others."*

A Heart That Forgives

SCRIPTURE READING: Matthew 18:33

Our Scripture text today comes from Jesus' parable on forgiveness. In the parable, one man had forgiven another man for a debt he could not pay. The forgiven man then went to demand money from someone who owed him. When the man could not pay, the forgiven man had him thrown into prison. Jesus' said, "Shouldest not thou also have had compassion on thy fellowservant, even as I had pity on thee?"

A heart that loves is a heart that forgives. Forgiveness exercises the love of Christ in our lives. The whole world stands forgiven through Christ's death on Calvary's cross. Jesus is forgiveness, and if He lives in us then we, too, must forgive.

Unforgiveness in our hearts can be deadly to our spiritual growth. Continued unforgiveness puts us in a place where we will be chastened by the Lord for our disobedience (Hebrews 11:6). Sometimes we don't want to forgive because we don't feel like others deserve forgiveness. This thought stems from our sinful flesh and from Satan. Galatians 5:17 says, "For the flesh lusteth against the Spirit, and the Spirit against the flesh: and these are contrary the one to the other: so that ye cannot do the things that ye would." If you can't forgive, then you can't exercise God's unconditional love for mankind. You have allowed your flesh to control you rather than being controlled by the Spirit of God.

Jesus is our example of forgiveness. He forgave a woman in adultery (John 8:3–11), Peter's denial (John 18:15–18, 25–27, and 21:15–19) and the thief on the cross (Luke 23:39–43). My friend, a heart that loves forgives. Don't let unforgiveness hinder you from having a heart that loves.

> *"A heart that loves is a heart that forgives."*

Unconditional Love

SCRIPTURE READING: Ruth 1:16

In the book of Ruth, we read about the love Ruth had for her mother-in-law, Naomi. Naomi was down on herself and God because of the losses she had suffered. Naomi had faced the loss of loved ones, financial ruin, insecurities and depression. We, too, often face these same battles.

Like Naomi, we often want to be left alone when we are down, discouraged, bitter and angry. These emotions so overwhelm us that we aren't sure of anything. One moment we want to be left alone, and the next moment we want to cry out for help or comfort. One day we feel positive and able to cope, but the next day we feel unable to cope at all. Often, like Naomi, we hurt others because we are hurting. Our countenance drops, and everyone becomes our enemy. We find fault in everything and everybody. We reject encouraging words because we don't want advice. We just want to be left alone. We can't pray or read God's Word, and when we do it seems dry and useless. Is this familiar to you?

Naomi couldn't understand why Ruth insisted on staying with her under such unpleasant circumstances. Ruth exemplified true Christ-like love by comforting and encouraging Naomi with an unconditional love. A heart that truly loves will go the distance, even taking rejection from those for whom it loves and cares.

The only love that helps and heals when one is hurting is God's love, and the only way it is given is through people like you and me. Unconditional love understands someone who may be hurting or bitter. Are you willing to stand by those who are hurting or suffering, even if it means rejection? Be like Ruth and say to that person what she said in today's Scripture text, "And Ruth said, Entreat me not to leave thee, or to return from following after thee: for whither thou goest, I will go; and where thou lodgest, I will lodge: thy people shall be my people, and thy God my God."

> "Unconditional love understands someone
> who may be hurting or bitter."

A NEW DESIRE

Vessels of God's Love

SCRIPTURE READING: 2 Corinthians 4:7

We are vessels of the Lord. When we love others, whether it be in word or in deed, we love as vessels of God's love. God loves others through us. Our Scripture text for today says, "But we have this treasure in earthen vessels, that the excellency of the power may be of God, and not of us."

Jesus taught the importance of love. In Matthew 22:37–40, He reminds each of us to "love the Lord thy God with all thy heart, and with all thy soul, and with all thy mind. Thou shalt love thy neighbour as thyself." In the 21st chapter of John, Jesus asked Peter three times for a confession of love. Jesus stressed that love, for God and for others, should be our only motive for serving the Lord.

If we truly love the Lord, we will gladly share His love with others. We share God's love with others by serving them with the truth of God in our hearts. If we love others only for what we can get out of them, then our love is vain, counterfeit and meaningless. Christ loves at all times, unconditionally and with absolutely no hesitation. First Corinthians 13:1 says, "Though I speak with the tongues of men and of angels, and have not charity (love), I am become as sounding brass, or a tinkling cymbal." You can do good deeds and speak kind words forever, but if your words and actions do not impress God's love upon another's life, then you have nothing that will last to offer.

Being a vessel of God's love isn't always easy. A heart that loves must, in many cases, take up its cross to follow Jesus. Nevertheless, we must continue to share God's love. If you're not willing to be a vessel of God's love, someone may never know the true love of God.

"When we love others, whether it be in word or in deed, we love as vessels of God's love."

Carrying the Cross of Love

SCRIPTURE READING: Matthew 16:24

A heart that loves often must take up its cross to follow Jesus. Loving hearts, hearts that are truly vessels of God's love, are always looking out for everyone else's needs over their own. A heart that truly loves is willing to sacrifice in order to share the love of God with a hurting or needy soul.

Our Scripture text for today says, "Then said Jesus unto his disciples, If any man will come after me, let him deny himself, and take up his cross, and follow me." Sometimes we are called to love those who seem like hopeless cases, but Jesus never gave up, and neither should we. Human nature grows tired of the repetitive circumstances we must face in our relationships with others. However, we must endure our feelings and continue to pray for and help others just like Jesus did.

A heart that loves is stable and compassionate in the Lord. Even though it is sometimes hard to be a vessel of God's love, someday it will pay off. God will eventually bless you by allowing you to see how your repetitive words or deeds have helped someone. You may grow tired now of constantly reassuring that hurting heart that God really cares and that He is in control. You may be ready to give up on that one you have to bail out of trouble over and over again, but your constant, unconditional love will eventually pay off, and God will allow you to see how it was productive in someone's life.

Don't ever stop loving or sharing your love. You are the only Jesus that some may ever see. Lawrence Pearsall Jacks once said, "Nobody will ever know what you mean by saying that 'God is love' unless you act it as well." Take up your cross, and be a vessel of God's love.

"A heart that loves is stable and compassionate in the Lord."

Witness of the Heart

SCRIPTURE READING: 1 Peter 3:4

True godliness in our lives is recognized by the witness of our hearts. Godliness can't be seen through our wealth or our outward beauty. It is our heart that makes a bold statement for righteousness.

Our Scripture text for today says, "But let it be the hidden man of the heart, in that which is not corruptible, even the ornament of a meek and quiet spirit, which is in the sight of God of great price." This Scripture defines for us the witness of the heart: humility, compassion and Christ-likeness.

A willingness to separate yourself from this world and its ways is of great value in the work of the Lord. A quiet, meek spirit is far more precious than a loud, aggressive personality. God will use a woman of quietness and sincerity in ways she can't comprehend.

The witness of the heart is an overflow of the Holy Spirit into one's daily life. A woman of witness is active in the work of the Lord. Her serious studies are seen through her actions. The light of Christ shines to those around her in many ways. Her manner of dress reflects godliness. She controls both her language and her topic of conversation. She does not subject herself to dirty jokes, vicious gossip or indecent flirtations. Even when she is facing hard times, others see the peace of God in her life. Her happiness and contentment in Christ is evident.

Does the work of the Holy Spirit overflow your heart and shine through your life? Get into God's Word and let it change your life. Let your light shine and make a difference in someone's life. Let us not compromise as Christians, but let us contend to make a statement for Jesus Christ.

"Scripture defines for us the witness of the heart: humility, compassion and Christ-likeness."

God's Unconditional Love

SCRIPTURE READING: Psalm 106:1

Satan likes to deceive us into thinking that God's love is like our own fleshly love for one another. Satan focuses our attention on our past sins, recurring sins and the destructive habits that seem to control our lives. He uses these things against us to make us feel beyond forgiveness and worthless to ourselves, to others and to God. Then, he offers us alternatives that will eventually draw us back out into a sinful world. The result is spiritual defeat and self-destruction.

Satan couldn't care less what you become. His intentions are to turn you from God. Satan can't offer you love. He only offers things and relationships that appear to be love but eventually end in destruction. God's love, on the other hand, is real. It is unconditional and nondestructive. Jesus revealed this love on the cross. He loved those who crucified Him, even asking the Father to forgive them for what they were doing. Jesus knew that His death would be the atonement for His tormentors. God loved them in spite of their behavior.

God's love is often revealed through His chastening. When the correction is past we can look back and see that God was not punishing us, but that He was loving us. What we view as punishment and hardship is often simply God's love in action.

How can God love a drug addict, an adulterer, a drunk or a murderer? Just like He loves His only begotten Son. Just like He loved David when He committed murder and adultery. Just like He loved Judas Iscariot, who betrayed the Lord for thirty pieces of silver. God's love is a merciful love. Today's Scripture text says, "Praise ye the LORD. O give thanks unto the LORD; for he is good: for his mercy endureth for ever.

*"God's love is real. It is unconditional
and nondestructive."*

Love's Joy

SCRIPTURE READING: Luke 15:7

God's unconditional love is the door to love's joy. Love's joy is defined for us in today's Scripture text: "I say unto you, that likewise joy shall be in heaven over one sinner that repenteth, more than over ninety and nine just persons, which need no repentance."

Because love's joy is in seeing sinners saved, it can only be found in God's unconditional love. God's love doesn't end when we feel like we have disappointed or shamed Him. When Jesus hung on the cross, He took disappointment and shame with Him. We mistake our own disappointment with ourselves for God's. We let our viewpoints blind us from seeing God's mercy. When you can't love yourself, you must remember that God loved you so much that He gave His Son that you might have life more abundantly. If God can forgive you, then you must forgive yourself also. God loves and forgives others, and He expects us to do the same.

The drunkest drunk, the dopiest drug addict, and the most well-known adulterer, even the meanest murderer are all valuable to God. He still loves them to the point of changing their lives to the likeness of His Son if they will only believe. God loves the sinner just as much as He loves the righteous.

Don't be so quick to condemn others. Be willing to overlook their faults and reach out to their needs. We should be able to love others regardless of our differences with them. Challenge yourself to have the same love toward yourself and others that Jesus had when He said, "Father, forgive them; for they know not what they do." Open the door to love's joy by loving others with God's unconditional love.

"Love's joy is in seeing sinners saved."

The Love of the Spirit

SCRIPTURE READING: Galatians 5:22

When Paul listed the fruit of the Spirit, the first mentioned was love. Our Scripture text for today says, "But the fruit of the Spirit is love . . ." The purpose and strength of this fruit is recorded in 1 Corinthians 13. Each time we see the word charity in 1 Corinthians 13, it refers to love.

In the first three verses of the chapter, the author reminds us that love is the superior fruit of our Spirit. Regardless of what we perform or pursue, it is invalid and profits nothing without love. Even from the slightest to the greatest of spiritual gifts, they are nothing if not motivated by love. How do we arrive at the point where our actions are motivated by and our gifts are used in love? We must first accept God's love by accepting Jesus Christ as our Savior. First John 4:10 says, "Herein is love, not that we loved God, but that he loved us, and sent his Son to be the propitiation for our sins." Without Christ in our lives, we cannot obtain true love.

The character of love is revealed in 1 Corinthians 13:4–8. "Charity suffereth long, and is kind; . . . envieth not; . . . vaunteth not itself, is not puffed up, Doth not behave itself unseemly, seeketh not her own, is not easily provoked, thinketh no evil; Rejoiceth not in iniquity, but rejoiceth in the truth; Beareth all things, believeth all things, hopeth all things, endureth all things. Charity never faileth." These characteristics were embodied by Jesus Christ alone. Jesus alone can teach us how to love.

Today and everyday, your prayer should be: "Lord, fill me with your love, and teach me how to magnify this love in the lives of others. Lord, teach me to look beyond my opinions and attitudes in order to love others with your never-ending love."

"Regardless of what we perform or pursue,
it is invalid and profits nothing without love."

Love That Never Fails

SCRIPTURE READING: 1 Corinthians 13:8–10

Yesterday, we saw briefly that God's love is never-ending. It is a love that never fails. We find this clearly taught in today's Scripture text: "Charity never faileth: but whether there be prophecies, they shall fail; whether there be tongues, they shall cease; whether there be knowledge, it shall vanish away. For we know in part, and we prophesy in part. But when that which is perfect is come, then that which is in part shall be done away."

Today's Scripture text tells us that all things will eventually end, including half-hearted love. The point is, God's love is a perfect, constant love. "Charity never faileth." It will stand when everything else fails.

There are many things in this life that we don't understand. Some things we may never comprehend, but one thing is certain. When we love others with God's love, we go beyond our own thoughts. We escalate to the thoughts of God. Only when we have put on the mind of Christ can we love others unconditionally with a love that never fails.

Wouldn't we all like to possess this fruit? The truth is, we can. Those who have accepted Christ as their Savior already possess the fruit of love. We may not always act on the love that is within us, but as children of God, we can rest assured that this love does abide somewhere deep within. Today, pray again that prayer that we prayed yesterday, "Lord, fill me with your love, and teach me how to magnify this love in the lives of others. Lord, teach me to look beyond my opinions and attitudes in order to love others with your never-ending love." Continue to pray that prayer daily until you see your life bearing the fruit of God's love that never fails.

"Only when we have put on the mind of Christ can we love others unconditionally."

"How Can He Love God?"

SCRIPTURE READING: 1 John 4:20

Often it is not easy to love others just as they are. Does that mean that we don't have the love of God within us? Absolutely not. Even though we have been born again, we still live in our fleshly bodies.

This body of flesh is a body of sin. Daily, we live with a nature that is prone to disobedience and rebellion. Paul said in Galatians 5:17, "For the flesh lusteth against the Spirit, and the Spirit against the flesh: and these are contrary the one to the other: so that ye cannot do the things that ye would." The flesh will always aid in finding fault in others. Being conformed into the image of Christ is a day by day, step by step process. It does not happen overnight.

It is our fleshly nature to love ourselves before we love others. It is our fleshly nature to complicate true love. If you are unable to love others unconditionally, examine yourself. It is possible that God's love is not in you. However, it is also very possible that you are a child of God with God's love dwelling within you. It may be that you have allowed your fleshly life, attitude, spiritual condition or some other hindrance to prevent you from loving others for who they are.

Only you and God know for sure whether or not the love of God is dwelling within you. Today's Scripture text gives us the answer: "If a man say, I love God, and hateth his brother, he is a liar: for he that loveth not his brother whom he hath seen, how can he love God whom he hath not seen?" Do you hate your brother (or that other person who you just can't seem to love unconditionally), or are you just having a hard time accepting them for who they are? The answer will reveal God's love, or lack of it, within you.

"The flesh will always aid in finding fault in others."

A NEW DESIRE

The Marks of God's Love Within

SCRIPTURE READING: 1 Corinthians 13:4–8

Sometimes we wonder if the love within our hearts is truly God's love. We can know if the love in our hearts is God's love by testing it for the marks of God's love. These marks are found in today's Scripture text.

Verse 4 says, "Love suffereth long . . ." In other words, true love, God's love, is not quick to resent. Then, true love ". . . is kind . . ." The Greek form of the word "kind" means to be useful. True love will be distributed to others. It is not going to sit inside a person and not be effective.

Next, it ". . . vaunteth not itself . . ." True love doesn't lift itself up with praise. It ". . . is not puffed up . . ." It does not dwell in pride. Love "doth not behave itself unseemly." This means that love is always exercised in decency and self-control. Love "seeketh not her own." Those who have the marks of God's love within will seek to edify others over self.

True love "is not easily provoked, thinketh no evil." True love is enduring and righteous. It "rejoiceth not in iniquity, but rejoiceth in the truth." Any person who thrives off of gossip, lies and confusion rather than the truth is less likely to be a person who truly possesses God's love within.

Do your actions toward others hold any of these values? These are the marks of God's love within. If your actions toward others reflect these characteristics of love, then you are allowing God to love others through you. If your actions toward others do not hold true to these values, you are either hindering God's love from shining through you or you do not have God's love within. Examine yourself and seek God's Word for counsel.

"True love will be distributed to others."

Positive Christian Love

SCRIPTURE READING: 1 Corinthians 13:7–8

We studied the marks of God's love within yesterday. Today we will see what it takes to have a positive Christian love toward others.

Today's Scripture text says, "[Charity] beareth all things, believeth all things, hopeth all things, endureth all things. Charity never faileth: but whether there be prophecies, they shall fail; whether there be tongues, they shall cease; whether there be knowledge, it shall vanish away." This can only mean that godly love overlooks the worst and continues to love unconditionally.

This is the standard of a positive Christian love. If we can give others the benefit of the doubt rather than having a critical or negative attitude, we can become very positive influences in the lives of others. We become positive Christians.

The only way to be sure you have a positive Christian love is to examine yourself once again. If your love is anything other than what has been defined here, and in the preceding days, seek God's Word for counsel. First John 4:16–17 says, "And we have known and believed the love that God hath to us. God is love; and he that dwelleth in love dwelleth in God, and God in him. Herein is our love made perfect, that we may have boldness in the day of judgment: because as he is, so are we in this world."

Are you able to love others regardless of their lifestyle? Are you able to love them even when they do things you don't like? Most of all, are they able to see that your concern for them is truly out of a deep, godly love for them? The answers lie within our own hearts.

"The only way to be sure you have a positive Christian love is to examine yourself once again."

A NEW DESIRE

Loving Like God Loves

SCRIPTURE READING: Matthew 22:37–39

How can we overcome the hindrances of our flesh and love others the way God loves them? First, you must get yourself into God's Word in order to learn of Him and His ways. Then, you must prayerfully seek to become more like Him. You will find that the closer you get to God, the more like Him you become. God's love is not based on feelings or performances. God's love is a decision. Once we make the decision to love with God's love, nothing will be able to stop or separate that.

We can overcome the flesh by looking at every person and every circumstance through the eyes of God. We must learn to deal with our feelings and emotions through the power of the Holy Spirit within rather than reacting with the reflexes of our fleshly nature. Overcoming the flesh requires sacrificing our own thoughts in order to put on the mind of Christ. We must deny our own wants in order to be what God wants us to be.

Most importantly, in order to love with God's love, we must obey the two greatest commandments. We find these commandments in today's Scripture text: "Thou shalt love the Lord thy God with all thy heart, and with all thy soul, and with all thy mind. This is the first and great commandment. And the second is like unto it, Thou shalt love thy neighbour as thyself." Obeying these two commandments will transform us from self-love to self-denial, from conditional love to unconditional love. We will go from walking in the flesh to soaring in the Spirit.

Are you loving others like God loves? If not, set aside the flesh and get in His Word. Allow Him to transform you into a vessel of God's love.

> *"We can overcome the flesh by looking at every person and every circumstance through the eyes of God."*

Compassionate Love

SCRIPTURE READING: 1 Peter 3:8

Compassion is one of the characteristics of Jesus Christ. Jesus wept at the loss of a loved one. He understood the desperate attempt of the woman with the issue of blood who was determined to touch His garment. He lovingly faced Peter after he denied Him three times. Most of all, He had compassion as He hung on the cross of Calvary dying for the sins of a world that hated Him.

Compassionate love is all of this and nothing less. You can't compromise it, and you can't water it down. Compassion runs from deep within the heart, and it stems from an unlimited love. Compassion means to feel sorry for someone. Jesus certainly felt sorry for us as He went to the cross. He had so much compassion for us that He took our place.

Today's Scripture says, "Finally, be ye all of one mind, having compassion one of another, love as brethren, be pitiful, be courteous." We must care about other people and the lives they are living. We must show them compassion by helping and praying for them. You can never do someone good by judging them. Let God do the judging, and let us show them compassion. It is time for us, as Christians, to have sympathy for and feel sorry for one another and for this lost and dying world.

Compassion can be demonstrated by the smallest of things. A simple prayer, a short phone call or a brief visit to someone can brighten their day. Perhaps you could send someone a card with words of encouragement or even a bouquet of flowers just to let them know you were thinking about them. Any simple gesture made out of a sincere love for the person you're dealing with is an act of compassionate love.

Have you shown compassion today?

"Compassion can be demonstrated by the smallest of things."

Love or Lust?

Scripture Reading: 1 John 4

The world shares its love in special ways, but sometimes I think the world paints more of a picture of lust than love.

We often base our love for others on the way they treat us. We "love" others as long as they buy us things and cater to our wishes. When things don't go as planned, we doubt our love for that other person. Chances are, what you felt for that person was lust, not love.

Today's Scripture text teaches us that true love is of God. If God doesn't live in us, then we can't know true love. If you can't love someone in both good times and bad, reconsider why you first loved this person. Was it love or lust? Fulfilling the lust of the flesh can be a great deception in our lives. This is why so many relationships are being torn apart. They are based on lust instead of love.

True love isn't based on pretty gifts, financial security, looks, fame or prosperity; it is an unconditional decision based on God. True love doesn't leave when the gifts aren't coming in or the bills get behind. It doesn't stop loving when feelings get hurt; it heals the hurt.

We've studied love for several days. Now examine every doubt of love you may have in your heart and make sure that your love is of God, not of this lustful flesh. Ask yourself these questions: Am I saved? Do I have God's love in me? Was God included in my relationships from the start? If your answer to any of these questions is no, then you must seek the Lord. Seek Him for salvation, and put Him first in your life. Let His love mend your relationships, and build your future relationships on the foundation of God's love.

> *"True love doesn't leave when the gifts aren't coming in or the bills get behind."*

God Still Cares

SCRIPTURE READING: Hebrews 13:5

Spiritual barriers can interfere with our ability to have an intimate relationship with the Lord. Spiritual barriers are thoughts and attitudes that slow down our spiritual development. Are you worried or afraid? Are you struggling financially, or battling a physical illness or some other insecurity? If you are facing any of these spiritual barriers, you need to go back to the promises of God's Word and renew your faith.

The Bible gives us promise after promise to stand on. These promises are so strong and unbelievable to our flesh that we can't even begin to comprehend the fullness of them. Still, in our trying times we find it difficult to trust in these promises. We allow our fears and anxieties to control our hearts and minds until we become engulfed with feelings of doubt about God's realness and His almighty power.

How do we overcome this dilemma, and where do we begin? The answer is found in today's Scripture text: "Let your conversation be without covetousness; and be content with such things as ye have: for he hath said, I will never leave thee, nor forsake thee." We must learn to sit still in the Lord. Even though our understanding is blurred, we can learn to rest in the Lord and wait upon Him. In that time of waiting and resting, God will bring to our remembrance the many times and situations when we were delivered by His power alone.

When you get to the point of defeat and you wonder if God really cares about you and the condition you're in, don't give up. God is still there, He knows about your situation, and He still cares.

"We must learn to sit still in the Lord."

A Way of Escape

SCRIPTURE READING: 1 Corinthians 10:13

As we learned yesterday, God still cares about our problems, but it's easy to fall into the trap of thinking He doesn't. We often become so stressed and doubtful that we begin to feel like we're in this world all alone and no one cares about the state we're in. Others quickly change the subject when we share our burdens, and we feel they're not concerned. This rejection pushes us into a cell of solitary confinement, and we dare anyone to open the door and free us from this wrenching condition. We become bitter and cold to the people and circumstances around us, eventually losing all hope that anyone cares or that things will ever get better.

The first step to victory is sitting still in the Lord and letting Him remind us of the many times He's delivered us before. Paul faced many conflicts and sufferings during his ministry; others sought to take his life because of the message he preached. God delivered Paul from would-be assassins, and God loves you and me just as much as He loved Paul. You see, God always provides a way of escape for His children.

God longs for us to depend on Him for all things and to trust Him to provide the impossible things. God's joy is being able to reveal Himself to us in trying situations. First Corinthians 10:13 says, "There hath no temptation taken you but such as is common to man: but God is faithful, who will not suffer you to be tempted above that ye are able; but will with the temptation also make a way to escape, that ye may be able to bear it." God cares enough about us to provide a way of escape; give Him the chance to provide that care.

"God longs for us to depend on Him for all things."

Casting Your Cares

Scripture Reading: 1 Peter 5:6–7

God longs to provide us with things which seem impossible. Matthew 6:26 says, "Behold the fowls of the air: for they sow not, neither do they reap, nor gather into barns; yet your heavenly Father feedeth them. Are ye not much better than they?" If God so cares for those things which neither sow nor reap for Him, how much more does He care for those who serve Him? We must never lose hope in Christ. When hope is lost, defeat is in control of every area of our lives.

To have hope is to have faith. When we lose our faith, we close the door for God to show us He still cares. Hebrews 11:1 says, "Now faith is the substance of things hoped for, the evidence of things not seen." Sometimes it's hard to completely trust in someone we've never seen with the eye, but we have the Spirit of God within us to reveal to us the things our flesh can't comprehend. If we'll rely on the power of the Holy Spirit within, our hope and faith can be renewed and strengthened in life's trying times.

God's care for us neither started nor stopped at Calvary. God has always cared for His people, and He always will. He started caring for Adam and Eve, and He hasn't stopped caring yet. The cross was the way for everlasting care for each of us. God still cares, and He's still working in your life. He is never too busy to care about you. Today's Scripture text reminds us of this fact. "Humble yourselves therefore under the mighty hand of God, that he may exalt you in due time: Casting all your care upon him; for he careth for you."

"God has always cared for His people, and He always will."

A NEW DESIRE

Our Source of Strength

SCRIPTURE READING: Romans 4:20–21

Abraham, an old testament prophet, had faith so strong he was found righteous in the eyes of God before God ever made provision for man's righteousness. Abraham's faith was so strong that he was willing to offer up his only son, Isaac, as a sacrifice to God. Today's Scripture text says, "He staggered not at the promise of God through unbelief; but was strong in faith, giving glory to God; And being fully persuaded that, what he had promised, he was able also to perform."

Our source of strength depends on the amount of faith we have in God. Our faith in God calms our fears, gives us peace in troubled times and reassures us of the promises of God's Word. Believing in God is our only hope of a victorious Christian life. Without faith it is impossible to please God. Prayers are answered by faith. The Word of God is understandable only by faith in God and the leadership of the Holy Spirit in your life.

Exercising our faith is the key to releasing its strength and power in our lives. Abraham exercised his faith through action, by offering up his son as a sacrifice. When we, without hesitation, act on our faith we grow in spirit and in truth, and we allow others to see the power of God at work in our lives. When we choose to exercise our faith we reflect godliness, and our source of strength becomes excitingly real inwardly and outwardly. We, in return, spread our joy, peace and happiness in such a way that others know it could only come from God.

Let's follow in the footsteps of Abraham. Let us love the Lord so much that the power we have through faith in Him will become our source of strength, and we can demonstrate His power to a lost and dying world.

"Our source of strength depends
on the amount of faith we have in God."

You Are What You Want to Be

SCRIPTURE READING: Galatians 4:9

Bgut now, after that ye have known God, or rather are known of God, how turn ye again to the weak and beggarly elements, whereunto ye desire again to be in bondage? (Galatians 4:9)" As born again believers, we are sons of God through our adoption in Jesus Christ. We have the Spirit of God's Son within us. We have as much access to God and His power as we want.

There is no limit to what we can do or be for the Lord according to His will for our lives. Don't limit God and His power. We accept salvation freely, but we don't want to serve God wholeheartedly. We even try to tell the Lord what we can and can't do for Him according to our own lifestyles. We limit God's power in our lives this way. Rather than letting God lead us into service for Him, we tell Him what we're comfortable doing.

A great example of limiting our service for the Lord is found in Mark 10:17–22. This is the story of the rich young ruler who wanted eternal life until he found out what he had to do to get it. The rich young ruler didn't understand that he hadn't been asked to give up all he had. He was told to give it to the poor so he would have treasures in heaven. He couldn't understand that giving up the temporal things of the world would give him eternal things that hold so much more value. His choice sent Him away grieved.

We are much like the rich young ruler. We want the benefits of Christianity, but we don't want to sacrifice for them. We don't want to labor or repent. We get so caught up and comfortable with the things of this world that we don't want to give them up.

Remember, we are what we want to be!

"There is no limit to what we can do or be for the Lord."

A NEW DESIRE

No Excuses

SCRIPTURE READING: Romans 8:35–36

Often we come up with excuses for our failure to be all that God wants us to be. "You don't understand what is going on in my life right now." It may be true that others can't understand your situation, but God's Word says in today's text, "Who shall separate us from the love of Christ? shall tribulation, or distress, or persecution, or famine, or nakedness, or peril, or sword? As it is written, For thy sake we are killed all the day long; we are accounted as sheep for the slaughter." This should be a consolation to you, regardless of your circumstances.

Today's text teaches that we should never allow anything to keep us from being all that God wants us to be. Perhaps you're having financial problems, and you're ashamed to go to church to pray and worship because of this. God has not stopped loving you; He is still there. Maybe you're having marital problems that you're afraid will end in divorce, so you feel you shouldn't serve God publicly due to your situation. Friend, these excuses are not accepted by God. Regardless of your circumstances, God loves you and He longs for you to serve Him in spite of the situation.

Your problem is no excuse for your failure to be all that God wants you to be. Instead, your excuses simply become sin. Your situations can't separate you from the love of God. Rather, such tribulations and distresses should provoke us to total dependence upon God. He is the only one who can deliver us from these circumstances. Romans 8:37 says, "Nay, in all these things we are more than conquerors through him that loved us." Don't defeat yourself in your life for Christ; give Him control and conquer your circumstances.

"We should never allow anything to keep us from being all that God wants us to be."

MARCH   ~ 75

Overcoming Bondage and Deception

SCRIPTURE READING: Galatians 6:7–8

What do you do when hard times come your way? Many times we fail to see that God has allowed our circumstances for a reason. We become so angry and rebellious in our circumstances that we miss the benefits of our suffering. Paul tells us in Romans 8:37 that victory is ours if we will only claim it: "Nay, in all these things we are more than conquerors through him that loved us." If we fail to seek God in our circumstances, we reject victory. When we reject victory, we choose to be in bondage. We feel unworthy of God's love and deliverance. Satan takes advantage of these feelings to deceive us into sin. He tempts us with the pretty and pleasurable things of the world in which we can bury our pain. Falsely believing that these things have alleviated our pain or changed our circumstances, we start slipping out into the world again. We try to justify our habits and desires by claiming that God sent them as a way of deliverance. Our Scripture text for today reminds us that there are consequences for our actions: "Be not deceived; God is not mocked: for whatsoever a man soweth, that shall he also reap. For he that soweth to his flesh shall of the flesh reap corruption; but he that soweth to the Spirit shall of the Spirit reap life everlasting."

You will reap what you have sown if you allow yourself to fall into this deception. How can you overcome deception and bondage? Simply pray to God, "Father, I quit. I can't come out of these circumstances. They have destroyed me spiritually. Lord, I can't do it; please do it for me."

> *"If we fail to seek God in our circumstances,*
> *we reject victory."*

A NEW DESIRE

Recognizing Deliverance

SCRIPTURE READING: Matthew 12:33

Overcoming deception and bondage requires complete dependence upon God. How do we recognize deliverance when it comes? How can we be sure we are depending completely upon God? Our Scripture text for today says, "Either make the tree good, and his fruit good; or else make the tree corrupt, and his fruit corrupt: for the tree is known by his fruit." We can recognize true deliverance by evaluating the activities of our Christian lives.

Do you read and study God's Word on a regular basis? Do you sacrifice for Christ's sake? Are you easily distracted from Christian activities? Do you pray regularly? Do you publicly proclaim Christ as your Savior? Are you disciplined for spiritual maturity in any way? Are you easily influenced by the opinions of others and easily persuaded to do worldly things for pleasure?

The Bible teaches us that God's mercy endures forever. It says that we love Him because He first loved us. The Bible teaches us that if we confess our sins, He is faithful and just to forgive our sins. The Bible teaches us that Jesus died for all the sins of the world, including mine and yours. The Bible also teaches us that there is no power but that of God. Scripture after Scripture reminds us that we, as children of God, are more than conquerors.

God wants to help you through your hard times, but you must want His help. Let God help you, because He is your only hope. We can't do it without Him, but Paul reminds us that we can do all things through Him. Are your fruits showing dependence upon God?

"God wants to help you
through your hard times."

Perfected Forever

SCRIPTURE READING: Hebrews 10:14

Our Scripture text for today says, "For by one offering he hath perfected for ever them that are sanctified." It is hard to comprehend this infallible truth. We know that this flesh will never be perfect, so what is Paul trying to tell us in this verse?

Perfect, in the original Greek language, means to mature or to be complete. In our Scripture text, perfection is spoken of in a spiritual sense. It refers to our relationship with Christ. In order to understand what it means for us to be perfected, we must first understand what the word "sanctified" means. Sanctification is a twofold experience in salvation.

First, sanctification is the work of Christ that makes us worthy to be saved. His blood cleanses us from all unrighteousness. This part of our sanctification is permanent and instant. The second part of our sanctification is also permanent, but it is progressive rather than instant. This part of our sanctification means to be set aside for the work of Christ. We will never be fully perfected in this flesh, but we should be growing in spiritual maturity daily. Our perfection will be completed in Heaven where we can give only the Lord honor and glory for it.

Finally, notice that our Scripture text says that we are perfected forever. We are eternally perfect in Christ. In other words, the part of us that has been born again is already perfected by the indwelling of Christ Jesus. First John 3:9 says, "Whosoever is born of God doth not commit sin; for his seed remaineth in him: and he cannot sin, because he is born of God."

Thank God today that He is alive and working in your life, perfecting you for His service.

"We will never be fully perfected in this flesh, but we should be growing in spiritual maturity daily."

A NEW DESIRE

Growing in Perfection

SCRIPTURE READING: 2 Timothy 4:8

As Christians, we should seek to grow in the Lord by humbling ourselves before Him and seeking His will for our lives. It then becomes our responsibility to be obedient to His will. Obedience is the seed to growing in holiness and perfection. Exercising obedience allows us to grow in faith and righteousness.

Obedience, faith and righteousness are the three main ingredients for spiritual maturity. As we grow in these three areas, we are made aware of our sins, hindrances and weaknesses. Repenting of these as we recognize them is the foundation for growth in Christ Jesus. Refusal to turn from these faults and hindrances will stunt our spiritual growth and drain us of spiritual effectiveness.

Spiritual growth is a lifelong process. We grow daily as we pray, study, seek and submit to God's will for our lives. We must pray for the Lord to reveal those things that prevent us from giving our all to Him. As we do this we become wiser in the Word, and we experience new heights of our Christianity. The more we experience the power and presence of God in our lives, the closer we grow to Him. The joy of it all is to look back to where we first started and realize how much the Lord has taught us while we were being planted and watered by the truths of His Word and the leadership of His Spirit.

Our Scripture text for today reminds us of the joys of growing in the Lord. It says, "Henceforth there is laid up for me a crown of righteousness, which the Lord, the righteous judge, shall give me at that day: and not to me only, but unto all them also that love his appearing."

Let's start experiencing this joy today by being obedient to God.

"Obedience is the seed to growing in holiness and perfection."

From Buds to Blossoms

SCRIPTURE READING: Isaiah 55:10–11

For the next several days, we are going to learn about the process of growing in the Lord. Our Scripture text for this entire study will be the same. Isaiah 55:10–11 says, "For as the rain cometh down, and the snow from heaven, and returneth not thither, but watereth the earth, and maketh it bring forth and bud, that it may give seed to the sower, and bread to the eater: So shall my word be that goeth forth out of my mouth: it shall not return unto me void, but it shall accomplish that which I please, and it shall prosper in the thing whereto I sent it."

Our Scripture text for this study explicitly defines the Word of God as the seed that gives increase in our lives. It is the food that strengthens and prepares us for growth. It comforts us in troubled times, and it will neither lie nor let us down. We must trust the Word of God for all the answers to our problems.

As children of God, we have a responsibility to fulfill. We must run the race for maturity in Christ. We should strive to grow in the knowledge and wisdom of God. We should want to know more about Him every day. We should strive to be witnesses for the sake of the Gospel.

In order to fulfill our responsibilities, we must first realize (after being born again) that Christ is the sower of the seed, and our hearts are the fields where the seeds are sown. Our self-will is the soil that allows the seed planted by Christ to produce fruit. Self-will is the key factor in Christian growth. Once we have received Christ, our maturity is based on our self-will.

What is your self-will? Do you desire to grow in Christ, or are you complacent in your walk with God?

"We should strive to grow in the knowledge and wisdom of God."

A NEW DESIRE

Fertile Soil

Scripture Reading: Mark 4:8

Our self-will, as we learned yesterday, is the soil in which our Christian fruit grows. Mark 4:1–20 is the parable of the sower. In this parable Jesus gives us several examples of Christian maturity. Today's text verse gives us the definition of a broken self-will that has been made fertile soil. "And other fell on good ground, and did yield fruit that sprang up and increased; and brought forth, some thirty, and some sixty, and some an hundred." Our theme unfolds right here. This Scripture reminds us that we can grow from "buds to blossoms."

We became buds when we accepted Christ as our Savior. The opening or unfolding of that bud into a blossom is left up to us. Today's Scripture text reminds us that, according to our desire, we can produce thirty, sixty or even a hundred fold. It is all based on our willingness to know and live for Jesus Christ. To blossom into full bloom, we must have full dependence on God.

Many of us are already blooming and producing thirty or sixty fold because we have been obedient in the Spirit's leadership in studying God's Word. However, we must never stop striving for the complete unfolding of that bud. We may never achieve a hundred fold, but we should always strive for it. The continuous releasing and submission of ourselves to Him matures us spiritually and opens us up to see God's presence and power at work in our lives.

Over the next few days, we will examine ourselves to see where we are on our journey from buds to blossoms. As we go through this examination, determine in your heart to become a full blossom who reveals the beauty of Christ to all who behold you.

"Determine in your heart to become a full blossom who reveals the beauty of Christ to all who behold you."

Bud or Blossom, Step One

SCRIPTURE READING: Isaiah 55:10–11

Today's questions all focus on our relationship with the Lord. As you examine yourself, be honest about your answers. If you find that the honest answer is not the one you would have hoped for, don't grow discouraged. God knows what you need and when you need it. Wait patiently on Him as you grow from a bud to a blossom.

Do you realize that had it not been for Christ you would already be dead because He is the breath of your life? John 3:36 says, "He that believeth on the Son hath everlasting life: and he that believeth not the Son shall not see life; but the wrath of God abideth on him."

Have you realized that God desires a personal, intimate relationship with you? John 10:14–16 says, "I am the good shepherd, and know my sheep, and am known of mine. As the Father knoweth me, even so know I the Father: and I lay down my life for the sheep. And other sheep I have, which are not of this fold: them also I must bring, and they shall hear my voice; and there shall be one fold, and one shepherd." See also John 10:26–30, and John 15.

Do you totally depend on God for all things? Second Corinthians 1:8–10 says, "For we would not, brethren, have you ignorant of our trouble which came to us in Asia, that we were pressed out of measure, above strength, insomuch that we despaired even of life: But we had the sentence of death in ourselves, that we should not trust in ourselves, but in God which raiseth the dead: Who delivered us from so great a death, and doth deliver: in whom we trust that he will yet deliver us." See also John 15:5.

> "God knows what you need and when you need it."

Bud or Blossom, Step Two

SCRIPTURE READING: Isaiah 55:10–11

Our focus today continues to be on our relationship with the Lord. Remember, answer these questions honestly, and then seek the Lord to help you change in areas where you feel you need growth.

Have you realized that your only purpose for being alive is to live for Jesus Christ? First Peter 2:9 says, "But ye are a chosen generation, a royal priesthood, an holy nation, a peculiar people; that ye should show forth the praises of him who hath called you out of darkness into his marvellous light." See also: Colossians 1:15–19, James 4:14–17, and 2 Corinthians 5:14–20.

Is serving God a privilege or a burden for you? Galatians 6:9–10 say, "And let us not be weary in well doing: for in due season we shall reap, if we faint not. As we have therefore opportunity, let us do good unto all men, especially unto them who are of the household of faith." See also 1 Corinthians 9:16–19.

Do you hunger to worship and praise God more often? John 4:24 says, "God is a Spirit: and they that worship him must worship him in spirit and in truth." See also Hebrews 13:15.

Do you get excited about sharing the Lord and what He is doing in your life with others? First Corinthians 1:18 says, "For the preaching of the cross is to them that perish foolishness; but unto us which are saved it is the power of God." See also Hebrews 6:10.

Hopefully, your answers have been mostly positive so far. If not, don't be discouraged. God wants to reveal your weaknesses so you can grow in those areas.

"Your only purpose for being alive
is to live for Jesus Christ."

Bud or Blossom, Step Three

SCRIPTURE READING: Isaiah 55:10–11

Today's examination will focus on the obstacles we face in our Christian walk and how we use God's Word to overcome.

Do you search to find the sins in your life? Isaiah 59:2 says, "But your iniquities have separated between you and your God, and your sins have hid his face from you, that he will not hear." See also 1 John 1:8–10 and Numbers 32:23.

Are you willing, once you've identified sin in your life, to turn from sin and turn to God (repent)? Acts 3:19 says, "Repent ye therefore, and be converted, that your sins may be blotted out, when the times of refreshing shall come from the presence of the Lord."

Do you go to the Word of God to find the answers to your problems? Second Timothy 3:16 says, "All Scripture is given by inspiration of God, and is profitable for doctrine, for reproof, for correction, for instruction in righteousness."

Have you realized that you need help in understanding and learning the Word of God? Luke 24:44–45 says, "And he (Jesus) said unto them, These are the words which I spake unto you, while I was yet with you, that all things must be fulfilled, which were written in the law of Moses, and in the prophets, and in the psalms, concerning me. Then opened he their understanding, that they might understand the Scriptures."

Let God show you a reflection of yourself in His Word, then seek His power to turn you from the works of the flesh.

"Let God show you a reflection of yourself in His Word."

Bud or Blossom, Step Four

SCRIPTURE READING: Isaiah 55:10–11

Today's focus is on growing strong through trials and temptations. Do you rejoice in the Lord when your battles overtake you? Second Corinthians 12:9–10 says, "And he said unto me, My grace is sufficient for thee: for my strength is made perfect in weakness. Most gladly therefore will I rather glory in my infirmities, that the power of Christ may rest upon me. Therefore I take pleasure in infirmities, in reproaches, in necessities, in persecutions, in distresses for Christ's sake: for when I am weak, then am I strong." See also Romans 5:1–4.

Do you realize that trials and temptations are an opportunity for growth? James 1:12 says, "Blessed is the man that endureth temptation: for when he is tried, he shall receive the crown of life, which the Lord hath promised to them that love him." See also Romans 8:28 and 1 Peter 1:7.

Do you believe that everything in your life is in God's control? Hebrews 12:1–2 says, "Wherefore seeing we also are compassed about with so great a cloud of witnesses, let us lay aside every weight, and the sin which doth so easily beset us, and let us run with patience the race that is set before us, Looking unto Jesus the author and finisher of our faith; who for the joy that was set before him endured the cross, despising the shame, and is set down at the right hand of the throne of God."

Do you feel you are growing stronger in faith? Romans 10:17 says, "So then faith cometh by hearing, and hearing by the word of God." See also Colossians 1:21–23; 2:6–7.

"Rejoice in the Lord when your battles overtake you."

Bud or Blossom, Step Five

SCRIPTURE READING: Isaiah 55:10–11

Today's focus is your desire for God. Do you desire to spend time with God, or are you just going through the motions?

Are you aware of God's increasing presence and power in your life? Romans 12:2 says, "And be not conformed to this world: but be ye transformed by the renewing of your mind, that ye may prove what is that good, and acceptable, and perfect, will of God." See also Romans 13:1 and Philippians 4:19.

Do you have a greater desire to pray and obey God? Matthew 6:33 says, "But seek ye first the kingdom of God, and his righteousness; and all these things shall be added unto you." See also James 1:22–25 and Philippians 4:7–9.

Do you find yourself being zealous over the time you spend in studying God's Word? Second Timothy 2:15 says, "Study to show thyself approved unto God, a workman that needeth not to be ashamed, rightly dividing the word of truth." See also Hebrews 4:12.

Can you truthfully say that you prefer to spend time with God above all others? Exodus 20:5 says, "Thou shalt not bow down thyself to them, nor serve them: for I the LORD thy God am a jealous God, visiting the iniquity of the fathers upon the children unto the third and fourth generation of them that hate me." See also Matthew 6:33.

How have you done so far? Are you satisfied with where you are with the Lord, or have you found areas in your life where the soil is not so fertile?

"Are you satisfied with where you are
with the Lord?"

A NEW DESIRE

Sure Growth

SCRIPTURE READING: John 3:30

John the Baptist revealed the secret to sure growth in John 3:30: "He must increase, but I must decrease." Regardless of how small the bud or how large the blossom, we will eventually wilt away if we're not depending on God's power rather than our own. Self-will is infertile soil, and it can not sustain our spiritual growth.

Some buds never open at all. They stay tiny and then wilt away. Some buds only open half way, and their full beauty is never known. Other buds open to full bloom, and their strength and beauty are revealed to every eye that beholds them.

Which stage would you place yourself in based on your self-examination? If you answered positively to some or most of the questions, you are definitely blossoming. Regardless of where you found yourself on the spiritual growth chart, you must not become discouraged. Remember, spiritual growth is a lifelong process. You will not grow from bud to blossom overnight.

The self-examination you have gone through was designed to help you find the areas of strength and weakness in your Christian life. Positive answers reveal areas of strength, and negative areas indicate possible areas of weakness. Now that you know what your strengths and weaknesses are, you can seek the Lord's guidance in the areas where you feel you need to grow.

The two greatest things you should remember in this process of growing from buds to blossoms is: 1) wait patiently on the Lord, and 2) "He must increase, but I must decrease."

"Seek the Lord's guidance in the areas where you feel you need to grow."

Am I in God's Will?

SCRIPTURE READING: 1 John 3:22

How can we know whether or not we are in God's will? The key to finding the answer lies in today's Scripture text: "Keep his commandments, and do those things that are pleasing in his sight."

How can we know God's commandments and what is pleasing in His sight? Study the life of Christ. Seek to know His personality and the intentions of His actions while on this earth. Seek to comprehend His motives for everything He said and did. Each book of the Bible, from the old testament to the new, presents Christ's purposes and personality in some form. There is nothing about the life of Christ that we can't find out about if we will study the Word of God.

We must be like Jesus in order to keep God's commandments and do those things pleasing in His sight. We must seek Him and listen to His counsel. We must know what He requires of us and trust Him for guidance. God's Word is our only sure way of knowing if we're in God's will. The counsel of others, the fleeces we put out, and our gut feelings can deceive and mislead us, but the Word of God was given to guide our steps. The Bible encourages us to seek the counsel of others, but not over the Word of God.

God's Word lays down three requirements for being in God's will. First, you must be born again. Second, you must depend totally upon God. Anything that is not of faith does not please God (Romans 14:23). Finally, you must be willing to serve Him. We must be willing to live for Jesus if we are ever to know we are in His divine will. If you are fulfilling these three requirements, you are pleasing to the Father. Therefore, you are in His will.

> *"God's Word is our only sure way of knowing if we're in God's will."*

A NEW DESIRE

Keeping His Commandments

SCRIPTURE READING: Matthew 22:37–40

We learned yesterday that part of being in God's will is keeping His commandments. The commandments we are exhorted to keep are the commandments Jesus spoke of in our Scripture text: "Jesus said unto him, Thou shalt love the Lord thy God with all thy heart, and with all thy soul, and with all thy mind. This is the first and great commandment. And the second is like unto it, Thou shalt love thy neighbour as thyself. On these two commandments hang all the law and the prophets."

Many people tell us that being in God's will and keeping His commandments means obeying the ten commandments. Jesus disproved this theory in His words above. I'm not telling you to go out and break the Commandments. I'm just saying that Jesus came to fulfill the law for us, and when He hung on the cross all of the law and prophets hung with Him.

The principle for the Ten Commandments today is this: Christ came to redeem the law through His unconditional love for us. He bore the sins of the law for us. However, if we are born again and fulfilling this same love for Him, then we will automatically, out of righteousness, fulfill the keeping of the Ten Commandments. Our love for God, our desire to live righteously and our dependence upon the Holy Spirit will teach us to flee from adultery, fornication, murder, worshipping graven images, etc . . .

Remember, we learned yesterday that anything that is not of faith does not please God. If you're trying to keep the commandments by your own power, you will fail every time. Put God first, others second, and then yourself last. This is the key to keeping God's commandments and being in His will.

> *"Christ came to redeem the law through*
> *His unconditional love for us."*

God's Will in Christian Service

SCRIPTURE READING: 1 John 5:14

Can you be in Christian service outside of God's will? Keep in mind what we've learned for the last two days. Hebrews 11:6 says, "But without faith it is impossible to please Him." Satan seeks to devour those who are unsure about their service for the Lord. Often we take a job in the church just because someone asked, and we never seek the Lord for His direction. This can cause us to lose our peace and joy in service. How can we be sure that our service is in God's will?

Pray and seek God, then listen attentively for His voice. Activate your will to work according to His voice. Often, God's will requires sacrifice. Therefore, we must be sure we are rooted and grounded in God's Word. When our service calls for sacrifice, Satan will be on hand to remind us of what we're giving up. Be sure you are secure enough in God's Word that you are able to stand against the wiles of the devil.

If you are uncertain about God's will for your service, take some time to slow down and listen for His voice. Ask Him to reassure you about what you're doing and whether it is pleasing in His sight. If you still can't find peace, perhaps it's time to take greater measures. If necessary, seek God through fasting and prayer until you've positively heard from Him. Fasting may be a challenge for you, but sometimes we must lay aside this flesh for the cleansing of the soul.

Remember, our Scripture text for today assures us that God will reveal His will to us: "And this is the confidence that we have in him, that, if we ask any thing according to his will, he heareth us."

"Pray and seek God; listen attentively for His voice. God's will requires sacrifice."

A NEW DESIRE

Living for God

SCRIPTURE READING: Philippians 2:8

What does it mean to say that we are living for God? Is it defined by our moral beliefs or our religious activities? Living for God goes beyond our moral beliefs and patterns of tradition. Living for God pushes us to reflect sacrificing for the sake of Jesus Christ.

There are many ideas about true sacrifice, and until we can separate truth from opinion we will be deceived by traditional and opinionated thoughts. True sacrifice is plainly defined for us through the life of Jesus Christ. He was the ultimate sacrifice for all sin, and He was the ultimate demonstration of a life of sacrifice.

As the Son of God, Jesus left His heavenly abode with the Father, a place of pure delight, for a place of torment and rejection. He exchanged His royal position for that of a servant. As a man, Jesus was born of a poor, peasant woman from a city despised by men. John 1:46 reveals the distaste people had for those from Jesus' hometown, "And Nathanael said unto him, Can there any good thing come out of Nazareth?" Throughout His earthly life, Jesus resisted the lust of the eyes, the lust of the flesh and the pride of life to become the sinless and perfect One. Jesus could have had it all at just His command, but He chose to humble Himself. Our Scripture text for today says, "And being found in fashion as a man, he humbled himself, and became obedient unto death, even the death of the cross."

Living for God requires this type of sacrifice. We are always looking for something better or greater, wasting the time we could be spending with God in prayer and study. All of our labor is in vain if we are not sacrificing any of our time to truly live for the Lord. Don't just live; live for the Lord.

"All of our labor is in vain if we are not sacrificing any of our time to truly live for the Lord."

True Sacrifice

SCRIPTURE READING: Philippians 4:19

Yesterday we learned that living for the Lord requires sacrifice. Unfortunately, many of us don't know what true sacrifice is. Many of us are convinced that working every day is a sacrifice because we have to give up our own pleasures to provide for the needs of our families. What we fail to realize is that work is a responsibility God gave us as a result of Adam's sin. Therefore, with this truth in mind, we must not use work as an excuse not to live for God.

Compromise has put us in the position where we are forced to work so many hours. Satan has deceived us into believing that God wants us to have the finest things the world has to offer. I'm not saying that God doesn't want us to have nice things, but He doesn't want us to compromise a dedicated Christian life to get them.

Lot is a prime example of a godly man who compromised. He chose to dwell in a land of wicked sin in order to gain a worldly advantage. His compromise resulted in his own back-slidden condition, the moral destruction of his daughters and even the death of his wife. If Lot had chosen a land that was less suited for his livestock, yet not so wicked, God would have supplied his every need. We, too, can choose a lower worldly reputation for a life dedicated to Christ, and God will supply all of our needs. Philippians 4:19, our Scripture text for today, says, "But my God shall supply all your need according to his riches in glory by Christ Jesus."

Don't compromise your walk with God for the things of this world. Sacrifice those hours of overtime for hours of prayer and study, and watch God supply your needs according to His will for your life.

"Don't compromise your walk with God
for the things of this world."

A NEW DESIRE

Coming Out of Compromise

SCRIPTURE READING: 2 Corinthians 6:17

Compromising puts us in a state of sin. Through our compromises, we become workaholics, social fanatics and finally sinful people. We choose temporal things over things eternal. We choose anxiety over joy, and we usually end up spiritually defeated with no happiness in our lives at all.

We give up the greatest years of our lives trying to amass worldly treasures. Before we know it, we are too old and too tired to enjoy all the things we've worked so hard to gather. We find ourselves with everything the world has to offer, yet there is still a void in our lives. Depression sets in because we've realized that everything we've devoted our lives to now means nothing. When these symptoms arise, don't compromise your walk with God for the things of this world. Our Scripture text for today says, "Wherefore come out from among them, and be ye separate, saith the Lord."

God bids us to come to Him through our unhappiness and depression. Our worldly lusts have made us unclean, and God wants us to sacrifice all of our compromises to come to Him for cleansing, joy, peace and happiness. If we will separate ourselves, we can find contentment in knowing that we are sons and daughters of God. Second Corinthians 6:18 says, "And [I] will be a Father unto you, and ye shall be my sons and daughters, saith the Lord Almighty."

Sacrifice is a demonstration of our love for God. Those who truly love the Lord will eventually have to sacrifice their will for His will. We don't like the idea of going against our own wills, but following the Lord always means victory! Come out of compromise and claim the victory God has waiting for you today!

"Sacrifice is a demonstration of our love for God."

The Studied Christian

SCRIPTURE READING: Acts 17:11

Our Scripture text for today gives us the key to being a studied Christian. It says, "These were more noble than those in Thessalonica, in that they received the word with all readiness of mind, and searched the Scriptures daily, whether those things were so." The key to being a studied Christian is receiving the Word.

The people at Berea were responsive to Paul's teaching and preaching. They were open-minded enough to study along with Paul rather than simply rejecting him and his message. They sought the Scriptures daily to confirm the message Paul preached. They respected and trusted Paul's messages, but he exhorted them to search out his teachings so they could rely on God's Word for themselves and see how it related to their own lives.

We, too, should do the same. A studied Christian will go beyond the teaching and preaching of the Sunday school teacher and the pastor. The studied Christian will search the Scriptures on the subject taught or preached. It is important to understand that teachers and preachers do not have the final authority on the Scriptures. We must let what they say be the seeds which are watered by God's Word through our personal study time outside of the church.

We, as individuals, are responsible for how much we learn about God and the plan that He has for our lives. There are golden nuggets hidden in the pages of God's Word, and the only way to find them is through personal, in-depth study. Don't miss out on your blessings by taking someone else's word on what God has to say about your life. Today, challenge yourself to make and keep a daily, personal study time.

"The key to being a studied Christian is receiving the Word."

Take the Sword

SCRIPTURE READING: Ephesians 6:17

The benefits of personal Bible study are too great to be numbered. Studying is the only sure way to know the mind of Christ and His will for our lives. Studied Christians are not easily confused or unstable in their walk with God. They are ready to give an answer for their beliefs, and they are able to help those in need.

The studied Christian becomes very disciplined in her relationship with God and is willing to follow wherever He leads. Studied Christians are willing to sacrifice for the Gospel's sake. One of the most important things studied Christians know is how much God loves them, and they have come to love Him in return. A studied Christian knows how valuable she is to the Lord because she knows that God gave His only begotten Son to redeem us from our sins.

One of the greatest benefits of being a studied Christian is that in times of spiritual warfare, we are able to fight back. Today's Scripture text says, "And take the helmet of salvation, and the sword of the Spirit, which is the word of God." That sword of the Spirit is the same weapon Jesus used during His spiritual warfare with Satan. Each time Jesus was faced with a temptation He used the Word of God as His weapon in order to resist the temptation. Matthew 4:4 says, "But he answered and said, It is written, Man shall not live by bread alone, but by every word that proceedeth out of the mouth of God." Verse 7 says, "It is written again, Thou shalt not tempt the Lord thy God," and again in verse 10, "Get thee hence, Satan: for it is written, Thou shalt worship the Lord thy God, and him only shalt thou serve."

Take the Sword that Jesus took in spiritual warfare by studying God's Word.

*"Studying is the only sure way to know
the mind of Christ and His will for our lives."*

Accept Forgiveness

SCRIPTURE READING: John 3:16

A daughter came to her father one day to confess a fault. She approached him with fear and resentment, dreading the punishment she had imagined. As she confessed her wrong, she awaited his harsh reaction of uncontrolled anger and aggressive punishment. She felt shame, guilt and sorrow for what she had done, but she knew she deserved whatever she got in return. Quietness filled the room as she awaited his reaction. Slowly and patiently he responded, "My child, because you recognize your wrongs and have confessed them openly, I forgive you with love and understanding. I expect you to refrain from doing this again. Go, now, and let this be a lesson for you, and remember, you are forgiven, and you must forgive yourself."

She left the room bewildered and unsure of her father's reaction. She knew she deserved a greater punishment, yet her father hadn't even raised his voice. She thought, "I'll hear about this again when he gets mad about something else. He'll wait until then and throw it up in my face. I'll not get off this easy." Days, weeks, months and years went by, yet her father never mentioned her wrong doing. She waited to hear it from him every day, but she only heard it from herself.

The father, in love and compassion, had forgiven his daughter forever, but she refused to accept his forgiveness. She couldn't accept the fact that forgiveness could be that easy. Our heavenly Father bestows this same forgiveness upon us. John 3:16 says, "For God so loved the world, that he gave his only begotten Son, that whosoever believeth in him should not perish, but have everlasting life."

Stop holding your past over your head, and accept God's unconditional, free pardon.

"Stop holding your past over your head, and accept God's unconditional, free pardon."

A Disciplined Prayer Life, Step One

SCRIPTURE READING: Matthew 6:6

Today's Scripture text says, "But thou, when thou prayest, enter into thy closet, and when thou hast shut thy door, pray to thy Father which is in secret; and thy Father which seeth in secret shall reward thee openly." In this passage of Scripture, and in many more throughout the Bible, God teaches us the important principles for our prayer life. Prayer is essential in the life of every believer. Prayer must become the very breath of our lives, and we must discipline ourselves to pray everyday. A healthy prayer life always has great rewards; we are told this in the verse above. When we pray with discipline, God is able to speak to us about matters that we wouldn't think He cared about.

God is concerned about the most minute and even the material things in our lives. God always wants the best for His children, but until we get personal with Him, He is not going to be able to teach us this principle.

Prayer is given to us for many reasons, but the most important is to know God more intimately. God already knows all about us. Our prayer life is for us to learn about His will for our lives and for us to draw closer to Him.

A disciplined prayer life requires us to do several things. First, we are to "enter into thy closet." Your closet is anywhere that is a private place, away from all distractions. Our closet is a place where we can get alone with God. We must form very private prayer lives with the Lord. It is time we, as Christians, develop this type of intimacy with Christ. Find a place to call your closet and get personal with God today.

> ## "Prayer is given to us so we can know God more intimately."

A Disciplined Prayer Life, Step Two

SCRIPTURE READING: Matthew 6:6

Yesterday we learned to find a secret place of prayer. Today's Scripture text says ". . . When thou hast shut thy door. Pray to thy Father which is in secret . . ." A disciplined prayer life requires oneness with God. Giving Him our undivided attention produces a very personal relationship. When we get personal we get results from our prayers.

The second step to a disciplined prayer life is to apply our Scripture verse, "When thou hast shut thy door, pray to thy Father which is in secret." You must "shut the door." The door here refers to closing our minds from all other thoughts while opening our hearts to the presence of God.

When we shut the door of our minds, we allow God room to come in and saturate our hearts with His love and instructions. Many times when we pray, we pray from our minds instead of our hearts. This is why people's prayers are seldom effective; they pray with a mind full of vain and selfish requests.

God will never honor selfish, gain-seeking prayers. When we pray with an empty mind and an open heart, then we get results. God is able to transform our minds.

How long has it been since you have examined your prayer life? Start today praying with your door shut. Close your mind to your circumstances. Pray to the Father with an open heart. You will surely be blessed by His presence as well as His provision for you.

> *"A disciplined prayer life requires oneness with God."*

A NEW DESIRE

A Disciplined Prayer Life, Step Three

SCRIPTURE READING: Matthew 6:6

Today's Scripture text says, "Pray to thy Father which is in secret; and thy Father which seeth in secret shall reward thee openly." The final thing we need to do for obtaining a disciplined prayer life is to pray in secret. This means to be concealed. Our prayer lives are the most effective when we keep it between us and God. When we keep our prayer lives concealed then we are fully trusting God to provide. This does not mean we can't ask others to pray for us. Intercessory prayer is very important in our lives.

The concealed prayer life I am speaking of is praying without broadcasting it. A concealed prayer life is what makes you personal with the Father. When you see answers to prayers that only you and God know about, it automatically draws you closer to Him. You realize that He hears your plea and that He cares about all of your life and your needs.

Praying in secret develops an intimacy with God like nothing else can. You will recognize Him as your loving, caring Father. You will have confidence that He is hearing and seeing you pray secretly before Him. You will then understand today's Scripture verse. "Pray to thy Father which is in secret; and thy Father which seeth in secret shall reward thee openly."

Start today with a secret prayer life. Pray for God to show you the importance of prayer. Discipline yourself to praying daily.

"Praying in secret develops an intimacy with God."

Unworthiness, Burden or Blessing?

SCRIPTURE READING: 2 Corinthians 3:18

Unworthiness humbles us into seeing God's mercy. However, Satan also uses it to destroy our confidence in every area of life, including our walk with God.

If Satan can destroy our self-confidence through feelings of unworthiness, our self-esteem will eventually fade away. Over a period of time, depression becomes our best friend. Each morning as we see ourselves in the mirror, we see someone who is broken and in need. We struggle to find the problem and correct it. We cry within ourselves, we cry out to others, and we cry out to God for help. Our feelings of inadequacy blind us from the hope God freely offers.

Today's Scripture text says, "But we all, with open face beholding as in a glass the glory of the Lord, are changed into the same image from glory to glory, even as by the Spirit of the Lord." Our victory rests in the Lord. We, as children of God, are being changed into His image. Grasping this truth allows God to deliver us from the burden of unworthiness.

Examine the feelings of insecurity and unworthiness that you are struggling with. Determine where these thoughts and attitudes are coming from. I think you will find these to be your own fleshly thoughts and weaknesses which Satan has used against you to steal your joy, kill your spirit and destroy your walk with God. John 10:10 says, "The thief cometh not, but for to steal, and to kill, and to destroy: I am come that they might have life, and that they might have it more abundantly."

Our victory is knowing that we, although unworthy, have been given life abundantly through Jesus Christ. This is the blessing of unworthiness; don't let Satan make it a burden.

"Our victory is in knowing that we have been given life abundantly."

Face to Face

SCRIPTURE READING: Galatians 5: 24–25

Today we will expound on what we began yesterday: the person we see face to face in the mirror. We often see a broken person in need; we see failure when we see ourselves face to face. These eyes of flesh don't allow us to see beyond ourselves. Therefore, we see in the mirror a reflection of who we are in the flesh—rejected, failed, unconfident, and disappointed.

Our victory rests in the Spirit of the Lord. We receive His Spirit when we are born again, and His Spirit allows us to overcome all things. Learning to walk in the Spirit is the key to a healthy face to face encounter with ourselves. Today's Scripture text says, "And they that are Christ's have crucified the flesh with the affections and lusts. If we live in the Spirit, let us also walk in the Spirit." If we live and walk in the Spirit, then we will see what God sees in us each time we see ourselves face to face. We will see power, peace and eternal security. The fear will be conquered, the doubts must vanish and Satan must flee. James 4:7 says, "Submit yourselves therefore to God. Resist the devil, and he will flee from you."

We must exercise our victory in Jesus by remembering to look at ourselves through the eyes of God. When He sees us, He sees the life of His only begotten Son. He sees cleansing through His Son's blood. He sees us as His children through the new birth. He doesn't see what we see—the bad, the failures, the unworthiness.

In His eyes, you are everything. God doesn't see you in disappointment and shame, and you shouldn't see yourself that way either. When you see yourself face to face, look for the reflection of Jesus.

> *"We must exercise our victory in Jesus by remembering to look at ourselves through the eyes of God."*

The Principles of Suffering

SCRIPTURE READING: 1 Peter 2: 20–21

We expect correction when we know we have done something wrong. We are quick to admit our faults, and we are prepared to suffer the consequences. This is what today's Scripture text refers to as "taking it patiently." We know we deserve whatever we get for our wrongdoing. However, this principle of suffering often makes it hard to understand why we should suffer for our godliness or well-doing. We can't comprehend the fact that true Christianity requires suffering; it seems unfair to our flesh because we have always been taught that well-doing should bring praise and pats on the back. This principle of suffering is very misleading and deceiving.

Christian suffering is rarely seen today. We are willing to go so far for God, but the line is drawn where our service would require us to sacrifice or suffer. Why should living for God require suffering? Our Scripture text says, "For what glory is it, if, when ye be buffeted for your faults, ye shall take it patiently? but if, when ye do well, and suffer for it, ye take it patiently, this is acceptable with God. For even hereunto were ye called: because Christ also suffered for us, leaving us an example, that ye should follow his steps." First Peter 3:17–18 says, "For it is better, if the will of God be so, that ye suffer for well doing, than for evil doing. For Christ also hath once suffered for sins, the just for the unjust, that he might bring us to God, being put to death in the flesh, but quickened by the Spirit."

Jesus is the reason we should be willing to suffer for our well-doing and godliness. We must understand that God knows all about our sufferings and that He is in control. Your suffering is working toward your salvation just as Christ's suffering gave you access to salvation.

"Jesus is the reason we should be willing to suffer for well-doing."

A NEW DESIRE

Overcoming Persecution and Suffering

SCRIPTURE READING: Hebrews 4:12

T hink about the times you have suffered because of your good intentions. Think about the hurt and the thoughts that went through your mind. Think about the bitterness that welled up within you toward the one who caused your pain or hurt you. Didn't you want revenge? Didn't you want to take back all of the good things you had done?

In our attempts to deal with the pain, our flesh becomes weak. Satan uses this against us to divert our attention from God and His principle of suffering. Satan corrupts our minds with thoughts of being forsaken by a so-called loving and holy God. These thoughts are from the devil and the petty feelings of our flesh. God is holy and loving, and He has mercy in our times of bitterness and questioning.

Hebrews 4:12 says, "For the word of God is quick, and powerful, and sharper than any two-edged sword, piercing even to the dividing asunder of soul and spirit, and of the joints and marrow, and is a discerner of the thoughts and intents of the heart." God's Word is our weapon for fighting off the thoughts of the flesh and the doubts planted in our minds by Satan.

When Jesus was tempted in the wilderness, His weapon was the Word of God. God's Word is His voice in our lives. It will explain our sufferings and show us what lies ahead. It destroys Satan's powers and delivers us from all evil. God's Word teaches us the greatest principle of suffering. First Peter 4:14 says, "If ye be reproached for the name of Christ, happy are ye; for the spirit of glory and of God resteth upon you: on their part he is evil spoken of, but on your part he is glorified."

"God's Word is our weapon for fighting."

Glorifying God by Denying Self

SCRIPTURE READING: 1 Peter 4: 1–2

Our last thought yesterday was of glorifying God by suffering for godliness. The ability to glorify God through our suffering requires the ability to deny self. Our example of this principle is Christ in the Garden of Gethsemane.

When Jesus was in agony in the Garden the Bible says, "His sweat was as great drops of blood (Luke 22:44)." Such suffering has never come our way. Sure, we have suffered to the point of tears, stress, depression, and maybe even nervous breakdown. Some of us have even gone back out into the world because we couldn't stand under the pressure, but suffering to the point of sweating blood and hanging on a cross is beyond our comprehension.

Jesus was a man in the flesh. He was tempted, weak and tired, but He denied Himself to glorify God. He prayed, "Father, not my will, but thine be done." When Jesus cried out, "My God, My God, why hast thou forsaken me? (Matthew 27:46)," His suffering had gone deeper than the flesh; as He hung upon the cross with the sins of the world upon Him, the pain pierced His heart for He was without God's love and presence in His life.

Jesus suffered a pain and rejection we will never have to know. He was forsaken by God so that we never would be. The only way we can bring glory to God in our sufferings is to deny ourselves just as Jesus did. Today's Scripture text says, "Forasmuch then as Christ hath suffered for us in the flesh, arm yourselves likewise with the same mind: for he that hath suffered in the flesh hath ceased from sin; That he no longer should live the rest of his time in the flesh to the lusts of men, but to the will of God."

> *"The ability to glorify God through our suffering requires the ability to deny self."*

Thank God for Your Sufferings

SCRIPTURE READING: 1 Peter 4:16

Yet if any man suffer as a Christian, let him not be ashamed; but let him glorify God on this behalf." How can we apply the words of our Scripture text and glorify God for our sufferings when they're so hard to endure? Acts 5:40–41 gives us a good example: "And to him they agreed: and when they had called the apostles, and beaten them, they commanded that they should not speak in the name of Jesus, and let them go. And they departed from the presence of the council, rejoicing that they were counted worthy to suffer shame for his name." A few days ago we discussed our feelings of unworthiness, but we see today that we are worthy if we are chosen to suffer for His name.

It's hard to thank God for our sufferings, but we must remember that God sees all of our sufferings, and our reward is in Heaven. Romans 8:18 says, "For I reckon that the sufferings of this present time are not worthy to be compared with the glory which shall be revealed in us." The benefits of suffering make it all worthwhile. Suffering puts us in close fellowship with our Lord and Savior Jesus Christ. We learn to walk in the Spirit rather than in the flesh. We increase in faith, knowledge and wisdom. Our hope in Christ gives us the strength to cross the next bridge.

Do you love God enough to suffer for Him? Are you truly being a light to others in your suffering? Suffering for Christ may require you to endure many things, "But the God of all grace, who hath called us unto his eternal glory by Christ Jesus, after that ye have suffered a while, make you perfect, stablish, strengthen, settle you (1 Peter 5:10)." Find your comfort in these words, and thank God for your sufferings.

> *"Suffering puts us in close fellowship with our Lord and Savior Jesus Christ."*

Emotional Control

SCRIPTURE READING: Hebrews 4:15

We live most of our lives based on feelings and emotions. We weep, we smile, we shout, and we clap. Sometimes we get angry, and we may even curse or get violent. We mourn, we get depressed, and then sometimes we feel nothing at all. Every thought we have forces one of these characteristics to surface.

Our emotions express our thoughts and beliefs on every circumstance we are confronted with. When something good happens, we react with excitement. We can't wait to tell others about what has happened. On the other hand, when something bad happens, we react with anger, fear or disappointment. These feelings surface when things aren't going the way we think they should. Eventually they take control of our thoughts and actions if we don't get a hold on them.

Eventually our negative emotions, if uncontrolled, will transform from feelings into a condition. We become very cold, troubled and hurt. Feeling that it would be better to deal with this on our own rather than allowing others to find out what kind of state we're in leads to pride. Emotions are feelings, but pride is a condition. Emotions must be controlled; pride must be broken. We build a wall of pride only God can break down. If you allow your emotions to transform into a condition, they become beyond your control.

Jesus knows how you feel in every circumstance you face. Our Scripture text says, "For we have not an high priest which cannot be touched with the feeling of our infirmities; but was in all points tempted like as we are, yet without sin." For the next few days, let's see how Jesus controlled his emotions and used them for the glory of God under different circumstances.

"Jesus knows how you feel in every circumstance you face."

A NEW DESIRE

Moved with Compassion

SCRIPTURE READING: Matthew 9:36

Emotions lead to actions whether the emotion is controlled or uncontrolled. Our Scripture text for today reveals Jesus' reaction to His emotions. "But when he saw the multitudes, he was moved with compassion on them, because they fainted, and were scattered abroad, as sheep having no shepherd."

The key emotion in this example is compassion. Compassion means "to have sympathy for or to pity." Jesus yearned to be the Shepherd of this flock. He expressed His emotions in this situation through His actions and words of instruction. The text goes on to say, "Then saith he unto his disciples, The harvest truly is plenteous, but the labourers are few; Pray ye therefore the Lord of the harvest, that he will send forth labourers into his harvest."

Jesus' feelings of compassion put Him in a condition of service and prayer. There is no greater condition to be in than that of unhindered fellowship with our Lord. Service and prayer are the two greatest assets in a personal relationship with God. These were the actions caused by Jesus' feelings of compassion.

As we walk through the emotions of Christ, let's examine ourselves to see how our emotions affect us. How would you have reacted seeing this crowd of people going astray? Would you have had compassion that led to service like Jesus did, or would you have been overwhelmed by the size of the work ahead of you and despondent about your abilities to carry it through?

Remember, your emotional reaction to circumstances reveals your thoughts and beliefs about the situation you face. Would your reaction have reflected trust in God or defeat in the flesh?

"There is no greater condition to be in than that of unhindered fellowship with our Lord."

Too Big to Cry?

SCRIPTURE READING: John 11:35

How often do we forbid ourselves to cry? Our tears are shed for many reasons, and each reason reflects an emotion. We shed tears of sorrow, joy, anger and pain. Tears are a way of dealing with our thoughts and feelings. Psalm 56:8 says, "Thou tellest my wanderings: put thou my tears into thy bottle: are they not in thy book?" Our tears are precious to God because they represent a humble and broken condition.

Jesus knew tears were created and given to us by God. Our Scripture text for today simply says, "Jesus wept." Tears shed by Jesus in front of all the people at Lazarus' graveside reveal that even Jesus, the human, felt and suffered the loss of loved ones. His emotions revealed His sorrow and love for Lazarus. Verse 36 reveals to us how others interpreted Jesus' tears: "Behold, how he loved him."

Jesus didn't intend to hide his tears or the pain that He felt at the loss of His dearly loved friend. He used this for an example of true love for all those who are too prideful to cry in situations such as this. We must remember that Jesus was a man in the flesh just as we are. He cried, He sorrowed, and He hurt just like you and I do. He wasn't prideful to the point that He didn't want anyone to see a grown man cry. Jesus knew that tears reveal the sincerity of our hearts and that "they who sow in tears shall reap in joy (Psalm 126:5)."

Are you too big to cry? Jesus wasn't. Jesus didn't give in to the theory that grown men don't cry. He didn't try to hide His hurt or deal with it on His own. What action did Jesus' emotions lead to in this situation? Jesus' tears revealed His love and sincerity. Are you too proud to reveal love and sincerity through your tears?

"Our tears are precious to God because they represent a humble and broken condition."

Righteous Indignation

SCRIPTURE READING: John 2:13–16

Jesus' anger is revealed today's Scripture text. Verse 15 says, "And when he had made a scourge of small cords, he drove them all out of the temple, and the sheep, and the oxen; and poured out the changers' money, and overthrew the tables."

The people in the temple were making a mockery of God's place of worship. Jesus found their dishonesty and greed disgusting. Passover was a time for presenting a sacrifice for sins and worshipping God, but it had been turned into an opportunity to open a marketplace. Jesus' anger at such behavior led to righteous indignation.

Should we allow our anger to go uncontrolled? Jesus' angry actions were in response to the people's disrespect for God. We, on the other hand, get angry and violent over trivial things. Uncontrolled rage and righteous anger must be separated. It is okay to be angry about sin and evil, but we must be careful not to lose control and overstep the laws of our government and the authority of God.

Our anger should be dealt with and controlled in a Christian manner, respecting God's authority. Ephesians 4:26 says, "Be ye angry, and sin not: let not the sun go down upon your wrath." Anger does not become sin unless we refuse to deal with it. If we wallow in our anger, we begin to plot revenge and take the matter in our own hands. We deal with our anger righteously by confessing it to God and allowing Him to deal with the situation. Romans 12:19 says, "Dearly beloved, avenge not yourselves, but rather give place unto wrath: for it is written, Vengeance is mine; I will repay, saith the Lord." Let God deal with your anger instead of allowing it to hinder your relationship with Him.

"Anger does not become sin unless we refuse to deal with it."

Trial or Temptation?

SCRIPTURE READING: 2 Timothy 2:15

Many times in warfare, we confuse trial and temptation as meaning the same things. We are often deceived by Satan into believing that our trials are punishment from God and that temptations are merely a part of our growth process. If Satan can convince us of this, he gets away clean and clear while we become angry with and rebel against God for allowing such unpleasant circumstances to come our way.

We must put forth the effort to know the difference between trials and temptations. We will never be able to stand against the wiles of the devil until we get into God's Word and search it with diligent prayer and complete attention. Ignorance of God's Word sets us up for Satan's deceptions. Our Scripture text for today says, "Study to show thyself approved unto God, a workman that needeth not to be ashamed, rightly dividing the word of truth." Studying is the only way to learn the difference between trials and temptations.

The Bible makes a clear distinction between trials and temptations and the source of each. Trials are put upon us by God to advance us into Christian maturity. Trials are overcome through our faith in and dependence upon God. Trials are sent our way to increase our faith, turn our attention toward God, reveal God's presence and power in our lives and show us our victory in Jesus. Temptations, on the other hand, are sent by Satan to entice our flesh and draw us away from God and into the world. They are overcome by relying on God. One of the greatest differences between trials and temptation is the outcome of each. Trials always leave us with benefits while temptations offer only consequences.

Are you facing trials or temptations?

*"We will never be able to stand against the wiles
of the devil until we get into God's Word."*

A NEW DESIRE

Escape Temptation

SCRIPTURE READING: 1 Corinthians 10:13

Giving in to temptations has consequences for both us and those around us. Eve gave in to Satan's temptations, and it has affected us even to this day. Exodus 34:7 says that the consequences of our sin will be visited upon our children to the third and fourth generations. It is important, therefore, that we escape temptation before we give in to it.

We see in Matthew 4:1 that temptation is not sin, for even Jesus was tempted, but He escaped temptation using the Word of God. God's Word is the greatest weapon we can use to escape the temptations that come our way. God's Word promises us that we can have victory over temptation. Today's Scripture text says, "There hath no temptation taken you but such as is common to man: but God is faithful, who will not suffer you to be tempted above that ye are able; but will with the temptation also make a way to escape, that ye may be able to bear it."

God is faithful. In the Greek, faithful means true or sure. The words "will not suffer" literally mean will not permit. God is sure not to permit you to be tempted above that ye are able. "Wherefore, my dearly beloved, flee from idolatry." Wherefore means "to this very account;" because God is being sure not to permit you to be tempted without giving in to it, you have no excuse not to flee from it. We can't flee idolatry alone, but God in us can. Philippians 4:13 says, "I can do all things through Christ which strengtheneth me."

In temptations, let's remember James 1:12: "Blessed is the man that endureth temptation: for when he is tried, he shall receive the crown of life, which the Lord hath promised to them that love him."

"God's Word promises us that we can have victory over temptation."

How to Resist Temptation

SCRIPTURE READING: 2 Timothy 2:22

Temptation is Satan's invitation to a life of sin. As he entices us, we must be prepared to resist his invitation. To resist Satan's temptations, we must:

- Remember that temptation is not a sin. Even Jesus was tempted, yet He did not sin. Don't let Satan deceive you into believing that you have already sinned just because you have been tempted.
- Sincerely pray for God to make a way of escape. Everyone is tempted. Others have resisted it, and so can you. God will see you through.
- Run from temptation. Paul told Timothy in today's Scripture text: "Flee also youthful lusts: but follow righteousness, faith, charity, peace, with them that call on the Lord out of a pure heart." To run from temptation is to protect yourself from evil thoughts that eventually control your actions. If you find yourself giving in to a recurring temptation, take Paul's advice and run from it as fast as you can.
- Recognize and avoid the things and situations that tempt you. Be prepared to suffer the consequences if you subject yourself to temptation.
- Reject temptation by surrounding yourself with Christian friends who will help you overcome. Find yourself a spiritual mentor with whom you can share your temptations in confidence as you pray together for deliverance. Ecclesiastes 4:9–11 says, "Two are better than one; because they have a good reward for their labour. For if they fall, the one will lift up his fellow: but woe to him that is alone when he falleth; for he hath not another to help him up. Again, if two lie together, then they have heat: but how can one be warm alone?"

"Temptation is Satan's invitation to a life of sin."

Enduring Trials

SCRIPTURE READING: 1 Peter 4: 12–13

Endurance is the key to receiving the benefits of our trials. Today's Scripture text says, "Beloved, think it not strange concerning the fiery trial which is to try you, as though some strange thing happened unto you: But rejoice, inasmuch as ye are partakers of Christ's sufferings; that, when his glory shall be revealed, ye may be glad also with exceeding joy."

Trials are part of our Christian walk. Growth comes through trials. Paul and John speak strongly about their trials. Anytime they speak of these sufferings, they explain that it worked out for their growth and the glory of God.

Trials can truly become treasures if we will patiently endure them by trusting in God to see us through. Just like Paul and John, we must face trials for the good news of Jesus Christ. Second Timothy 2:9–10 says, "Wherein I suffer trouble, as an evil doer, even unto bonds; but the word of God is not bound. Therefore I endure all things for the elect's sakes, that they may also obtain the salvation which is in Christ Jesus with eternal glory." Anytime we are being a light to others and spreading the Gospel there will be hardships, but we are being molded into Christ-likeness through them.

Second Timothy 3:10–11 reveals the treasure of enduring trials. "But thou hast fully known my doctrine, manner of life, purpose, faith, longsuffering, charity, patience, Persecutions, afflictions, which came unto me at Antioch, at Iconium, at Lystra; what persecutions I endured: but out of them all the Lord delivered me." Through trials we experience the power and presence of God through His deliverance.

> *"Trials can truly become treasures*
> *if we will patiently endure them."*

Hoping or Hurting?

SCRIPTURE READING: Psalm 16:9

As Christian women, we often find ourselves feeling more burdened than blessed and feeling more hurt than hope. In our attempt to find the cause, we become more confused than content in our spiritual condition.

In our efforts to overcome the confusion we become very doubtful about our service, wondering if it's truly what the Lord would have us to do. Through our explorations, we find that there are positive and negative feelings within us that either give us hope or leave us hurting. More often than not, it leaves us hurting and results in a negative attitude about ourselves and our Christian life. Many of us may find that we experience feelings of both hope and hurt. Regardless of the state we find ourselves in, our only hope for progressing in Christ comes through trusting in Him.

Over the next few days, let's analyze our condition and learn what we must do to prevail. We will contrast a hoping woman with a hurting woman in five areas. Be honest with yourself as you go through these evaluations. You can only be transformed from hurting to hoping if you're willing to admit your hurt.

A woman of hope is willing, obedient, meek, active and noble. A woman of hurt it weak, oppressed, miserable, absent and negligent. Which are you? Perhaps you're a little of both. Let's examine them in detail and see.

As you go through the examination, keep today's Scripture text in mind: "Therefore my heart is glad, and my glory rejoiceth: my flesh also shall rest in hope." If you're not a woman of hope now, let's identify the hurt and overcome it through Christ so that you can be.

> ### *"Our only hope for progressing in Christ comes through trusting in Him."*

Willing or Weak?

SCRIPTURE READING: Matthew 16: 24–25

Our Scripture text for today defines the willingness of a woman of hope. "Then said Jesus unto his disciples, If any man will come after me, let him deny himself, and take up his cross, and follow me. For whosoever will save his life shall lose it: and whosoever will lose his life for my sake shall find it."

A willing woman is a woman of hope. She is ready to serve Christ regardless of the sacrifice. She willingly works in the church. Without complaint she lays aside her needs for the needs of others. A woman of hope graciously shares Christ with others and studies God's Word with excitement. She is dependable whatever the need may be. She is an encourager, a prayer warrior and a witness to all. A willing woman serves Christ out of love for Him. She knows her risen Savior in an intimate way. She "presses toward the mark for the prize of the high calling of God in Christ Jesus (Philippians 3:14)." She is known most of all because she excels above the realm of an average Christian.

A weak woman, on the other hand, is often lazy in Christ. She judges others in order to justify herself. She can easily find an excuse not to serve, and she is hindered at home because she is preoccupied with her own needs. A weak woman quickly finds fault in others, complains often and has a hard time studying God's Word. She rarely prays and is not one to bear other's burdens. She only attends church when it is convenient for her. Her light shines dimly to other Christians and the lost. Her desires are of the world, and she easily turns back to them for pleasure.

Which woman do you identify more with, the willing or the weak?

"A woman of hope graciously shares Christ with others."

Obedient or Oppressed?

SCRIPTURE READING: 1 Peter 1: 13–14

Today's Scripture text defines an obedient woman for us. "Wherefore gird up the loins of your mind, be sober, and hope to the end for the grace that is to be brought unto you at the revelation of Jesus Christ; As obedient children, not fashioning yourselves according to the former lusts in your ignorance." Are you an obedient or oppressed woman? Check yourself against the characteristics of each below.

An obedient woman is anxious to hear the voice of God in everything she does. Her obedience allows her joy to be seen by others. She is happy and excited about the Lord, and she is always waiting to do what God bids. She is anxious to serve God in any way she can. She prays for the smallest of things, and her prayers get answered. She is a witness for the sake of Christ because she glorifies God even in the bad times. She is praised not only by God, but also by others because she seeks to please God rather than men (Acts 5:29).

An oppressed woman, on the other hand, is held down by depression because she does things by the power of her own will. She is easily deceived by Satan. The oppressed woman wants to work for God, but she fails in her attempts. She seldom finishes what she starts, and her oppression puts her in a backslidden condition.

It is important to note that oppression is not always the result of sin or failures. Isaiah 53:7 says that Jesus was oppressed and afflicted, but His oppression was for our sakes. If we should be oppressed, let it be for His sake rather than because of our hurt and doubt.

Are you finding yourself to be a woman of hope or hurt? Be honest with yourself. If you asked someone else to evaluate you, what would they find?

> "An obedient woman is anxious to hear
> the voice of God."

Meek or Miserable?

SCRIPTURE READING: Psalm 25:9

God seeks women of meekness. Today's Scripture text says, "The meek will he guide in judgment: and the meek will he teach his way." Are you the meek woman God is seeking, or are you a miserable woman?

A woman can only become meek by staying planted in the Word of God. A woman of meekness is willing to reach out to others in love. A meek woman portrays Christ-likeness because she has the heart and mind of Christ implanted within her. She is at peace with herself and God's will for her life. She can listen without judgment, and she loves without expecting to be loved in return. She forgives and forgets. She is a disciple, a burden bearer and an example of true Christianity. In Matthew 5:5, Jesus said that she was blessed: "Blessed are the meek: for they shall inherit the earth."

A miserable woman is described in Romans 3:11–18: "There is none that understandeth, there is none that seeketh after God. They are all gone out of the way, they are together become unprofitable; there is none that doeth good, no, not one. Their throat is an open sepulchre; with their tongues they have used deceit; the poison of asps is under their lips: Whose mouth is full of cursing and bitterness: Their feet are swift to shed blood: Destruction and misery are in their ways: And the way of peace have they not known: There is no fear of God before their eyes." A woman without hope is a woman of confusion, misleading others as a Christian. She is unstable in her ways, wanting to live for Christ while living in the world. She is never content, always searching for happiness in the wrong places. She has no hope for the rewards of her eternal life (1 Corinthians 15:19). Can you identify with her hurt?

"God seeks women of meekness."

Active or Absent?

SCRIPTURE READING: 2 Timothy 4:5

A woman of hope is active as defined in today's Scripture text: "But watch thou in all things, endure afflictions, do the work of an evangelist, make full proof of thy ministry." The hurting woman, on the other hand, is absent (Hebrews 10:25). Do you hold the characteristics of an active or an absent woman?

An active woman is a positive Christian, confident in the Lord's direction for her life. She has no doubt about her service; she is dependable in whatever the Lord leads her to do. She truly loves the Lord, and she makes the necessary sacrifices to do her job well. She faithfully attends church. She has a servant's heart.

The absent woman is quick to jump to the conclusion that others are judging her. She is automatically placed under conviction by her own conscience. She is in bondage to her own thoughts about not being in church regularly. This makes it easier and easier for her to excuse herself from the next service, and she can become a lazy Christian if not careful. The absent woman becomes a target for Satan's temptations because she is easily persuaded to do other things.

Some absent Christians actively attend church, yet they are not actively serving Christ. Attendance without activity doesn't make an active woman of Christ. Others who are not always in attendance are still active in service on another mission field. Paul said in 2 Corinthians 5:9, "Wherefore we labour, that, whether present or absent, we may be accepted of him."

Are you actively serving Christ or are you absent from service? A woman of hope is an active woman; a hurting woman is absent. Which are you?

"A woman of hope is an active woman."

Noble or Negligent?

SCRIPTURE READING: Luke 21:36

Nobility is defined in our Scripture text. "Watch ye therefore, and pray always, that ye may be accounted worthy to escape all these things that shall come to pass, and to stand before the Son of man." A noble woman is constant in watching and prayer that she may be found worthy. The negligent woman, on the other hand, neglects the gifts that God has given her for service (1 Timothy 4:12–14). Are you noble or negligent? Check yourself against the characteristics of each lady below.

The noble woman finds favor in God's eyes. She is respected by those around her because of her Christ-likeness; she is a pillar for the weak. She is full of knowledge and wisdom. Her moral standards for life are based on God's Word and applied steadfastly by the Spirit. She is unmoveable and abounds in the work of the Lord. She puts God first and is a leader in furthering the Gospel. She is content in whatever state she is in, and she fulfills the roles of both the Titus 2 lady and Ruth. Her presence radiates the peace of God.

The negligent woman has low self-esteem and little or no concern for her testimony or the example she sets as a child of God. She is not dependable in service because she only does things at her own convenience. She is not rooted in God's Word, nor does she try to be. She is jealous of the service of other Christians, and she is quick to intimidate them in order to free herself of guilt. The negligent woman forsakes God for the world and takes her Christianity lightly. She overlooks the dangers of her negligence. Hebrews 2:3 says, "How shall we escape, if we neglect so great salvation; which at the first began to be spoken by the Lord, and was confirmed unto us by them that heard him."

Are you noble or negligent?

"The noble woman finds favor in God's eyes."

Hope in Him

SCRIPTURE READING: Psalm 31:24

Over the past few days we have examined ourselves to find out if we are hoping or hurting. You may have discovered that you are experiencing some of the symptoms of both hoping and hurting. Hopefully you found yourself with more hope than hurt.

Did you find yourself identifying more with the willing woman or the weak woman? Are you obedient or oppressed? Are you meek or miserable? Are you active in service for the Lord, or are you absent in service to Him? Are you nobly serving the Lord each day, or are you neglecting God and the example you are setting of Christianity? Are you hoping, or are you hurting? If you found some hurt in your life, pinpoint the problem that is causing it. Confess it to God and allow Him to deliver you from the hurt into the hope that He promises to those who will obey Him.

We serve a God who created hope, love and understanding. We can freely go to Him at any time for rest, assurance and refreshment. When we feel pain, failure and despair, it is usually because we are not allowing God to control our problems. We are hoping in ourselves instead of hoping in Him.

Today's Scripture text shows the key to being delivered out of our hurt and into His hope. "Be of good courage, and he shall strengthen your heart, all ye that hope in the LORD." Whatever your hurt is, God cares. He will give you the strength to overcome if you'll only hope in Him.

> *"We serve a God who created hope, love, and understanding."*

Assumptions

SCRIPTURE READING: John 8:7

When the scribes and Pharisees brought the adulterous woman to Jesus in John 8, they assumed He would condemn and reject her. They truly hoped Jesus would assume the worst and act upon those assumptions, but Christ never assumed anything because He always knows the truth.

Jesus did not approach this woman with accusations. Instead, He used their assumptions about this woman to assure them that He knew all about her sin and theirs, too. Jesus said in today's Scripture text, "He that is without sin among you, let him first cast a stone at her."

Assumption is drawing conclusions without facts. We draw our conclusions based on only part of the story. We then act negatively upon our conclusions as if they were facts. We, like the scribes and Pharisees, take information and use it to our own advantage. We feel better about ourselves when we assume the worst about others.

God works on assurance rather than assumption. We, too, should seek the truth for assurance. We must not allow ourselves to become prey to the attitude of assumptions. We must seek the truth about those things we assume to be true. We must seek God for the truth of the matter before we hurt someone or end up being hurt ourselves by the assumptions we've made.

Whether you have positive or negative assumptions about a situation, you need to find out the true facts so that your assumptions will not mislead you. A sincere Christian will not act upon their assumptions, but will, like Christ, seek assurance in all things.

"Assumption is drawing conclusions without facts."

Underneath the Rubble

SCRIPTURE READING: 2 Corinthians 4:7

Our lives are controlled by feelings and emotions, especially negative ones. Depression, loneliness, weariness, sickness, financial strain, time restraints, boredom, worry, fear, doubt, confusion, rejection, marital problems and insecurities have us buried underneath the rubble of our lives. We pray for help, but we feel no relief. The rubble just grows deeper with anger, bitterness and despair. We feel hopeless and weary.

Friend, you are God's earthen vessel. Today's Scripture text says, "But we have this treasure in earthen vessels, that the excellency of the power may be of God, and not of us." You must realize that God made you to depend on His power, not your own. At your strongest moments, your power is powerless because it is not God's power. You will never see daylight shining through your rubble if you're trying to get out on your own. Our victory lies in the power of God alone. He is the crane that can remove the pieces of our rubble. His is the light that shines in your darkness, and He is the hope that breaks your hopelessness. The victory is already won for God's children. We have been delivered from the debris of fleshly hindrances and moved to a place of spiritual peace through the death, burial and resurrection of our Lord Jesus Christ. Through God's power we can overcome all of the negative emotions, fears and insecurities that bury us underneath the rubble.

What negative feelings have you buried underneath the rubble? What has kept the light of victory from shining in your hour of darkness? Identify it today; tomorrow we'll learn how to come out from underneath the rubble of our lives and walk in victory.

"Our victory lies in the power of God alone."

Coming Out from Underneath the Rubble

SCRIPTURE READING: 2 Corinthians 4:8–9

Today's Scripture text show us our victory in Jesus, giving us the power to come out from under life's rubble. It says, "We are troubled on every side, yet not distressed; we are perplexed, but not in despair; Persecuted, but not forsaken; cast down, but not destroyed." We will have trials, but we need not have defeat. Philippians 4:13 says, "I can do all things through Christ which strengtheneth me."

Serving God brings with it suffering. Through suffering we learn obedience, just as Christ did. Hebrews 5:8 says, "Though he were a Son, yet learned he obedience by the things which he suffered." Jesus knows what you're going through, and He knows how you feel. He gave His life to give you victory over the things that trouble you. Now you must choose to walk your way out or to stay underneath. You must die to self and live in God's power.

If you are willing, God will reach down and lift you out from underneath your rubble and put you in a place of spiritual peace where He can mature you. There will be times of trouble, but because you belong to Him you can never be crushed (in distress). You will be perplexed (have fear and doubt), but you need never despair (lose hope). You have hope in Christ. You will often be persecuted, but you can rest assured that God will never leave you forsaken. You will be cast down, but you will never be cast out. God will never turn His back on you; His love is unconditional.

Don't give up now! Your circumstances, regardless of what they are, can be overcome with God's power. Though our outward man is perishing, our inner man is being renewed day by day.

"God will reach down and lift you out from underneath your rubble."

God's Authority in Prayer

SCRIPTURE READING: Psalm 139:1–4

O LORD, thou hast searched me, and known me. Thou knowest my downsitting and mine uprising, thou understandest my thought afar off. Thou compassest my path and my lying down, and art acquainted with all my ways. For there is not a word in my tongue, but, lo, O LORD, thou knowest it altogether." What more could we learn about God's authority in our prayer lives?

In verse one David confessed God's all-knowing power in his life. In verse two, he admitted that God knew all about his sin, doubts, fears and confusion as well as his accomplishments, desires, sincerity and deep love for Him. David makes a revelation in verse three that many of us allow to cause doubt and uncertainty in our own prayer lives: God truly knows our every way, including our feelings of doubt and unworthiness.

We must take on David's attitude in our prayer lives. David didn't begin this prayer with a negative attitude about himself. He didn't allow his doubts and feelings of inadequacy to separate him from his prayer life with God. David began his prayer with praise to God because God knew David's heart greater than even he did.

David had absolute confidence in God's authority in his prayer life. David knew that God was with him in whatever he did or wherever he went. In the honest, humble and specific prayer of Psalm 139, David introduces us to God's omniscience, omnipotence and omnipresence. God is all-knowing, all-powerful and present everywhere. David knew that, and he made it known to us in today's Scripture text. Let's continue to study these attributes of God as David knew them and see how David came to be so confident in God's authority in prayer.

> *"God is all-knowing, all-powerful and present everywhere."*

A NEW DESIRE

Omniscient, Omnipotent and Omnipresent

SCRIPTURE READING: Psalm 139:7–8

Psalm 139:7–8 reveals the relief David found in knowing that God would never be shocked by his actions regardless of where he went or what did. "Whither shall I go from thy spirit? or whither shall I flee from thy presence? If I ascend up into heaven, thou art there: if I make my bed in hell, behold, thou art there." David knew that God was all-knowing, all-powerful and everywhere; therefore, He would never be caught off-guard by David's actions. David knew that God would love and hear him in every circumstance, regardless of his spiritual, physical or fleshly condition.

David could have this confidence in God because he knew that God had chosen Him to be king over Israel. We are also God's chosen people if we have accepted Christ as our Savior. Shouldn't we have the same confidence? David was a man after God's own heart, yet he had fears, doubts and feelings of unworthiness. He also committed murder and adultery. Does this sound anything like your life? The only difference between David and us is that David refused to let hindrances defeat him in his walk with God. David simply came to God openly and honestly, knowing that he was nothing without God's leadership.

David's confidence came from resting in God's promises. He rested in the fact that God was in control, and he knew that God was the great deliverer in all situations. David always poured his heart out to God, including his doubts, fears and insecurities, and in doing so he protected himself from spiritual defeat.

Let's learn, like David, to conquer the things that defeat us in prayer by recognizing God's authority.

"Let's learn to conquer the things that defeat us in prayer by recognizing God's authority."

Hindrances in Prayer

SCRIPTURE READING: 1 Timothy 2:8

Wrath and doubting are major hindrances in our prayer lives. Today's Scripture text says, "I will therefore that men pray every where, lifting up holy hands, without wrath and doubting." Knowing this, we must conquer what defeats us.

We conquer wrath and doubting by coming to the Lord in confidence and humility with a complete willingness to surrender ourselves to God. God bestowed upon us, in the book of Psalms, the keys to communicating with Him. We find in Psalms three keys to effective communication with God through prayer. Those keys are openness, sincerity and honesty with God. These three attributes make our prayers priceless to God.

Don't let feelings of defeat defeat you. Place your feelings in the hands of your Heavenly Father; He already knows all about them. God can free you from the guilt and hindrances of your feelings if you'll confess them to Him. David said in Psalm 139:23–24, "Search me, O God, and know my heart: try me, and know my thoughts: And see if there be any wicked way in me, and lead me in the way everlasting."

Your prayer life is the most essential part of an intimate relationship with God. It is the water for your spiritual growth. Without water, all things begin to wither and fade away. Your relationship with God is no different.

We serve the same God David did, and we can talk to Him as openly, frequently and freely as David did. Don't be defeated in your prayer life by trying to hide things from God. Like David, make your prayer life one of consistence, confidence and courage.

"Place your feelings in the hands of your Heavenly Father; He already knows all about them."

A NEW DESIRE

Praying Effectively for Others

SCRIPTURE READING: Colossians 1:9–14

For the next few days, we'll study how to pray effectively for others. Several years ago, God placed a heavy burden on my heart about praying for others, but as much as I prayed I failed to see any results in their lives. In my attempt to find the reason for my ineffectiveness, God revealed His will in our prayers for others through today's Scripture text.

"For this cause we also, since the day we heard it, do not cease to pray for you, and to desire that ye might be filled with the knowledge of his will in all wisdom and spiritual understanding; That ye might walk worthy of the Lord unto all pleasing, being fruitful in every good work, and increasing in the knowledge of God; Strengthened with all might, according to his glorious power, unto all patience and longsuffering with joyfulness; Giving thanks unto the Father, which hath made us meet to be partakers of the inheritance of the saints in light: Who hath delivered us from the power of darkness, and hath translated us into the kingdom of his dear Son: In whom we have redemption through his blood, even the forgiveness of sins."

This was Paul's prayer for the people of Colosse. Paul took his prayers for these people very seriously, and he watched as the results unfolded in their lives. We find seven principles of effective prayer for others in the words of Paul's prayer. If we will apply them to our lives we can begin to see lives transformed by the power of praying according to God's will.

The seven principles are found in verses 9–12 of today's text. Reread them and prepare your heart for tomorrow.

"See lives transformed by the power of praying."

Principles of Effective Prayer, Part One

SCRIPTURE READING: Colossians 1:9–12

The first principle of effective prayer is found in Colossians 1:9: "For this cause we also, since the day we heard it, do not cease to pray for you, and to desire that ye might be filled with the knowledge of his will in all wisdom and spiritual understanding." Prayer for others is almost useless if they never come to the knowledge and understanding of God's will for their life. Without it, the ones we are praying for will never be able to overcome their circumstances. We can't give others knowledge, wisdom and spiritual understanding, so we must pray that God will give them the desire for it and lead them to it by teaching them the importance of studying, praying and seeking God's direction instead of asking others to seek it for them.

"That ye might walk worthy of the Lord unto all pleasing, being fruitful in every good work, and increasing in the knowledge of God." It is important that we pray for others to walk worthy of the Lord and be found pleasing unto Him; this will help protect them from adversities brought on through God's chastening. We walk worthy of God when we realize we can do nothing without Him and that He must increase and we must decrease. Applying this concept makes us pleasing to God as well. We should also pray that their inward position will be outwardly fruitful. If the ones you are praying for are not seeking God and professing Him in their lives, they will be spiritually defeated.

We should pray for others to be filled with the knowledge of God's will in all wisdom and spiritual understanding. Then we should pray that they walk worthy of the Lord, being pleasing unto Him and fruitful in every good work. Start praying this today!

"We walk worthy of God when we realize we can do nothing without Him."

Principles of Effective Prayer, Part Two

SCRIPTURE READING: Colossians 1:9–12

Verse 10 of our Scripture text reveals the fourth principle of effective prayer for others. "That ye might walk worthy of the Lord unto all pleasing, being fruitful in every good work, and increasing in the knowledge of God." The Bible is filled with gems that can fill our hearts with the knowledge of God. Stress the importance of Bible study to those you're praying for. Knowledge of God begins by getting in His Word.

The fifth principle is found in verse 11. "Strengthened with all might, according to his glorious power, unto all patience and longsuffering with joyfulness." Weakness is the reason most people can't get beyond the daily grind. Pray for God to reveal the availability of His strength to others so they can rest in His power rather than struggling in their own.

Verse 11 also teaches us to pray for the patience of others. People are defeated spiritually all the time because they have a problem waiting on God. They take matters into their own hands because they don't have the patience to wait on God who has all things under control. Pray that those you love will learn to wait on God with joy.

The seventh and final principle of effective prayer is found in verse 12. "Giving thanks unto the Father, which hath made us meet to be partakers of the inheritance of the saints in light." You must always come to God with a thankful heart. God is the giver of all things and through Him we obtain all things. He deserves our thanks and praise.

As you pray for yourself and others today, pray that God will grant you all to be filled with the knowledge of His will in all wisdom and spiritual understanding, to walk worthy of the Lord unto all pleasing, being fruitful in every good work, increasing in the knowledge of God, to be strengthened with all might, to be patient in waiting on Him, and be thankful for what He has given, and He will give in answer to your prayer.

"The Bible is filled with gems that can fill our hearts with the knowledge of God."

Transforming the Mind

SCRIPTURE READING: Galatians 5:24–25

Sometimes our hearts and minds seem to be in constant battle with one another. Our hearts tend to know what the right thing to do is, but the mind seems to lean to its own understanding. We usually allow the flesh to take over and wind up doing the wrong thing. Our flesh acts on the thoughts of the mind which Satan has defiled with evil and sinful thoughts.

We can transform our minds from evil thoughts to thoughts of righteousness by walking in the Spirit. Romans 12:2 says, "And be not conformed to this world: but be ye transformed by the renewing of your mind, that ye may prove what is that good, and acceptable, and perfect, will of God." Our Scripture text also says, "And they that are Christ's have crucified the flesh with the affections and lusts. If we live in the Spirit, let us also walk in the Spirit."

Walking in the Spirit requires a personal relationship with God. It means that we pray, study and seek God for everything. Humbling ourselves in this manner allows God to transform our minds according to His will. When our minds are transformed we are actually activating the intents of the heart. We are in one mind and one accord with the Lord.

Transforming our minds is a daily process as we draw closer to the Lord. As we learn more about God, our minds are transformed and our habits begin to change from our old sinful ways to God's ways. In order to transform our minds, we must be willing to make sacrifices and deny ourselves of the worldly things we put before God. We must use everything in our lives for the honor and glory of God rather than for personal gain.

If you have things in your life that are sin and evil, turn from them by turning to God. This is transforming your mind!

"Transforming our minds is a daily process as we draw closer to the Lord."

A NEW DESIRE

Making a Difference

Scripture Reading: Jude 21–23

What does it take to make a difference in the lives of others? The answer is found in today's Scripture text. "Keep yourselves in the love of God, looking for the mercy of our Lord Jesus Christ unto eternal life. And of some have compassion, making a difference: And others save with fear, pulling them out of the fire; hating even the garment spotted by the flesh."

In our walk with the Lord we should strive daily not to conform to this world or to partake in its enticements. We should be challenged to stand out in the crowd by wearing a smile and an attitude that presents Jesus as the authority in our lives. Our Scripture text gives us three principles for doing just that.

The first principle is "keeping ourselves in the love of God." We can do everything through love by following the mind of Christ within us. Second, we must be "looking for the mercy of our Lord Jesus Christ." We must realize that we are nothing without God's love and mercy. We must also realize that we could not make it as Christians without His mercy toward us. Finally, we must "have compassion." When we have compassion for those around us, we are truly on our way to making a difference in this world. When we apply these three principles we begin to see the results promised in our Scripture text; we begin to make a difference in the lives of others.

I challenge you to meditate on this Scripture throughout this month. Read it daily or weekly and act upon the principles set forth in these Scriptures in order to make a difference in the lives of others.

"We can do everything through love by following the mind of Christ."

Rejoicing with Joy

SCRIPTURE READING: 1 Peter 1:8

We get so excited about the things in life that bring us happiness, especially the things we can see. New cars, a sparkling diamond ring, money in the bank and other such things that are pleasing to the eye bring us great joy. Yet what about the things we can't see?

Do you find that things that are intangible or that do not produce some type of fleshly pleasure fail to have such a strong effect on you? For example, true love is usually felt rather than seen, and we often take it for granted. Good health is not always appreciated until we are afflicted with some type of illness.

Our Scripture text for today reveals perhaps the most often overlooked thing over which we should be rejoicing with joy. "Whom having not seen, ye love; in whom, though now ye see him not, yet believing, ye rejoice with joy unspeakable and full of glory." We often take Jesus for granted more than any other aspect in our lives when He should be proclaimed above all else.

Jesus is the Creator of our happiness. No, we can't see Him, but in the hard times He's the first we call on for help, and He's always so faithful to come through for us. Jesus gives us grace for every need, and He loves us unconditionally. It's time we get back to Jesus and rejoice with joy for all that He has done.

Rejoice in the Lord today, and for the rest of this week. Make it a daily habit to rejoice with joy for what the Lord has done in your life. Let's get as excited about Jesus as we do about these other things that we can see. After all, Jesus has blessed us with all we have.

> *"Make it a daily habit to rejoice for what*
> *the Lord has done in your life."*

Rejoicing in All Things

SCRIPTURE READING: 1 Thessalonians 5:16–18

Rejoicing is both a benefit and a privilege for Christians. Rejoicing comes free along with salvation. It is an outward expression following an inward happening.

We should rejoice simply because we are saved. Luke 10:19–20 reminds us that many benefits come with salvation, but salvation alone is the reason for rejoicing. "Behold, I give unto you power to tread on serpents and scorpions, and over all the power of the enemy: and nothing shall by any means hurt you. Notwithstanding in this rejoice not, that the spirits are subject unto you; but rather rejoice, because your names are written in heaven."

Being saved doesn't mean that we will no longer have financial or physical problems. It doesn't mean that we won't have to face the storms of life. However, through our faith and dependence upon God, we can greatly rejoice in all things. Today's Scripture text says, "Rejoice evermore. Pray without ceasing. In every thing give thanks: for this is the will of God in Christ Jesus concerning you."

For most of us, the word rejoice means to be inwardly happy and thankful. We think of rejoicing as something calm and personal. First Peter 1:6–7 says, "Wherein ye greatly rejoice, though now for a season, if need be, ye are in heaviness through manifold temptations: That the trial of your faith, being much more precious than of gold that perisheth, though it be tried with fire, might be found unto praise and honour and glory at the appearing of Jesus Christ." The word rejoice here means to jump for joy. Can you jump for joy simply because you're saved? Can you jump for joy in the hard times because you know they're making you stronger in Christ?

Life will not always be easy, but we are always more than conquerors through Christ. Rejoice in all things!

"We should rejoice simply because we are saved."

Learning to Rejoice

SCRIPTURE READING: Philippians 4:4

"Rejoice in the Lord always: and again I say, Rejoice." Those words are hard for us to comprehend and accept because there are many things in our lives we have no control over. Regardless of the effort we put into smoothing things out, nothing we can do makes the problem any better. Doubt and confusion make us angry. We begin to question ourselves and God.

God allows us to get in this state for a reason. God knows what it takes to get our attention, and He is in control of every situation. God wants us to be unhindered and wholehearted. If we will only trust Him with our problems, knowing that He is in control of our circumstances, then we can rest in the words of Matthew 11:28–30. "Come unto me, all ye that labour and are heavy laden, and I will give you rest. Take my yoke upon you, and learn of me; for I am meek and lowly in heart: and ye shall find rest unto your souls. For my yoke is easy, and my burden is light."

We allow our joy to be smothered by trying to control the circumstances in our lives. We are our own worst enemy in most situations. When God has humbled us to the place where we are willing to listen to Him, then we will learn that we can rejoice even in these situations because we have the blessed assurance that God will not allow us to be tempted to the point of destruction (1 Corinthians 10:13). Wow, what a reason to rejoice!

Each time we make a mountain out of a molehill, God is there making a way for us to handle the situation. He is there to renew our strength when we feel like strength is gone. He will make a way of escape, and He will lead us out of temptations. That alone is a reason to rejoice. The whole principle to rejoicing is trusting in God. Rejoicing comes naturally when we're trusting in Him.

"God knows what it takes to get our attention. God wants us to be unhindered and wholehearted."

"The Lord Hath Need of Him"

SCRIPTURE READING: Luke 19:30–31

Today's Scripture text emphasizes our Lord's interest in things of seemingly no value. Jesus said, "Go ye into the village over against you; in the which at your entering ye shall find a colt tied, whereon yet never man sat: loose him, and bring him hither. And if any man ask you, Why do ye loose him? thus shall ye say unto him, Because the Lord hath need of him."

In verses 34–36 of this same passage we see the people of Jerusalem throwing their garments in the donkey's pathway as Jesus made His triumphant entry into Jerusalem. The people wanted to give Jesus what they could to help Him complete His journey. They expected Him to come as a king. They wanted to show Him complete reverence and royalty. Spreading their garments before Him was similar to our modern tradition of rolling out the red carpet.

To you and me, the donkey and the garments don't seem like much to offer a king, but to Jesus they helped Him to make His journey smoothly and on time. Jesus needed these people and what they had to offer.

What do you have to offer the Lord? You must realize that you are very important to Jesus. His work cannot be effectively completed without your participation. Your gifts and talents may seem insignificant to you, but to the Lord they are very important and essential. We can't all be pastors, deacons, teachers and authors, but we can all be vessels for the Master's use.

God can make something great out of something small. That's how Jesus fed a multitude with one little boy's lunch. It wasn't much to offer for such a great need, but in God's hands it was more than enough. Let Jesus use your gifts and talents in a mighty way to further the Gospel, regardless of how small and insignificant they may seem.

"You must realize that you are very important to Jesus. God can make something great out of something small."

The Widow's Mite

SCRIPTURE READING: 2 Corinthians 8:12–15

In Luke 21, we find the story of the Widow's Mite. What this woman gave, two mites, was equal to about fifty cents. Can you imagine how little that is? Notice, though, Jesus' response to her offering in verses 3–4. "And he said, Of a truth I say unto you, that this poor widow hath cast in more than they all: For all these have of their abundance cast in unto the offerings of God: but she of her penury hath cast in all the living that she had." She may have only given a little in man's eyes, but in God's eyes she gave a lot.

Satan seeks to destroy your self-esteem, defeat you spiritually and make you feel inadequate about your abilities. There are many things we can do for the Lord. Our time and undivided attention are the two things He desires most from us, and they don't even require being talented or gifted. It doesn't matter how big or small you think your gifts and talents are; they are just perfect for what God desires to use them for. You must simply be willing to let the Lord use you. Today's Scripture text says, "For if there be first a willing mind, it is accepted according to that a man hath, and not according to that he hath not. For I mean not that other men be eased, and ye burdened: But by an equality, that now at this time your abundance may be a supply for their want, that their abundance also may be a supply for your want: that there may be equality: As it is written, He that had gathered much had nothing over; and he that had gathered little had no lack."

Whatever we offer the Lord means just as much to Him as what we thought was the greater gift someone else gave. Don't let Satan deceive you into thinking that what you have to offer the Lord isn't enough. Proverbs 15:16 says, "Better is little with the fear of the LORD than great treasure and trouble therewith."

"You must be willing to let the Lord use you."

A NEW DESIRE

"Cast Thy Burden Upon the Lord"

SCRIPTURE READING: 1 Peter 5:7

Jesus not only wants your great and small abilities, but He wants your problems as well. This is confirmed in today's Scripture text and many other places throughout God's Word. Our Scripture text says, "Casting all your care upon him; for he careth for you."

Why would Jesus want your problems and cares? He wants them because He died for them. He provided a way of escape for you when He went to the cross. He simply wants you to reverence that sacrifice by trusting Him with all of your cares. He wants to make you free from your burdens and cares so you can serve Him effectively.

The Lord needs you and everything about you. He longs to deliver you from all of your fears and burdens so that nothing can hold you back. Psalm 34:4 says, "I sought the LORD, and he heard me, and delivered me from all my fears." Fear is not of God. It makes you insecure and unsure of your position in Him, but God can use your fears for His honor and glory by delivering you from them. There is nothing about your life God can't use.

You don't have to be a millionaire, someone famous or near perfect for God to use you. All you have to be is willing. If you feel like you don't have anything else to offer God, offer Him your praise. He is worthy to be praised.

What are you offering the Lord? Are you sincere in your desire to be of service to Him? God wants to use all of you, including your anxieties, insecurities and temptations for His honor and glory. You need the Lord, and He needs you. He cares about your circumstances, and He wants to use them for His honor and glory. Won't you give Him your circumstances today?

"Jesus not only wants your great and small abilities, but He wants your problems as well."

From Troubles to Triumphs

SCRIPTURE READING: Psalm 46:1

Each day we see Satan confronting homes, families, marriages and churches more than ever before. His attacks have become stronger and more damaging. Why must it be this way?

Today's Scripture text says, "God is our refuge and strength, a very present help in trouble." The reason we have so many troubles and trials, the reason our battles are so hard to win, is that we don't allow God to be our refuge and strength. Instead, we allow ourselves to think that we are strong enough to handle everything on our own.

Our refuge has become feeding our flesh instead of trusting God. Maybe we buy something expensive that we don't really need, take a vacation or commit a sinful act that we refer to as pleasure instead. In the end, the troubles are still there, and we've only added to them by giving in to our flesh.

God wants to be your burden bearer. He doesn't want you to depend on your own strength; He wants you to trust His strength instead. Our only true place of refuge is at His throne. The only strength we'll find is in His arms.

Life is troublesome because we allow it to be. If we'll only learn to turn to God, our troubles will turn to triumphs. This is when God become a "very present help in trouble." Psalm 73:26 says, "My flesh and my heart faileth: but God is the strength of my heart, and my portion for ever." Habakkuk 3:19 says, "The LORD God is my strength, and he will make my feet like hinds' feet, and he will make me to walk upon mine high places."

Give God everything you face, and let him turn your troubles to triumphs.

"God is the strength of my heart."

Effectively Studying Our Bibles

SCRIPTURE READING: 2 Timothy 2:15

Today's Scripture text says, "Study to show thyself approved unto God, a workman that needeth not to be ashamed, rightly dividing the word of truth." Bible study is a fundamental part of our Christian growth. The word study in our Scripture text refers to intensive intellectual effort.

Acts 17:10–11 explains why it is important for us to study God's Word. "And the brethren immediately sent away Paul and Silas by night unto Berea: who coming thither went into the synagogue of the Jews. These were more noble than those in Thessalonica, in that they received the word with all readiness of mind, and searched the Scriptures daily, whether those things were so."

How can we be better students of God's Word? I have found seven basic principles to go by in studying God's Word. We will study the principles listed below in detail over the next several days:

- Pray before you study.
- Get away to a quiet place to study.
- Seek the Scriptures until you find something that interests you.
- Never get frustrated over what you don't understand.
- Use tools such as a dictionary, concordance, etc. to help you understand what you're studying.
- Apply what the Holy Spirit teaches you to your own life.
- Share what you learn with someone else.

Search the Scriptures daily with a readiness of mind to make sure what you're being taught is truth. Applying these seven principles of Bible study will help you do so easily.

Remember, an approved workman is not ashamed.

"Search the Scriptures daily with a readiness of mind."

The Principles of Studying, Part One

SCRIPTURE READING: 2 Timothy 2:15

The first few principles of effectively studying God's Word will help you to have an open and unhindered mind while learning God's Word. Today's Scripture text is the same as yesterday's, and it will remain the same for each day of this series: "Study to show thyself approved unto God, a workman that needeth not to be ashamed, rightly dividing the word of truth."

1. Pray before you study. Never try to study the Bible in the flesh. Pray sincerely for the knowledge and wisdom of God's Word. The Holy Spirit can protect you from frustration if you'll only pray for His guidance as you study.

There are several adverse effects to studying God's Word in the flesh. First, you will only frustrate the Scriptures you read. Second, studying in the flesh leaves room for deception because the flesh is subject to taking Scripture out of context. Finally, studying in the flesh leaves room for confusion. Make sure you always pray for the Holy Spirit to teach you the truth by removing you from all fleshly thoughts and attitudes.

2. Get away to a quiet place. You must give God your undivided attention when you study. Trying to study in a crowd or with distractions like the TV will only cause discouragement. Studying in one room while trying to listen to what's going on in another room will rob you of the knowledge and wisdom of God's Word. Shutting everything out around you gives the Holy Spirit room to teach you what God wants you to know. Remember, Jesus always found a quiet place to get alone to seek His Father's will.

Don't wait until we're through with this study to start applying these principles to your study time. Start today applying what we've learned, and then add to these new habits each day as we study these seven principles.

*"Jesus always found a quiet place
to get alone to seek His Father's will."*

The Principles of Studying, Part Two

SCRIPTURE READING: 2 Timothy 2:15

S tudy to show thyself approved unto God, a workman that needeth not to be ashamed, rightly dividing the word of truth."

Picking up where we left off yesterday, we'll start today's study with the third principle of effectively studying God's Word.

3. Seek the Scriptures until you find something that interests you. Opening your Bible and reading the page you opened to isn't always sufficient. When studying, ask yourself the five standard questions: who, what, when, where and why. This is rightly dividing the Word.

When studying, look for a personal message. God is willing to speak to us if we are willing to listen. There are three keys to understanding what God is trying to say to you personally. First, God may be trying to reveal something about Himself to you, or God may want to reveal something to you about yourself. Finally, God may reveal something that He wants you to do.

Don't study God's Word out of guilt or for your own personal gain. You should study God's Word out of a desire to know Him and His will for your life. Studying will help us to walk in His ways and be pleasing to Him.

4. Never frustrate what you don't understand. God doesn't always reveal things to us just as we're studying them. He often wants us to meditate on and ponder what we've studied. Just remember a few important points: never put a question mark where God puts a period, always ask God to give you the understanding of what you've studied in His time, not yours, and never stop studying just because you don't understand.

Study to show thyself approved unto God.

"Study God's Word out of a desire to know Him."

The Principles of Studying, Part Three

SCRIPTURE READING: 2 Timothy 2:15

S tudy to show thyself approved unto God, a workman that needeth not to be ashamed, rightly dividing the word of truth."

Today we'll study the fifth principle of effectively studying God's Word. Remember, start applying these principles now; don't wait until we're through studying all of them.

5. Use tools such as a dictionary, concordance, etc. to help you understand what you're studying. Our Scripture text says that we are workmen, and workmen need tools. There is absolutely nothing wrong with using Bible helps such as concordances, dictionaries, commentaries and encyclopedias to broaden your skills as a Bible student. If we are going to be effective Bible students we must have the proper tools and training from our heroes of faith.

Keep the following simple suggestions in mind if you want to use tools to assist you in your studies. If you don't understand a word, look it up in a concordance or dictionary. When using commentaries, be sure you know the background of the author. Make sure he's teaching you truth. Don't take man's word as truth. The Holy Spirit will reveal whether or not the author's comments are the truth. Commentaries are a great help in opening our eyes to other views, but we should never let them come above God's Word. Remember the words of Acts 17:10–11 from the first day of this study: "And the brethren immediately sent away Paul and Silas by night unto Berea: who coming thither went into the synagogue of the Jews. These were more noble than those in Thessalonica, in that they received the word with all readiness of mind, and searched the Scriptures daily, whether those things were so." Finally, take notes when you're studying so that you'll remember the important parts of your growth in the knowledge of the Word.

> "Take notes when you're studying so that you'll remember the important parts."

A NEW DESIRE

The Principles of Studying, Part Four

SCRIPTURE READING: 2 Timothy 2:15

"Study to show thyself approved unto God, a workman that needeth not to be ashamed, rightly dividing the word of truth."

Today we'll finish up our study of the seven principles of effectively studying God's Word.

6. Apply what the Holy Spirit teaches you to your own life. The job of the Holy Spirit, as defined in the book of John, is to convict us of our sin, righteousness and judgment. He convicts our hearts by showing us our sins. It is our responsibility to apply the convictions by repenting of the sins we've been shown (turning from the sin and toward God). If we refuse to heed this conviction, the Holy Spirit will not show us anything else about God's Word or His will for our lives.

Remember, knowing Scripture and living by the Word are two different things. Until you live and abide by the truth of God's Word, truth will only be a conviction rather than a conversion. Romans 12:2 says, "And be not conformed to this world: but be ye transformed by the renewing of your mind, that ye may prove what is that good, and acceptable, and perfect, will of God."

7. Share what you've learned with someone else. This is our greatest responsibility. First Peter 5:2 says, "Feed the flock of God which is among you, taking the oversight thereof, not by constraint, but willingly; not for filthy lucre, but of a ready mind."

Share the joy of the Lord with those who are watching your life. The greatest example of a knowledgeable Christian is one who shares the simplest things about God's Word. When we share God's Word with others, we are planting seeds in their hearts and minds for God to water in His perfect time.

Apply these seven principles and become a workman that needeth not to be ashamed.

"Share the joy of the Lord with those who are watching your life."

Crossroads of Decision

SCRIPTURE READING: John 8:32

At some point in time, each of us will come to a crossroad in our lives. It may be when we realize that our lives are nothing like we intended them to be, or it may be at a time of misery or adversity. Whenever or wherever it comes, this crossroad will force us to examine our hearts and lives. We must see ourselves as we really are and base our decision on what we see. If we see ourselves as failures, we will most likely make the wrong turn at the crossroad. If we apply the words of our Scripture text, we will make the right decision. Today's Scripture text says, "And ye shall know the truth, and the truth shall make you free."

Satan often reminds us of our past failures and mistakes. He deceives us into believing that our lives can't be anything more because of the mistakes we've made. The enemy does not want us to be overcomers. He wants us to make wrong turns at the crossroads, hoping that our lives will never reflect Christ's character. Satan doesn't want us to feel the freedom to live for and walk in Christ. The enemy wants to keep us in a constant state of confusion.

Jesus had to make decisions about His life just like you and I do. He, too, faced many crossroads, but He never made a decision prematurely. He always sought His Father's counsel. He never made a move without the power of the Holy Spirit. Jesus understood that without His Father's guidance and the Holy Spirit's leadership, He would not make the right turn at His many crossroads of decision during His earthly ministry.

What in your life has you at a crossroads of decision? What is preventing you from fully trusting the Lord in your circumstances? Have you sought the Lord and His mind? Search your heart; surrender to the Lord and He will show you the right turn to make at your crossroads.

"Search your heart; surrender to the Lord. He will show you the right turn to make at your crossroads."

Abiding in Christ

SCRIPTURE READING: 1 John 2:6

When we choose to live righteously, we have stepped into abiding in Christ. Righteousness is living according to God's Word and being a shining light in this dark world. We walk as Christ walked when we abide in Him. We love everyone; we forgive even our enemies. We go through suffering and persecution trusting in God's promises and hoping in Him. We reverence Him as the authority in our lives, and we give Him full control. We desire to be more for Him and less for the world; we are willing to sacrifice our wants and desires for His honor and glory.

Saying that we abide in Him means that we have committed ourselves to Him and His will for lives. It also means that we must remain in Him. We must stay in our relationship with Him regardless of our circumstances and situations. If we are truly abiding in Christ, we will allow Him to control everything about us. Today's Scripture text says, "He that saith he abideth in him ought himself also so to walk, even as he walked."

Jesus was and is righteousness. We enter into His righteousness when we receive Him as our Savior. Therefore, we should immediately walk as He walked. He forgave those who hurt Him. He loved those who hated Him. He is the light of the world and the living Word of God. He is the vine and we are the branches.

As we walk with Him we will become more like Him. Are you walking as Christ walked? Are you abiding in Him? Would those around you identify you as one who is abiding in Christ? Remember, if you are abiding in Christ, you should be walking as He walked.

"If you are abiding in Christ, you should be walking as He walked."

Decisions of Righteousness

SCRIPTURE READING: 1 Corinthians 10:13

If we study Jesus' prayers in the Word of God, we see a picture of weariness in the flesh, a burden for the lost and a sincere concern for the spiritual state of the few who were believers at that time.

Jesus mentions in the Bible those who had gone back to their old ways and those who were steeped in religious laws and refused to forsake religion for righteousness. All of these people had evidently come to a crossroads of decision at some point, but they had chosen the wrong direction. They had been taught the truth, but they rejected it. They allowed their lust, their flesh and the influence of the world to override the truth of Jesus Christ.

We, too, are guilty of making the wrong choices in life. We build up dreams and fantasies of what we think life should be like, and we set out on our own journey to make it happen without even considering God's will for our lives. Our Scripture text reveals the importance of God's presence and control in our decision making. It says, "There hath no temptation taken you but such as is common to man: but God is faithful, who will not suffer you to be tempted above that ye are able; but will with the temptation also make a way to escape, that ye may be able to bear it." If we don't allow God to make a way of escape in our times of temptation, we will constantly make unrighteous decisions.

God is so understanding of our faults and the weaknesses of our flesh. He gives us chance after chance to choose a life of righteousness rather than a life of fading dreams and worldly ambitions. God understands the lust of the flesh, the pride of life and the lust of the eyes. He says that these three things are common to man, but choosing not to walk in them is the key to making decisions of righteousness.

"If we don't allow God to make a way of escape in our times of temptation, we will constantly make unrighteous decisions."

Making Decisions

SCRIPTURE READING: Galatians 5:17

Jesus was appointed by His Father to complete His mission for a lost and dying world. He left His glory in Heaven; He never looked back or wondered how bad His mission would get. He willingly went to do the Father's will. He knew He would have to be born as a man in the flesh; He knew all of the sin of the world would be put upon Him. Jesus knew He would be rejected, homeless, mocked, beaten and cursed. However, He still made the decision to die for the sins of the world.

The Word of God teaches us that man failed in every avenue of escape for sin that God offered. Therefore, God appointed His Son to be the sacrifice for our sin. Jesus knew the only way for sin, death and hell to be conquered was through His death. He made the decision to die regardless of the consequences.

We, too, through the shed blood of Christ, have a decision to make. As born again Christians, we must decide just how closely we want to walk with God. Until this decision is made, we will live in a constant state of warfare between the flesh and the Spirit. Today's Scripture text says, "For the flesh lusteth against the Spirit, and the Spirit against the flesh: and these are contrary the one to the other: so that ye cannot do the things that ye would." This Scripture teaches us the importance of making decisions in our relationship with God. If we decide to walk in the flesh, then we will never be all God wants us to be.

What decisions have you made that you wish you could change? It is never too late to make new decisions or to use your past decisions as stepping stones instead of stumbling blocks. Make the decision today to be more for the Lord. Become more like Jesus regardless of the circumstances.

"As born again Christians we must decide just how closely we want to walk with God."

The Point of Decision

SCRIPTURE READING: Luke 22:42

As we've studied over the past few days, we've seen Jesus as our example of someone at the crossroads of decision. Our Scripture text for today shows Him choosing to do the Father's will: "Saying, Father, if thou be willing, remove this cup from me: nevertheless not my will, but thine, be done." Jesus had the power to walk away from the crucifixion, but at the point of decision, He chose to do the Father's will. In Matthew 26:53–54 He said, "Thinkest thou that I cannot now pray to my Father, and he shall presently give me more than twelve legions of angels? But how then shall the Scriptures be fulfilled, that thus it must be?" Jesus decided to die because of His love for us.

When Jesus was on the cross He could have changed His mind, but His decision was made and He would not come down. You see, Jesus was abiding in the Father. He was staying in His Father's will. It is one thing to make a decision, but it is another to make a decision and stick with it. Jesus never wavered in His decisions, and neither should we.

Christ is not the only Biblical example of someone who was firm in their decisions. Ruth could have left Naomi, but she chose to stay, leaving her own country. Ruth's decision was one she knew would require much hard work, sacrifice and patience. Rahab the harlot (Joshua 2) was another example. She recognized the spies as being sent by the Lord, and she had to choose between God and country. Rahab chose God, and God protected her and her whole family.

Rahab, Ruth and Jesus walked with God, and they trusted Him. As we walk with God in this life, we must make decisions. Making the right choice will depend on your knowledge and love for God. The Lord is our strength, and He will show us the way at our point of decision.

"Making the right choice will be based on your knowledge and love for God."

Great Is Thy Faithfulness

SCRIPTURE READING: Lamentations 3:22–23

M ost people in this world, even professing Christians, have no concept of who God is, even though their lives are operating and surviving under the mercy and grace of our Lord and Savior Jesus Christ. Isn't it a good thing that His mercy is new every morning? Today's Scripture text reminds us of God's patience in our lives. It says, "It is of the LORD'S mercies that we are not consumed, because his compassions fail not. They are new every morning: great is thy faithfulness."

The professing Christians mentioned earlier are those who have made a profession of salvation, yet their lives show no reflection of Christ-likeness. They attend the local assembly and show up at special meetings and fellowship activities. However, they're also dabbling in sin, wanting the best of both worlds. They're struggling between what God wants for their lives and what they desire for themselves. These are people who need to become more faithful to God.

God is faithful to love us and provide for us according to His will. Our problem with being faithful to God surfaces when we reject God's will in order to fulfill our own desires. If we were only half as faithful to Him as He is to us each day, our lives would be so much easier.

Notice that our Scripture text says, "It is of the LORD'S mercies that we are not consumed." God is so faithful to love us with a boundless love. It is His love for us that extends His mercy to us. In all of our sin, our daily battles of the flesh and the temptations of the enemy God's mercy is what protects us from death and destruction.

We must challenge ourselves to be more faithful to living a life of righteousness. He should be able to say of us as we stand before Him, "Great is thy faithfulness." What areas of your life do you need to be more faithful to God in?

"We must challenge ourselves to be more faithful to living a life of righteousness."

The War Within

SCRIPTURE READING: 2 Chronicles 20:15

"What's wrong with me? Why can't I escape this? I don't like what I feel. I want this to go away. God help me." Does this sound familiar to you? Are you wondering what's going on inside?

This is common for many people. The chains of life are so heavy, binding and painful. We know something isn't right, and when we examine ourselves to find the problem, we discover that we are emotional and spiritual wrecks. We worry instead of trusting God. We live with fear instead of resting in the power of the Lord. We fret constantly about things we can't do anything about rather than giving God control of our circumstances. We become paranoid and nervous about life, people and our future. We find ourselves constantly trapped by feelings of inadequacy because we want to be like others instead of being happy with who God created us to be. We withdraw from everyone, feeling alone even in a crowd, because we forget that with God we are never alone.

All of these are symptoms of an inner battle that leaves you feeling totally defeated. The war within has taken its toll, and you feel that God is nowhere near. The Bible teaches us that in Christ Jesus we are never alone. Hebrews 13:5 says, "For he hath said, I will never leave thee, nor forsake thee." Jesus Himself tells us in Matthew 6 that He knows the things we stand in need of.

God promises to lead His children out of the battle and to provide for their every need. Our Scripture text for today tells us the truth of the whole matter for the battles we are facing. The victory of the war within is won in this verse; trust in the Word of God: "And he said, Hearken ye, all Judah, and ye inhabitants of Jerusalem, and thou king Jehoshaphat, Thus saith the LORD unto you, Be not afraid nor dismayed by reason of this great multitude; for the battle is not yours, but God's."

"God promises to lead His children out of the battle and to provide for their every need."

A NEW DESIRE

Battles, Battles and More Battles

SCRIPTURE READING: 2 Timothy 2:12

Battles, battles and more battles. The closer you grow to God, the harder the battle. Does this sound familiar?

Life for many of us has been or has become a struggle. This struggle has hindered us in some way. For some, you have grown hopeless, discouraged and tired. Others may feel abandoned and defeated. How do we escape this struggle? Where do we begin to fight?

First of all, we must realize what God's Word says. Today's Scripture text says, "If we suffer, we shall also reign with him: if we deny him, he also will deny us." The struggle you are facing is part of God's plan for your life. His plan will soon be revealed, so fight with faith in God.

Jesus struggled in His flesh just as you and I do. As He hung on the cross, He cried to God the Father, "My God, my God, why hast thou forsaken me?" He struggled in the garden as He prayed, "Father let this cup pass from me, nevertheless, not my will but thine be done." Jesus understands our battles, because He, too, struggled in His flesh. Jesus' weapons were faith in His Father's Word and the Holy Ghost. When He struggled, He remembered what His Father promised, and He depended upon the power of the Holy Spirit. He was too weak in the flesh to fight alone, and so are we.

Jesus was struggling to carry His cross to Calvary because He had been beaten, bruised and battered. His struggle was for you and me. He never gave up. He died to give us life everlasting. He knew His purpose for the struggle was for our gain. He willingly faced the battle.

Are you willing to face the battles that come your way? Just know that you are not alone. God is there fighting the battle for you as long as you turn the battle over to Him.

*"God is there fighting the battle for you
as long as you turn the battle over to Him."*

Endure Through Your Struggles

SCRIPTURE READING: 2 Timothy 2:1–3

The greatest lessons I have learned as a Christian have come from my struggles. I've learned that I struggle the most when I am trusting the least. We all have a tendency to take matters into our own hands. I am reminded of Peter when I do this.

Peter loved the Lord very much, but he was spontaneous in his walk with God. His struggle with self-control caused him to have hard times. Peter always wanted to fix things the way he thought they should be fixed. That sounds like all of us, doesn't it? However, God did not forsake him because God knew Peter better than Peter knew himself. God knew Peter's heart and intentions were meant for good, and God honored that. God always made a way of escape for Peter. Peter's tool for survival in his struggles was his love for God. It doesn't matter how bad we struggle or how tired we grow, our love for God should be enough to make us struggle on until we are delivered. It will be God's love that sees us through.

Your struggle will not only to teach you, but it will teach others also. As others see you endure through your struggles, they will see your faith, dependence and dedication to God. This will help them endure when it's their turn to struggle. Today's Scripture text says, "Thou therefore, my son, be strong in the grace that is in Christ Jesus. And the things that thou hast heard of me among many witnesses, the same commit thou to faithful men, who shall be able to teach others also. Thou therefore endure hardness, as a good soldier of Jesus Christ."

Our struggling is not in vain. If we struggle in hope and faith then we can endure hard times. Are you struggling with hope and faith? Are you trusting in God to help you endure your hard times?

"Our struggling is not in vain. If we struggle in hope and faith then we can endure hard times."

What Are You Struggling With?

SCRIPTURE READING: Hebrews 13:5–6

Each of us faces different struggles. Your struggle may be personal and private, just between you and the Lord. Someone else's struggle may be public and very obvious to others. Some people struggle with finances, marriage, children and/or church problems while others struggle with past sins, unforgiveness, fear, insecurities and doubts. These things become struggles because just when we think we have conquered them we find ourselves dwelling on them again.

There is hope for your circumstances. Today's Scripture text says, "Let your conversation be without covetousness; and be content with such things as ye have: for he hath said, I will never leave thee, nor forsake thee. So that we may boldly say, The Lord is my helper, and I will not fear what man shall do unto me." Struggling in life does not mean you are defeated. Defeat comes when you stop struggling and completely give up. You can say you are defeated when you have stopped calling upon the Lord, when you have no more hope in Jesus and the Word of God. You can say you are defeated when you go back to your old ways in the world, when you no longer fellowship with other Christians.

Examine your life and determine whether or not you have become defeated in your struggle. Where Jesus abides there is never defeat; He is victory, deliverance and strength for your struggle.

David struggled with the lust of his flesh. He committed great sin, but God still loved and used him. Hannah struggled with her inner feelings and envied the one who was able to conceive, but God loved her and heard her prayers. Job struggled with understanding God's intentions when he lost all he had, but God returned to him ten fold. When we can see struggling as a part of our growth in the Lord, then we, too, can be used and blessed by the Lord just as David, Hannah, and Job were.

"Struggling in life does not mean you are defeated."

Content or Discontent?

SCRIPTURE READING: 1 Timothy 6:6–8

Paul stated in today's Scripture text that he had learned to be content. He said, "But godliness with contentment is great gain. For we brought nothing into this world, and it is certain we can carry nothing out. And having food and raiment let us be therewith content." Through this statement he was explaining that contentment is gained in a process of time as we walk with the Lord. Paul was implying that contentment does not come overnight or as a free gift. Contentment comes as we see and experience God's sovereign power in our lives.

Contentment simply means to be satisfied or to have sufficiency. With our lifestyles, it's difficult to be satisfied. It's hard for us to grasp that what we have is sufficient enough. In this day and time we always want more or better. Paul said that simply having food and raiment was enough.

The secret to contentment is "godliness." What does "godliness" mean? It means to be pious or to show great respect towards God; it means to worship. Godliness is being devoted to God. If we are truly devoted to God we will be content; we will not get caught up in the competition of the world. We will not get in the frame of mind of thinking that more is better. God's provisions for your life will be sufficient for you. You will find yourself not only satisfied with what you have, but you will consider all things as blessings from God. Godliness is living in the righteousness of God. Often times we step outside of the righteousness of God in order to find some kind of contentment. This is where we make a mistake.

Let's learn to be content with what we have and to seek after godliness in our lives. Remember, "godliness with contentment is great gain."

"God's provisions for your life will be sufficient for you."

The Secret to Contentment

SCRIPTURE READING: Philippians 4:11

Discontented believers never know God for who He really is because their discontentment distorts the picture. My friend, if you suffer from discontentment, you need to find its cause. Discontentment can be caused by one of many things, or it could result from numerous different things. I have listed below a few causes of discontentment. You may find that one or more of them apply to you.

- Bad circumstances such as finances, marital problems, recurring sin, past failures, rebellious children, etc.
- Lost expectations when you just knew that God would work things out like you wanted it, but He didn't.
- Misunderstanding God when you feel like you have been abandoned by Him even though you did your best.
- Trying to control your environment and the people in it; trying to fix your problems.
- Allowing your emotions to attach themselves to your wants. For example: "Oh, I wish I could be like her." "I wish I could have a marriage like theirs." "I would love to have a car like his."

These causes of discontentment effect your life as well as the lives of everyone around you. We must refuse to blame our circumstances (or the people who make up our circumstances) for our lack of contentment. Real contentment hinges on what is happening inside of us rather than what is going on around us.

Paul gave us the secret to contentment in today's Scripture text: "Not that I speak in respect of want: for I have learned, in whatsoever state I am, therewith to be content." Are you content, regardless of the state you are in?

"Real contentment hinges on what is happening inside of us rather than what is going on around us."

Overcoming Discontentment

SCRIPTURE READING: Philippians 4:13

We learned yesterday that the secret to contentment is knowing that God is in control, regardless of the state we're in. When we focus on the circumstances around us instead, we suffer the effects of discontentment. I have listed these effects for you below:

- You are miserable with pretty much everything.
- You have broken fellowship with God because you feel like He doesn't care about your anger and hopelessness.
- You blame everyone around you for what is happening in your life.
- You lose all trust in God's love and concern for you.
- Relationships are eroded because you try to change the people around you rather than looking within for the cause of your discontentment.

Discontentment is your greatest enemy. It seeks to devour the very character of Christ in you. It forces you to act prematurely. It puts you in a state of bondage, and it will eventually destroy you spiritually. So, now we must learn how to become content.

Contentment is based on the truth of today's Scripture text. It says, "I can do all things through Christ which strengtheneth me." We can endure any circumstance without losing our peace and joy because of the strength we gain through our relationship with Christ. Contentment is achieved when we pinpoint the culprit of discontentment within ourselves and then rise to meet it. We must not be afraid to confront whatever is destroying our contentment. God will make a way of deliverance. Real contentment hangs on a very close, intimate relationship with Jesus Christ.

"Contentment is achieved when we pinpoint the culprit of discontentment."

A NEW DESIRE

Are You Aware of Your Struggle?

SCRIPTURE READING: Psalm 62:8

You may be struggling as a Christian, yet unaware of it. You may be deceived by Satan and your flesh. You may be blaming God and others for your circumstances when it's nothing more than God trying to reveal Himself to you through your struggles. How can you know if you are struggling as a Christian? Test yourself with the questions below.

- Are you easily distracted from fellowship with God (prayer, study, witnessing, etc)?
- Do you feel guilty because you don't pray, study, etc?
- Are you constantly reminded of your past?
- Do you feel unworthy, inadequate and/or ashamed to serve the Lord because of your past, your sin, your mistakes or even your present circumstances?
- Do you often feel like you are displeasing to the Lord and to others?
- Do you ever wonder if God has abandoned you and if He really cares about you and your problems?
- Are you searching for something to fill your void, but you keep coming up with nothing?
- Are you easily frustrated, burdened or depressed?
- Do you blame others or God for things going on within yourself?
- Are you more sensitive and easily offended lately?
- Do you find yourself to be on fire for God one day and discouraged the next?

If you answered yes to two or more of these questions, then it is very possible that you are struggling as a Christian. Don't give up on God or yourself. Heed the advice of today's Scripture text: "Trust in him at all times; ye people, pour out your heart before him: God is a refuge for us. Selah."

"Don't give up on God or yourself."

In His Time

SCRIPTURE READING: Job 23:10

But he knoweth the way that I take: when he hath tried me, I shall come forth as gold." These are the words of righteous Job. Faced with a life of total loss and adversity, Job still held to God's unchanging hand. I'm sure in his time of trouble it was hard for Job to make such a statement as we found in our Scripture text. The power behind such words, the source of his patience and endurance, was his faith and trust in God.

Job's flesh was just as weak as yours and mine. He was confused and down on himself and tired of the battle and the false accusations of those who were supposed to be his friends. He was a man full of sorrow with a mind full of questions. Job sought the Lord for answers and searched himself for sin and disobedience. He professed to be nothing more than a man of bitter complaint and full of trouble.

Job knew that only God could save him from the trenches of life. He was a man who feared God, and this manifested his knowledge and wisdom of God. Job 28:28 says, "And unto man he said, Behold, the fear of the Lord, that is wisdom; and to depart from evil is understanding."

Does your life reflect these same symptoms? Do you find yourself in the midst of uncontrollable circumstances? Are you questioning God's purpose and your position with Him? Are you wondering where God is in your circumstances? Are you wondering what happened to the good old days, when your life was trouble free and joyous? Do you feel in your heart that you will come forth as gold?

God knows the way you take, just as He knew the ways Job took. Trust Him in your circumstances, and know you will come forth as gold.

"God knows the way you take. Trust Him.
You will come forth as gold."

"By His Light I Walked Through Darkness"

SCRIPTURE READING: Job 29:2–3

Sometimes our greatest source for survival is reminiscing of the time of our first love with Jesus. We remember the days of excitement when we couldn't wait to share God's love and blessings with others. Job remembered those same things in today's Scripture text: "Oh that I were as in months past, as in the days when God preserved me; When his candle shined upon my head, and when by his light I walked through darkness."

Job was remembering when God's blessings flooded his life. He spoke throughout this chapter of times when he walked very close and intimate with God, a time when others respected Him. In verses 12–20, Job spoke of the effect he had on people in righteousness: he comforted the widows, cared for the lame and counseled those in trouble. Job was a man on fire for God, and he knew the Lord was allowing him to be tried and tested.

Without doubt, Job's trials and tests were hard for him. He was accustomed to feeling the presence of God and knowing God heard his prayers. Still, in Job 31:35–36, Job pleads for God to acknowledge Him: "Oh that one would hear me! behold, my desire is, that the Almighty would answer me, and that mine adversary had written a book. Surely I would take it upon my shoulder, and bind it as a crown to me." Job was a hurting man, yet even in his oppression he reverenced God as his great deliverer. He knew that God delivers in His time, not ours.

We often misunderstand God and His purpose in our lives. For every trial, there is a crown if we wait patiently for God's lesson. If we fold under the pressure, get mad at God, curse, reject and sin against Him, then our deliverance will only take longer. God will make a way of escape when He knows that you are ready to learn from the trial and apply the lesson to your life. This is the way all things come to pass in His time.

> *"For every trial, there is a crown if we wait patiently for God's lesson."*

Learning the Lesson

SCRIPTURE READING: 1 Corinthians 10:11

The way we respond to adversity teaches us just how much we trust God and how closely we walk with Him. God already knows how we'll respond. Therefore, He sets the lesson up according to what it will take to grow us up in Him. Our problem often stems from our refusal to learn the lesson. Instead, we just want to be delivered.

We often think Job was so righteous that we are not worthy to be delivered from our problems as he was. Our Scripture text tells us differently: "Now all these things happened unto them for ensamples: and they are written for our admonition, upon whom the ends of the world are come." Job was a righteous man, but he was not a perfect man. Job was a man born of flesh, just as we are. He loved God, but he, too, had to be taught the power of God. Job wasn't a perfect man, but he was a wise man. That's why he never cursed or gave up on God. Job knew that God knew the way he would take, and he knew that God would bring him forth as gold.

God knows the way you will take, and He knows the true intents of your heart. He understands your pain and agony, and He will deliver you. God will make you victorious in His time. When you learn to wait on God, you will come to a greater understanding of God's control in your life. God will do what He knows it will take to make you a teachable Christian.

God gave us Job as an example, to show us that enduring through disastrous times will make us more pleasing to Him. Job did the best he could do for his circumstances, and God honored that. In spite of the counsel of his friends (and his spouse), Job depended on God.

Stay with God and magnify Him in all things; you, too, will come forth as gold in His time. God will restore you and pour out His blessings upon you beyond measure.

*"God will do what He knows it will take
to make you a teachable Christian."*

The Lord Delivers

SCRIPTURE READING: Psalm 34:19

Are you stumbling through life in your own power? Are you in the midst of hardships, pain and turmoil? If your circumstances are hindering you from bearing fruit, then I challenge you to trust God. Run to Him for refuge and lean on Him for strength. You certainly will not find strength within yourself or in anyone else. Let God deliver you from the horrible pits of life. Let Him take your afflictions and make you effective in them.

God has chosen you to trust Him. He can't work in your life until you turn even the most minute problems in your life over to Him. How do you do that? Follow these three simple steps:

1. Reverence Him as Lord of your life.
2. Remember He is Lord over all things.
3. Recognize Him as the great Controller.

The Bible says in today's Scripture text, "Many are the afflictions of the righteous: but the LORD delivereth him out of them all." We can rest assured that what seems beyond repair, God will fix. What appears to be incurable, He will heal. What appears to be destroyed, He will rebuild.

Won't you trust today in the One who has divinely chosen you to be His?

"We can rest assured that what seems beyond repair, God will fix."

Magnify the Lord

SCRIPTURE READING: Psalm 34:3

In our Scripture text for today, David compels us to magnify the Lord. He says, "O magnify the LORD with me, and let us exalt his name together." David knew God's power, and he had experienced God in a very personal way. It is obvious through the Scriptures that God had delivered David from his adversity.

David was praising the Lord in spite of the fact that he was having a battle. He had experienced some hard trials, but he had no one to turn to but the Lord. David had faced enemy attacks, and he had fled from them because he feared for his life. In his time of trouble, David had run to God. He put his trust in the only One who could deliver Him. God was faithful to do just that for David.

David had learned the great lesson of trusting God. He knew that God would be the One whom he could always lean on. He learned that God would always protect Him. God will do the same for you today.

God's love for you is the same love David experienced. He will protect you and deliver you if you will only trust in Him. You, too, can sing David's psalm of praise: "O magnify the LORD with me, and let us exalt his name together."

> *"God's love for you will protect you and deliver you if you will only trust in Him."*

Chosen by God

SCRIPTURE READING: John 15:16

Close your eyes and imagine yourself as a little child without parents, an orphan in a home with many children, all looking for placement in a family where they will be accepted and loved. Imagine standing in a line of children being investigated by prospective adoptive parents.

You are worried that you may be overlooked or that your qualities will not be what the prospective parents are looking for. Suddenly, you reminisce of all your faults and failures, and you determine that you are too unworthy to even think about being chosen for adoption.

The prospective parents are now approaching you. Looking you over, they reach out and take your hand. You hear them say, "I choose you." Just as you are, you have been chosen. Your heart is flooded with joy, and you realize that someone has chosen to love you unconditionally.

Your relationship with God is identical to this situation. The Bible says in today's Scripture text, "Ye have not chosen me, but I have chosen you, and ordained you, that ye should go and bring forth fruit, and that your fruit should remain: that whatsoever ye shall ask of the Father in my name, he may give it you."

What an honor to be chosen by the Lord! We have been divinely selected and chosen out of this world to be His own. We didn't choose Him; He chose us. Now we must rest in His divine selection and trust Him.

He chose us and appointed us to go and bring forth fruit. He has purposed for us to be something for Him. Our responsibility as chosen ones is to love and trust Him. We must give ourselves over to Him so that He can produce fruit in us that magnifies Him. Give yourself to God today. Live as His chosen; He will never turn you away.

"We have been divinely selected and chosen out of this world to be His own."

A Special Person

SCRIPTURE READING: Deuteronomy 7:6

You are one of God's chosen people if you have received Christ as your personal Savior. That makes you a special person in the eyes of God. As God's child, you are given special benefits and privileges. Among your benefits, you have eternal life and forgiveness of sins. You have the privileges of access to the throne room through prayer, an intimate relationship with Jesus Christ our great redeemer and an eternal home in Heaven when life on this earth is said and done.

God sees us as very special people. Today's Scripture text reveals this truth to us. It says, "For thou art an holy people unto the LORD thy God: the LORD thy God hath chosen thee to be a special people unto himself, above all people that are upon the face of the earth."

The word special in this verse describes someone who is highly valued. Webster defines "special" as someone unique and highly favored, or someone chosen for a particular purpose.

Your heart should be honored at the thought that God has highly favored you to serve Him. He is your purpose, your reason for living. In His eyes, you are a special person. Make Him a very special person in your life today by telling someone of His great love.

"Your hearts should be honored at the thought that God has highly favored you."

A NEW DESIRE

Trusting the Lord

SCRIPTURE READING: Psalm 34:8

Trusting the Lord is a responsibility that comes with being one of His chosen. If we fail to trust God, we will never grow in Him; if we fail to grow in Him, then we will never be effective in His service.

So many of "God's chosen" have become much like the withered fig tree. We have become dried up with withered fruit simply because we refuse to trust God. God loves us, and He chose us to serve, love and trust Him. While we were lost and undone without hope, He chose, out of His great love, to die for us. He did not choose to die for us because we were famous or powerful personalities; He died for us simply because He loves us and He keeps His promises to us. The least we can do is love and trust Him.

Today's Scripture text reminds us that we are blessed if we choose to trust God. It says, "O taste and see that the LORD is good: blessed is the man that trusteth in him."

As you face the day, examine your circumstances. Identify the areas in your life where you are not trusting the Lord. Give those things to the Lord, trusting that He already knows about them. Trust Him to see you through it in His way, not yours.

"Trusting the Lord is a responsibility that comes with being one of His chosen."

Thou Art Worthy

SCRIPTURE READING: Revelation 4:10–11

Today's Scripture text gives us a description of the activity going on around the throne of God. It says, "The four and twenty elders fall down before him that sat on the throne, and worship him that liveth for ever and ever, and cast their crowns before the throne, saying, Thou art worthy, O Lord, to receive glory and honour and power: for thou hast created all things, and for thy pleasure they are and were created."

Oh, what a beautiful sight to behold! God's presence is so overwhelming that the four and twenty elders can only worship and honor the holiness of God. Nowhere in Revelation 4 do we read of hindrances or distractions. No material possessions are found to be worshipped as idols. The only thing the elders have are crowns, and their crowns were cast before the throne. They could not compare to the presence of the Lord. The elders were honored to lay their crowns at the throne, for they understood that God is worthy of all things. These crowns were a representation of the honor and glory of the elders, but once they approached the throne, they placed them around the One who alone was worthy saying, "Thou art worthy, O Lord, to receive glory and honour and power."

Do you see God as worthy of all honor and glory, or do you put all of your material possessions and fleshy goals ahead of your relationship with God? Could you lay your crowns around the throne of God like the elders did? These are questions that provoke us to examine our hearts and our relationships with God.

Examine your heart and relationship with God today. He is worthy of your all.

"God is worthy of all things."

Confessions of Love

SCRIPTURE READING: John 21:15–17

Today we see brokenhearted people on every hand. The news reports are of murder, wars and violence across the nation and the world. Sin abounds everywhere, and in a desperate fight to survive, hearts cry out for help. Confessions are being made of mistakes, sins and times of failure.

People are beginning to feel too unworthy to serve our risen Lord and Savior because of their past, or perhaps even their present, conditions. We must realize that God's love for us far exceeds all of our circumstances. God knows so much more about us than we will ever know about ourselves or others.

God knew Peter more than Peter knew himself. Our Scripture text for today shows us that Peter realized this. Having denied the Lord, just as the Lord had told him he would, Peter felt like a failure who was unworthy of God's love. Our Scripture text says, "So when they had dined, Jesus saith to Simon Peter, Simon, son of Jonas, lovest thou me more than these? He saith unto him, Yea, Lord; thou knowest that I love thee. He saith unto him, Feed my lambs. He saith to him again the second time, Simon, son of Jonas, lovest thou me? He saith unto him, Yea, Lord; thou knowest that I love thee. He saith unto him, Feed my sheep. He saith unto him the third time, Simon, son of Jonas, lovest thou me? Peter was grieved because he said unto him the third time, Lovest thou me? And he said unto him, Lord, thou knowest all things; thou knowest that I love thee. Jesus saith unto him, Feed my sheep."

Oh, what a great God we serve! Jesus didn't ask Peter to confess that he had denied Him three times. All Jesus wanted was Peter's confessions of love for Him. He knows the battles and unworthiness you face daily, and His desire is for you to confess your love for and dependence on Him through it.

"God's love for us far exceeds all of our circumstances."

Living Confessions of Love

SCRIPTURE READING: James 1:22

We are all able to confess our sins and problems without hesitation, but we are rarely quick enough to confess just how much we love God. Confessions of love for God do not come by mouth only. Confessions of love come through our actions and behavior as well. Today's Scripture text says, "But be ye doers of the word, and not hearers only, deceiving your own selves."

Confessions of love are spoken through our actions in many ways. Our love for God is openly confessed through our behavior when we:

- Are not ashamed of the Lord.
- Glorify Him in our trying times.
- Use unworthiness as a stepping stone rather than a stumbling block.
- Take a stand for righteousness in a world of compromise.
- Call sin like it is and refuse to join in with it.
- Obey the voice of God rather than giving in to the desires of the flesh.
- Resist the devil and flee his temptations.
- Await His appearing.

These, my friend, are things that demonstrate our love for God. As we learned yesterday, God simply wants us to make these confessions, just as He wanted Peter to. It is time for us to move out of our gloom and despair to rise and shine for Jesus. Let's confess our love for Him in all things and lift Him up in all we do.

> *"Confessions of love are spoken through our actions."*

A NEW DESIRE

Building Upon the Foundation

SCRIPTURE READING: 1 Corinthians 3:12–13

The Bible teaches us that God is a jealous God and that we cannot serve both God and mammon. God is the creator of all things, and He deserves to be glorified in all that we have and do.

Today's Scripture text says, "Now if any man build upon this foundation gold, silver, precious stones, wood, hay, stubble; Every man's work shall be made manifest: for the day shall declare it, because it shall be revealed by fire; and the fire shall try every man's work of what sort it is." The foundation this Scripture speaks of is the redemptive work of Christ; what we build upon this foundation is our works. Our works will be tried, and anything done for our own glorification will be burned as wood, hay and stubble.

It is easy to get caught up in the lust of the flesh and the pleasures of this world, but no one has ever taken anything of this world with them when they died. We won't take anything with us either. First Timothy 6:7–8 says, "For we brought nothing into this world, and it is certain we can carry nothing out. And having food and raiment let us be therewith content." It is time that we, as Christians, get busy about the Lord's work. It is time we strive to lay up treasures in Heaven so that we, too, have crowns to cast around God's throne.

God is worthy to be served, worshipped and praised not only in Heaven, but in this life also. God is the creator and giver of all things. Job 1:21 says, "And said, Naked came I out of my mother's womb, and naked shall I return thither: the LORD gave, and the LORD hath taken away; blessed be the name of the LORD."

What position are you in with God today? Whether He's giving to you or taking from you, He is worthy to be praised. What are you building upon the foundation?

"It is time that we, as Christians, get busy about the Lord's work."

Hearing the Voice of God

Scripture Reading: Deuteronomy 30:14

When God speaks, He speaks seriously with boldness and authority. He makes His plans known, and He expects the one to whom He has spoken to move in response. If God is faithful to speak to us, we should be faithful to hear and obey Him.

When God spoke to Moses from the burning bush, He left nothing undone. First, He revealed to Moses that He was the one, true God. When God speaks, you will know it's Him. He speaks in such a way that there is no denying Him.

God's voice is always one of truth, instruction, confirmation and comfort. Anything outside of this is not of God. We are often deceived by the voices of our minds. If in doubt, leave it out. God's voice is not one that produces doubt and confusion. A voice that produces doubt and confusion is the voice of the enemy.

There are times when God's voice may frighten us. Our flesh doubts, but the Spirit of God will calm that fear and replace our doubts with the excitement of seeing God do great things. God's voice is one of assurance, security and stability. You can be assured that what God says will stand forever.

Today's Scripture text says, "But the word is very nigh unto thee, in thy mouth, and in thy heart, that thou mayest do it." If we will hear the voice of God and obey it, we will not mistake God's will for our lives. Make sure you know the voice of God. Be quick to seek His guidance and heed His voice. God will faithfully bless us for obeying His voice.

"Be assured that what God says will stand forever."

God, Help Me

SCRIPTURE READING: Psalm 34:17

How many times have you found yourself saying, "God, help me"? This is a cry of desperation, and it is always comes when we are in a state of doubt and confusion. David had this same cry. Our Scripture text says, "The righteous cry, and the LORD heareth, and delivereth them out of all their troubles." David had called out to the Lord in doubt and desperation. David reveals here that he was both heard and delivered because of his relationship with God.

God is so faithful to help us. The problem with receiving God's help is that we want it our way and in our time. When we don't get the help we want when we want it, we start to doubt God and to get desperate for relief. Confusion overtakes us, frustration sets in and we begin to feel like God has let us down.

My friend, God promises to help you if you'll only come to Him with a sincere heart cry of, "God, help me." It does not matter what your cry may be. You may need salvation, you may need rededication or you may need comfort, confirmation or companionship. Regardless of what the need is, the Lord hears and delivers when the righteous cry.

Is your cry a cry of righteousness? Are you crying out to God because you love Him, or are you crying out to Him only because you need Him for the moment? God has never let us down. We blame God when he doesn't meet OUR expectations. When David cried, "God, help me," God knew that David would still uplift Him even without deliverance. That's the difference between David's cry and most of ours.

As you find yourself crying out to God for help, examine your situation to make sure your cry is a righteous cry. It is only the cry of the righteous that God hears.

"Regardless of the need the Lord hears and delivers when the righteous cry."

Confused?

SCRIPTURE READING: 1 Corinthians 14:33

Do you ever find yourself in a state of confusion? Do you struggle with doubt and uncertainties? Confusion is overtaking us more each day. Confusion is not of God. The Bible says in 1 Corinthians 14:33, "For God is not the author of confusion, but of peace, as in all churches of the saints."

Confusion is a weapon of the enemy. Confusion provokes its victims into disappointment and anger rather than leading them into God's guiding hand. Our bodies and minds grow tired and fragile, and our walk with God becomes weak and unimportant. When this happens we step completely into the flesh, and the enemy has us right where he wants us.

When our minds are controlled by Satan and our flesh, we find ourselves more and more confused. Before long we slip into depression. This doesn't mean that we've gone off of the deep end; depression happens to all of us. Some cases are more serious than others. Some cases of depression last for an extended period of time; some are over in a week, but we are all victims of depression at some point in time.

God is the only one who can bring us out of our confusion and depression. We must not allow our flesh or the enemy to steal our peace. Remember, God is peace, not confusion. There are five basic causes of confusion and depression. They are:

1) How we perceive ourselves.
2) How we perceive others.
3) How we perceive God.
4) How we choose to live.
5) What we expect out of life.

Search your heart. Determine today whether you are confused, depressed or at peace with God.

"We must not allow our flesh or the enemy to steal our peace."

Alive in Him

SCRIPTURE READING: Romans 6:11

The Word of God teaches us that, as children of God, we are no longer dead in our trespasses and sins. Christ has called us to live in righteousness through His redeeming blood. Through salvation, He has made us alive in Him.

Today's Scripture text confirms our newness of life in Christ. It says, "Likewise reckon ye also yourselves to be dead indeed unto sin, but alive unto God through Jesus Christ our Lord." Our hearts should rejoice without ceasing for being made alive in Christ. Christ took our place at Calvary, and the Bible says He became sin for us (2 Corinthians 5:21). He gave us access to life eternal through His body and blood.

We are dead in sin until we receive Christ as our Savior. The moment He calls our name and we receive Him, we become alive in Him. Jesus told Martha in John 11:25, "I am the resurrection, and the life: he that believeth in me, though he were dead, yet shall he live." At the moment of salvation, resurrection life takes place within us.

We are alive and well in Christ Jesus. Regardless of what life throws at us, we are safe in Him. The Bible assures us of our position. Romans 8:38–39 says, "For I am persuaded, that neither death, nor life, nor angels, nor principalities, nor powers, nor things present, nor things to come, Nor height, nor depth, nor any other creature, shall be able to separate us from the love of God, which is in Christ Jesus our Lord." Not even death can separate us from God's love.

Remember today that you are a child of God, and be alive in Him!

"As children of God, we are no longer dead in our trespasses and sins."

Hearts of Hope

SCRIPTURE READING: 1 Thessalonians 1:3

What is hope? It is not something we can see. Romans 8:24–25 says, "For we are saved by hope: but hope that is seen is not hope: for what a man seeth, why doth he yet hope for? But if we hope for that we see not, then do we with patience wait for it." Hope is the key to salvation, happiness, spiritual health and most of all holiness.

It is possible to be saved and lack hope. For many of us, our salvation and our hope is based on what we see, feel and receive. However, the true definition of hope reveals to us that hope is just the opposite of this. It is not what we see or feel. Hope means to expect, to have confidence or faith. Hope is having confidence in something or someone we can't see. It is expecting the unknown to carry us into the all-knowing; it is having faith when faith seems impossible.

Why do we need hope? Without hope, we become very unhappy, disappointed and defeated Christians. Hope is the essence of our salvation. Hope is pleasing to God. Second Thessalonians 2:16–17 says, "Now our Lord Jesus Christ himself, and God, even our Father, which hath loved us, and hath given us everlasting consolation and good hope through grace, Comfort your hearts, and stablish you in every good word and work." Our hope is Jesus Christ. Without Him, we have no hope. Today's Scripture text says, "Remembering without ceasing your work of faith, and labour of love, and patience of hope in our Lord Jesus Christ, in the sight of God and our Father."

Over the next few days, we will study in detail the elements of hope: the Holy Spirit, Obedience, Prayer and Endurance. If you find yourself lacking in any of these areas, ask God to help you overcome your lack of hope so you can grow in Him.

"Hope is having confidence in something or someone we can't see."

The Elements of Hope, Part One

SCRIPTURE READING: John 16:13

We need four things to obtain hope. Over the next few days, we'll study them. You can remember them easily through the acronym HOPE. They are:

- Holy Spirit
- Obedience
- Prayer
- Endurance

The first element of hope is the Holy Spirit. The Holy Spirit is within the heart of believers. He takes our needs, groanings and pleas to the Savior who's at the right hand of the Father. The Holy Spirit is the third person of God, and His job is to convict hearts, and to lead, guide, protect, direct, teach and comfort God's people.

The Holy Spirit is God within us. He not only convicts our hearts, but He also teaches us the righteousness of God. Our hope increases by Him, and we have the power to rest in hope through Him. He is the Spirit of Jesus Christ within us.

We must remember that the Holy Spirit is a person, not just an influence or being. Today's Scripture text refers to Him six times as "He", a personal pronoun. "Howbeit when he, the Spirit of truth, is come, he will guide you into all truth: for he shall not speak of himself; but whatsoever he shall hear, that shall he speak: and he will show you things to come."

The Holy Spirit yearns to reveal God's truths to you. He can teach you the deep things of God's Word if you'll give Him your undivided attention. The Holy Spirit will build your hope in Jesus on solid ground so you can grow into a mature, assured, stable child of God.

Let the Holy Spirit fill you today with His presence and power so that your hope can increase.

"The Holy Spirit will build your hope in Jesus."

The Elements of Hope, Part Two

SCRIPTURE READING: 1 Peter 1:13–14

Once we've allowed the Holy Spirit to fill us with His presence and power, we must learn to be obedient to His instructions. The Holy Spirit wants to lead us into righteousness so Jesus will be glorified in our lives.

The first thing the Holy Spirit will do is show us things in our lives that need to be corrected. When He shows us these things, we must choose how to react. We can either open our hearts and minds to accept and receive His instruction, or we can refuse His instruction and go our own way. If we choose to go our own way, we shatter the hope the Holy Spirit has built within us. When we open our hearts and allow Him to teach us and deal with us, then we become obedient.

Today's Scripture text tells us that hope and obedience must be applied together. It says, "Wherefore gird up the loins of your mind, be sober, and hope to the end for the grace that is to be brought unto you at the revelation of Jesus Christ; As obedient children, not fashioning yourselves according to the former lusts in your ignorance."

Obedience is the second step to obtaining hope. We must be willing to do what the Holy Spirit tells us to if we're ever going to rest in the Lord and live in His holiness. Obedience calls for a sacrifice of the flesh and a yielding to the Spirit of God.

When we open our hearts, we become willing to obey whatever God's plan for our lives may be. Is your heart open? You must remember that choosing to obey God doesn't always bring roses, but it will always bring righteousness and rewards. Are you obeying God or man? Your hope rests on your obedience to God.

> **"Choosing to obey God doesn't always bring roses, but it will always bring righteousness."**

A NEW DESIRE

The Elements of Hope, Part Three

SCRIPTURE READING: Psalm 55:17

Today's Scripture text shows us that David placed his hope in prayer. It says, "Evening, and morning, and at noon, will I pray, and cry aloud: and he shall hear my voice." David's hope was not only in communicating with God, but in knowing that God would hear his voice.

Prayer opens our hearts for God's instruction. It is also the key to an individual relationship with the Lord. As we come humbly to God, He is faithful to restore our hope by instructing us in how to overcome.

Prayer also develops faith. The more we talk with God, the greater our faith becomes. The greater our faith, the stronger our confidence and understanding in our Lord and Savior Jesus Christ. God honors nothing but our faith. Hebrews 11:6 says, "But without faith it is impossible to please him: for he that cometh to God must believe that he is, and that he is a rewarder of them that diligently seek him."

When we pray, we learn about ourselves as well as our Savior. Therefore, we must take prayer very seriously. David took prayer so seriously that he prayed morning, noon and evening. David learned that hope was found only in God as he fellowshipped with Him in prayer.

We must fellowship with God through prayer if we want hope restored to our lives. Today is the appointed day for your hope to be restored in and through God. Do your part; pray today.

"We must fellowship with God through prayer
if we want hope restored to our lives."

The Elements of Hope, Part Four

SCRIPTURE READING: 2 Timothy 2:3

Today's Scripture text says, "Thou therefore endure hardness, as a good soldier of Jesus Christ." This verse insinuates that a good soldier of Jesus Christ is identified by his endurance. The first part of the Scripture says we are to endure hardness.

What is hardness? Anything that strips us of our hope and confidence in God is hardness. Hardness comes in many forms. For some, hardness is spiritual. For others it is physical, financial or emotional. Whatever your hardness may be, God is your hope of endurance. God is the only one who can give you the strength to endure.

Many times in the heat of the battle, when all hope is gone, we find ourselves too weak to win. The hardness of the situation has stripped us of our strength. When our strength is gone, we want to quit and give up. We see no reason to carry on. Our expectations have been shattered and disappointment has overtaken us. How can God expect us to endure such hardships?

The answer lies in the hope we have in Jesus. The Bible teaches us that to endure we must place all of our faith and trust in the Lord. God promises to be all we need Him to be in our lives. He also promises to never leave nor forsake us. Through Him we can overcome anything.

God knows the weakness of our flesh and the hardness we face. However, God does not ask us to be strong warriors; He simply asks us to endure through the battle. All God wants is for us to fight the fight of faith. If we stand and endure in the midst of the battle, then we can rest assured that God will give us hope and victory. You, too, will have become a good soldier.

Whatever the battle is you are facing or may face today, just stand in it. Don't give up hope. God will see you through.

> *"If we stand and endure in the midst of the battle, then we can rest assured that God will give us hope and victory."*

Serving Christ Sincerely

SCRIPTURE READING: Ephesians 6:24

Christ, Nathanael and Paul are all found in the Scriptures as having no guile. This means they held the reputation of being sincere in every word and action. They were real examples of sincere Christians. They spoke, lived and loved God.

If Jesus told the sinners He loved them, they knew He meant it. When Nathanael testified as a disciple of Christ, those he witnessed to knew he was sincere and wholehearted. Nathanael had sincere faith in Jesus Christ, and he demonstrated it everywhere he went. Paul said in 1 Thessalonians 2:3–4, "For our exhortation was not of deceit, nor of uncleanness, nor in guile: But as we were allowed of God to be put in trust with the Gospel, even so we speak; not as pleasing men, but God, which trieth our hearts."

These men set examples for us to follow. They were so sincere that they suffered rejection and persecution for it. These men also stood for truth and righteousness regardless of the consequences. We, too, are commissioned by God to apply this same principle to our hearts. The Bible says in 1 Peter 2:21–23: "For even hereunto were ye called: because Christ also suffered for us, leaving us an example, that ye should follow his steps: Who did no sin, neither was guile found in his mouth: Who, when he was reviled, reviled not again; when he suffered, he threatened not; but committed himself to him that judgeth righteously."

We can't be sincere, God-loving, God-fearing Christians in front of people and then portray unconcern and worldliness at home or in private. God is someone we should be sincere about and conscious of all the time. Every second of every day He should be the head of our thoughts. Today's Scripture text says, "Grace be with all them that love our Lord Jesus Christ in sincerity. Amen."

"God is someone we should be sincere about and conscious of all the time."

How to Serve Sincerely

SCRIPTURE READING: 2 Corinthians 1:4

Serving Christ sincerely calls for laying aside of self and sacrificing our own wants for the needs of others. Christ made some great sacrifices for all the world, and He did it all out of love.

Love is the key to serving Christ sincerely. He loved us when we didn't love Him. When Christ went to the cross, unconditional, sincere love was demonstrated for the whole world to see. Can you say within yourself that you sincerely love Jesus? How can we know if our lives reflect sincerity?

There are many great biblical examples of sincere servants of the Lord. In 2 Corinthians 1, Paul explained to the people of Corinth that their actions were not to be looked upon to impress others. He said in verse nine, "But we had the sentence of death in ourselves, that we should not trust in ourselves, but in God which raiseth the dead." Paul explained the reason for their sufferings. They suffered for the benefit of the Gospel of Jesus Christ. Paul and Timothy were so sincerely concerned about the people of Corinth that they suffered to make sure they were taught and comforted of God. Their sincerity is revealed in today's Scripture text: "Who comforteth us in all our tribulation, that we may be able to comfort them which are in any trouble, by the comfort wherewith we ourselves are comforted of God."

Stand, as Paul and Timothy stood, in the blessed assurance that if we sincerely serve Christ and others with a godly love and concern, then we, too, will be comforted by God Himself. Let's be more like Nathanael, Paul and Timothy by letting Christ be seen in our words, our actions and our lifestyles.

God knows the true intent of your every thought and action. Be sincere about your life with God and your deeds for others.

"Be sincere about your life with God and your deeds for others."

A NEW DESIRE

Putting on the Sincerity of Christ

SCRIPTURE READING: Joshua 24:14

We will not always be sincere in our actions, and our flesh will always remind us of those acts of insincerity. Those who are not born again live in insincerity and fleshly motives daily. They boast about what they do for others and what they "do for God." They like to lift themselves up by bragging about their good deeds. On the other hand, Paul reveals the sincerity of Christ in 2 Corinthians 1:12, "For our rejoicing is this, the testimony of our conscience, that in simplicity and godly sincerity, not with fleshly wisdom, but by the grace of God, we have had our conversation in the world, and more abundantly to you-ward." In verses 21–22 of the same chapter, Paul reveals the power for putting on the sincerity of Christ: "Now he which establisheth us with you in Christ, and hath anointed us, is God; Who hath also sealed us, and given the earnest of the Spirit in our hearts."

Christ is genuine. His every thought and action is real and intended for our good. He only expects our love in return. True servants, in return, will promptly praise Him for His goodness. False, insincere servants will instead find a way to give themselves credit for any good done.

Serving Christ sincerely is truly a task for our fleshly minds. Put on the whole armor of God and walk in His Spirit to overcome the insincere thoughts and actions of the flesh. When we walk in the Spirit, wearing the full armor of God, we put on the sincerity of Christ. Today's Scripture text says, "Now therefore fear the LORD, and serve him in sincerity and in truth: and put away the gods which your fathers served on the other side of the flood, and in Egypt; and serve ye the LORD."

"Put on the whole armor of God and walk in His Spirit to overcome the insincere thoughts and actions of the flesh."

The Glory of God

SCRIPTURE READING: John 11:40

"Jesus saith unto her, Said I not unto thee, that, if thou wouldest believe, thou shouldest see the glory of God?" What is the glory of God that Jesus speaks of in today's Scripture text? Some would say it is the evidence of God's power or His blessings upon our lives. However, the glory of God in this verse can only mean one thing. It means to see and/or experience God's presence.

This passage reveals God's omniscience and omnipotence. Mary and Martha had questioned Jesus' delay in coming to the aid of their brother Lazarus. They were concerned because Lazarus had been dead for four days. Martha said to Jesus, "Lord, by this time he stinketh: for he hath been dead four days."

Mary and Martha knew that Jesus had power to heal the sick, raise the dead and cure all manner of infirmities. They had been with Jesus many times as He performed His miracles. Therefore, Mary and Martha needed a new experience with the Lord. They had never seen Him raise someone from the dead after four days in the grave. Jesus knew Mary and Martha needed to see Him in a whole new light. In John 11:4, when Jesus received news from Bethany that Lazarus was sick, Jesus said to His disciples, "This sickness is not unto death, but for the glory of God, that the Son of God might be glorified thereby."

You, too, can see the glory of God in your circumstances if you will heed to His voice and believe Him for the outcome. You may think He is nowhere near, but He is closer than ever before.

*"You, too, can see the glory of God in your
circumstances if you will believe Him
for the outcome."*

Come Forth

SCRIPTURE READING: John 11:43

In John 11, the Bible records the death of Lazarus as well as the heartache and grief that his loved ones experienced during this time. Word had been sent to Jesus that His friend was dying. Four days later, Jesus showed up at the tomb. We all know the rest of the story.

Martha questioned the delayed coming of Jesus. Jesus' simple reply to Martha was, "This is for me to be glorified." Everyone wondered what Jesus could do for Lazarus now; he had been dead for four days. In their minds, and in their time of grief, Jesus was too late to do anything. However, Jesus, in His almighty power, simply spoke for Lazarus to come forth, and up from the grave he arose. There was neither stench nor decay. Lazarus was alive and well. He came forth from the grave, and everyone present experienced the power of God in a whole new light.

God is at work in our lives in the same way. Everyday, He is revealing His presence to those who want to walk with Him intimately. God is saying to each of us, "Come forth. Live and shine for me. I am your God; you are my people."

Today's Scripture text says, "And when he thus had spoken, he cried with a loud voice, Lazarus, come forth." God wants the same for you. I challenge you today to take this Scripture and replace Lazarus' name with your own. Apply these words to your life. Come forth today for the sake of Jesus Christ.

> *"God is saying to each of us, 'Come forth.*
> *Live and shine for me.'"*

If Thou Would Believe

SCRIPTURE READING: John 11:40b

John 11:40b says, "If thou wouldest believe, thou shouldest see the glory of God." We find Jesus here scolding Martha for her lack of trust in Him.

So many times we miss the presence of God because of our own unbelief. Just like Martha, we allow the circumstances to cloud the presence of Almighty God in our lives.

Jesus reminded Martha that if she would believe Him, she could experience the glory of God through the death of her brother. God is saying to all who will listen that we, too, shall see the glory of God if we'll only believe.

Perhaps you are like Martha in her state of grief and turmoil. Perhaps you have lost hope in the midst of your trials. Maybe you're thinking there is no solution. If you are at this point in your life today, then it is very possible that you have collapsed in your despair.

Find strength in the Lord. Get in His Word and allow Him to speak to you just as He spoke to Martha. Believe what He tells you, and you will surely rise above the turmoil this day brings as you experience God's glory.

"Find strength in the Lord. Believe what He tells you. You will surely rise above the turmoil this day brings."

Come Forth As Gold

SCRIPTURE READING: Job 23:10

At different times throughout the year, we have spoken about trying circumstances, grief and despair. We've been reminded of the biblical examples of grief such as Mary and Martha's at the loss of their brother, the trials of the disciples, and the challenges of Bible prophets. We've recently, and frequently, studied Lazarus' death and resurrection.

Today, once again, we will examine a life of despair, the life of Job. Job had experienced it all. Job's life was a roller coaster of triumph, tragedy, triumph. However, his life was built on the foundation of God's promises. Job put his faith in the Almighty God. His response to his circumstances is found in today's Scripture text: "But he knoweth the way that I take: when he hath tried me, I shall come forth as gold."

At the proclamation of this Scripture, Job was revealing his dependence upon God. Job didn't quit and give up on God when surrounded by trials. Job did not allow himself to be distracted by the noise of His life. He kept his eyes and his ears on God. Job knew God was in control, and he wanted to come forth as gold.

Your prayers don't fall on deaf ears. Don't remain bound in clothes of despair. Allow God to put you through the furnace of affliction so you, too, can come forth as gold.

"Allow God to put you through the furnace of affliction so you, too, can come forth as gold."

A Sorrowful Spirit

SCRIPTURE READING: 1 Samuel 1:15a

Hannah was the first of two wives. The other wife, Peninah, could bear children, but Hannah was barren. In Hannah's time, a woman who couldn't bear children was considered to be useless. This alone brought Hannah much heartache. She was favored of the Lord, but why did she have to be sorrowful and doing without? Shouldn't it have been Peninah in this situation?

Peninah frequently reminded Hannah of her barrenness and apparent uselessness. I'm sure Hannah always felt like she was contending with the other wife and what she could offer the husband. Hannah felt insecure and inadequate as a woman and a wife. Today's Scripture text says, "And Hannah answered and said, No, my lord, I am a woman of a sorrowful spirit."

Hannah was being ridiculed and falsely accused by the other wife, her husband and even the high priest. She found herself confused, frustrated and even depressed. She was physically, spiritually and emotionally exhausted. Hannah had grown tired of trying to explain her condition to those closest to her. Therefore, in her state of sorrow, she turned to the only one who could help her. In her sorrow, she turned to God. God heard her prayer, and He intervened.

So many women today are silently suffering as Hannah did. We have withdrawn from our loved ones. We feel that no one understands us, and we feel there is no hope. We, too, must go to God weeping and praying, approaching our heavenly Father with all of our sorrows.

> "We must go to God, our heavenly Father,
> with all of our sorrows."

The Power of Forgiveness

SCRIPTURE READING: Ephesians 4:32

When Jesus Christ gave Himself on the cross, He died so we would have forgiveness of sin. While we were still sinners, He gave His life as a ransom (Romans 5:8). In nine hours of pure torture, Jesus paid the price for our sin. He forgave us, as unworthy as we are.

Nothing could have stopped the death, burial and resurrection of Jesus Christ. He was determined to be the final sacrifice for sin. He died for the ones who crucified and rejected Him. Jesus had walked with them for years, teaching and loving them, and telling them of what had to take place, yet they rejected His truth. Still, He loved them, knowing what they would do. Oh, what forgiveness!

Jesus never held a grudge. He never wanted revenge. He never hated anyone. The power of His forgiveness is awesome. Nothing can ever separate us from His forgiving love.

We receive God's forgiveness when we receive Him as our personal Savior. The next question we must ask ourselves is this: If Christ has forgiven me, then am I not to forgive others also? Am I not to love everyone, even my enemy, unconditionally as Christ loves? The answer to both of these questions is yes. Today's Scripture text seals this for us. It says, "And be ye kind one to another, tenderhearted, forgiving one another, even as God for Christ's sake hath forgiven you."

The power of forgiveness allows us to do this. Experience this power today by loving and forgiving others, even your enemies.

"Jesus never held a grudge. He never wanted revenge. The power of His forgiveness is awesome."

Forgiving Others

SCRIPTURE READING: Matthew 6:14

Our Bible verse for today tells us that in order to receive forgiveness, we must forgive. It says, "For if ye forgive men their trespasses, your heavenly Father will also forgive you."

Forgiving others who have hurt us is hard to do, even if the hurt was unintentional. We claim to forgive them, but we can't seem to get past what happened. We experience painful memories, and before we realize it we have a mass of unforgiveness harbored in our hearts. This puts us in a state of hindered fellowship with God.

When Jesus taught the disciples about effective prayer, He told them to forgive as they had been forgiven. Matthew 6:12 says, "And forgive us our debts, as we forgive our debtors." Jesus taught the disciples that the principle to being effective for Him is to forgive all who have hurt us.

If you are not willing to forgive others than you are not following Christ's principles, and you are in sin. God wants you to confess your unforgiveness. He is faithful to hear you. However, your prayers will not be effective until you become willing to forgive others.

Unforgiveness is a poison to the heart. It destroys any kindness, compassion and desire that you may have within you to live for God. Is there someone in your life whom you have not forgiven? You know what God wants you to do. Don't let unforgiveness destroy you.

"Unforgiveness is a poison to the heart."

A NEW DESIRE

Unforgiveness

SCRIPTURE READING: Matthew 6:15

In yesterday's devotion, we learned that unforgiveness is a poison of the heart. Unforgiveness also causes us to seek revenge and to retaliate with hatred and viciousness. We find ourselves paranoid about the genuineness of others. The greatest problem with unforgiveness is the bitterness and the wall we build to protect us from any more pain. We then end up in self-pity, wondering what we did to deserve such hurt.

In the Old Testament, Joseph is a great example of someone who was used, abused and hurt. He was one of the twelve sons of Jacob. He was hated by his brothers, thrown into a pit, sold for twenty pieces of silver, falsely accused by a woman and then thrown into prison. How many more reasons would a person need to have a spirit of unforgiveness? Joseph did not harbor unforgiveness. He had a love in his heart toward his enemies, and he forgave.

Joseph didn't want anything to stand in His way of receiving God's forgiveness. Joseph understood the principle of today's Scripture text. It says, "But if ye forgive not men their trespasses, neither will your Father forgive your trespasses."

I pray that you understand the message in this verse. Don't harbor unforgiveness in your heart. Confess and forgive today so you can receive the power and blessings of God's forgiveness.

"Confess and forgive today so you can receive the power and blessings of God's forgiveness."

A Beautiful Picture of Grace

SCRIPTURE READING: Isaiah 53:3–7

Today's Scripture text is longer than usual, but oh, what a beautiful picture of grace. It says, "He is despised and rejected of men; a man of sorrows, and acquainted with grief: and we hid as it were our faces from him; he was despised, and we esteemed him not. Surely he hath borne our griefs, and carried our sorrows: yet we did esteem him stricken, smitten of God, and afflicted. But he was wounded for our transgressions, he was bruised for our iniquities: the chastisement of our peace was upon him; and with his stripes we are healed. All we like sheep have gone astray; we have turned every one to his own way; and the LORD hath laid on him the iniquity of us all. He was oppressed, and he was afflicted, yet he opened not his mouth: he is brought as a lamb to the slaughter, and as a sheep before her shearers is dumb, so he openeth not his mouth."

This is a picture of Jesus on Calvary. Put yourself in His place for a moment. Imagine yourself literally loathed and rejected by those you have devoted your life to: your parents, your children, your companion, your friends, your co-workers, your fellow Christians, and even your dog. Could you hold up under the feelings of rejection? Jesus did!

God knew we couldn't and/or wouldn't pay sin's price, so He sent His Son, Jesus, the one perfect, sinless man, to die in our place. By His stripes we are healed. Our sins are forgiven. We have the free gift of salvation. Jesus did it all because He loves us. First John 1:9 says, "If we confess our sins, he is faithful and just to forgive us our sins, and to cleanse us from all unrighteousness." Oh, what a beautiful picture of grace!

> *"God knew we couldn't and / or wouldn't pay*
> *sin's price, so He sent His Son, Jesus."*

Bondage

SCRIPTURE READING: 2 Peter 2:19

Bondage is the nuclear weapon of Satan, the cancer of the flesh and the atomic bomb of one's spiritual destruction. It is brought into our lives by Satan, the flesh and our fellow man.

Bondage has many different faces. Perhaps it is brought on by past, present or recurring sin. It may be caused by an old habit or something that inhabits the heart and mind, preventing us from living a victorious Christian life. We are easily put into the shackles of bondage by worry, fear, stress, doubt and frustration.

Satan uses this nuclear weapon both to prevent unbelievers from coming to salvation and to prevent a believer from living effectively for God. Satan uses the bondage of guilt and shame over past sin to prevent unbelievers from coming to Christ. He convinces them that they are not worthy of God's love and that God could never accept them because of what they've done. He uses the same bondage trap against Christians whom God is calling into ministry. Satan tells us that God can't use us because of our past and that we could never live up to the standards that working for the Lord requires. If Satan can convince us of these lies and hold us in the bondage of guilt, shame and doubt, then he can destroy our stability, effectiveness and faith in Jesus Christ.

Satan is only one of our three enemies who seeks to bring us into bondage. As we study bondage, remember the words of our Scripture text: "While they promise them liberty, they themselves are the servants of corruption: for of whom a man is overcome, of the same is he brought in bondage." Whether you're in bondage to Satan, the flesh or man, you can have victory. Don't be overcome by the things of this world.

"Bondage is the nuclear weapon of Satan."

Obeying God

SCRIPTURE READING: Acts 5:29

We learned yesterday how and why Satan puts us in bondage. Today we'll see how we put ourselves into bondage and allow ourselves to be put into bondage by man.

We put ourselves into bondage to our flesh. The bondage of the flesh eats at our minds like a cancerous tumor. We don't like to think of the things that truly living for the Lord will require us to sacrifice. We'd much rather enjoy a sunny day on the lake than be in church on Sunday. Our flesh immediately starts throwing up shields to protect its desires, and Christ is rejected once again because of the spirit of bondage we have in the flesh.

We allow ourselves to be put into bondage by man in much the same way. We worry about what others will think if we sacrifice the things of this world to live for Christ. We don't want others to think that we're fanatics, and we don't want to lose our social standing. If you are unable to serve God because of the opinions or persecutions of others, you are putting more faith in man than you are in the power of God.

Our Scripture text for today teaches us that obedience to God can free us from bondage to both ourselves and man. When Peter spoke the words, "We ought to obey God rather than men," he was in the midst of being persecuted for living for Christ. As a matter of fact, Peter spoke these words to those who persecuted him and the other apostles for spreading the Gospel. Although they had ordered Peter to stop preaching the Gospel, Peter chose to obey God rather than living in bondage to man.

Don't give in to your flesh or to the opinions and persecutions of man. Choose to obey God instead.

> *"Don't give in to your flesh or to the opinions and persecutions of man."*

192 A NEW DESIRE

Life in Bondage

Scripture Reading: 2 Peter 2:19–20

Living in bondage gradually strips us of the peace, joy and contentment which Jesus Christ died for us to have. Bondage stunts our spiritual growth, strangles our strength, terminates our testimony and falters our faith.

Bondage provokes feelings of inferiority, insecurity and pressure in every area of our lives. These feelings, in turn, cause us to find fault in everything and everyone, including God. People lose their confidence in us because we have lost confidence in ourselves, and our testimony carries no weight. People don't like to be around someone under pressure because they are like a bomb waiting to go off, destroying everything around them.

In this state of weakness, we become prey to temptation, confusion and doubt. In an effort to satisfy our flesh and soothe our hurts, we go to extremes in pampering ourselves. We turn all of our attentions toward ourselves, hurting others and our testimony in the process. We also tend to neglect time in prayer and study of God's Word when we allow ourselves to get into this kind of bondage. Therefore, we lose faith in God.

Bondage is not of God. He gave His only begotten Son to free us from this disease. Today's Scripture text teaches us the consequences of living in bondage: "For if after they have escaped the pollutions of the world through the knowledge of the Lord and Saviour Jesus Christ, they are again entangled therein, and overcome, the latter end is worse with them than the beginning." How much has bondage affected your life?

> *"Bondage is not of God. He gave His only begotten Son to free us from this disease."*

Made Free

SCRIPTURE READING: Hebrews 10:16–17

We've seen how damaging bondage can be in our lives for Christ. The good news is that we have been made free from bondage. John 8:32, 36 says, "And ye shall know the truth, and the truth shall make you free. If the Son therefore shall make you free, ye shall be free indeed."

Jesus Christ made us free from all sin. The truth lies in Him, and the truth as taught in the Bible from Genesis to Revelation is that His blood cleanses us from all sin. Scripture after Scripture releases us from the chains of bondage. These Scriptures are more than truth; they are promises that we can stand on.

Our Scripture text teaches us that God no longer remembers the sins and iniquities of believers. John 3:17 says, "For God sent not his Son into the world to condemn the world; but that the world through him might be saved." Jesus neither condemns us, nor does He put us in bondage. Bondage gives us the fear of condemnation; Jesus delivered us from condemnation. First John 1:7 says, "But if we walk in the light, as he is in the light, we have fellowship one with another, and the blood of Jesus Christ his Son cleanseth us from all sin." There is nothing you have ever done or can do for which Jesus hasn't already made the atonement.

God's power is bestowed upon us for deliverance from failure and the attitude of unworthiness. Nothing can ever separate us from His love (Romans 8:38–39). Freedom from bondage is found in the love of God and the blood of Jesus which covers our sins and frees us from all hindrances. God wants to make us fruitful Christians by making us free through His truths so we can have the peace, joy and contentment that life with Christ produces.

"Jesus Christ made us free from all sin."

What Is Grace?

Scripture Reading: 1 John 1:7

Grace is our access to eternal life. Grace comes from Jesus Christ. Grace protects us from a literal hell. We have grace to live and grace to die. Grace is Jesus upon the cross with all our sins upon Him. Think about it; every sin you have ever committed was nailed to Calvary's cross.

Christ was the atonement for all sin. Today's Scripture text says, "But if we walk in the light, as he is in the light, we have fellowship one with another, and the blood of Jesus Christ his Son cleanseth us from all sin." This, my friend, is the definition of grace. He forgave not only yesterday's sins and today's, but tomorrow's and forever's. That is what the cross was all about.

Grace is being able to receive forgiveness without having to pay the price Jesus paid for it on Calvary. Grace is knowing that you may sin today, hurt someone's feelings, be rude, selfish or unloving, and you'll still be loved unconditionally by Christ. Grace is being able to confess such actions and know that God knew about it already; He was waiting for you to confess and repent. First John 1:9 says, "If we confess our sins, he is faithful and just to forgive us our sins, and to cleanse us from all unrighteousness."

Grace is knowing that in everything we face, we are not alone. Jesus has already been there, and He's there to help us through it. Hebrews 4:15–16 says, "For we have not an high priest which cannot be touched with the feeling of our infirmities; but was in all points tempted like as we are, yet without sin. Let us therefore come boldly unto the throne of grace, that we may obtain mercy, and find grace to help in time of need."

God's grace has made us free. Rest in His grace today.

"Grace is Jesus upon the cross with all our sins upon Him."

Fulfilling a Promise

SCRIPTURE READING: Hebrews 10:23

When someone makes a promise to us, we stand on that promise until it is performed. We put all of our faith and trust in this person, knowing they won't let us down. If that person fails to fulfill that promise, our trust is broken, our faith wavers and our confidence in that person is destroyed. We feel hurt, rejected and unwanted.

Jesus is our greatest example of promises fulfilled. He never once went back on His word. He performed everything He said He would. He has never lied to us or let us down.

We often make promises to God dependent upon His deliverance from a circumstance or situation we face. Almost as often, we fail to come through on these promises once we've been delivered. We break promises to friends, children and family without thinking twice about it.

Breaking promises is not of God, and it harms our Christian character. We shouldn't take promises so lightly. Jesus never took promises lightly. Jesus knew that breaking a promise would make Him a liar, and Calvary would have been of no effect.

Do you realize the importance of fulfilling the promises you make? It is essential to remain faithful to your promises. Life is rewarding because we can stand on the promises of God, so we must be just as faithful to others to enjoy the rewards of God's promises. Today's Scripture text says, "Let us hold fast the profession of our faith without wavering; (for he is faithful that promised)."

Grow in faithfulness by fulfilling the promises you make and by mending the promises you have broken.

"Jesus is our greatest example of promises fulfilled."

A NEW DESIRE

Learning to Behave

SCRIPTURE READING: Romans 12:1

Today's Scripture text says, "I beseech you therefore, brethren, by the mercies of God, that ye present your bodies a living sacrifice, holy, acceptable unto God, which is your reasonable service." Our bodies are to be an outward example of our inward life. If Christ lives in us, we have the power to present our bodies as this living sacrifice. We can choose to behave through our Spirit, or we can live in our flesh. The decision is ours to make.

If we choose to live in the flesh, we will not be good examples for Christ. We have failed to present our bodies as that living sacrifice. The flesh acts upon its own lust, not the direction of God's Spirit and power. The flesh does not know how to behave itself because we will not bring it under subjection to God.

The Holy Spirit is our power for good behavior and bringing our bodies under subjection to God. Our Scripture text reveals to us the three keys to good, pleasing behavior in the eyes of God. We must: become a living sacrifice, become holy, and become acceptable to God. How do we do these three things?

We become a living sacrifice by forsaking our fleshly lusts and sacrificing our own wants for what God wants. We become holy by setting aside our sinfulness and living in righteousness. Finally, we become acceptable unto God by walking in these ways every day and striving to behave like He does.

Jesus is our teacher for good behavior. Strive to be more like Him.

"Jesus is our teacher for good behavior."

A Sense of Belonging

SCRIPTURE READING: 1 Samuel 30:13

Today's Scripture text tells of the plight of a young man without a sense of belonging. It says, "And David said unto him, To whom belongest thou? and whence art thou? And he said, I am a young man of Egypt, servant to an Amalekite; and my master left me, because three days ago I fell sick."

This young servant had been stranded; he was left, sick and alone, by his master. His illness made him of no use to his master. He had no sense of belonging. We, like this young man, often feel abandoned and out of place with God. We feel like He doesn't hear us or care about our circumstances.

The devil loves for us to feel this way about God. He attacks our spiritual security by filling our minds with these insecurities. Satan doesn't want us to trust God's love. We can overcome these attacks by standing on the promises of God.

God wants us to have a sense of belonging to Him. His Word tells us that He knows our every need, thought and burden. If we can only rest in His promises, then we can feel forever safe as a part of the family of God. As born again children of God, nothing can ever separate us from His love, no matter how hard the battle gets.

In God, you should have and feel a sense of belonging. You are His, and He loves you very much. If you don't have this sense of belonging, Satan will use it to destroy the effectiveness of your service to God. Don't let this happen to you. If you know God wants you to do something, then claim your position with God and move forward in His service with the confidence that you belong to Him.

> *"God wants us to have a sense of belonging to Him."*

A NEW DESIRE

Negative or Positive?

SCRIPTURE READING: Matthew 12:35

How many thoughts do you have in a day's time that would be considered negative? What is a negative thought? A negative thought is any thought that degrades, denies or refuses a positive response or action. In other words, negativity is bad thoughts, actions or words toward one's self or toward another. Just how many bad thoughts do you have in a day about yourself or someone else?

How many thoughts do you have in a day's time that would be considered positive? What is a positive thought? A positive thought is any thought that uplifts, affirms and assures one's self or another. In other words, positivity is good thoughts, actions or words. How many positive thoughts do you have in a day about yourself or someone else?

It seems that most people have more negative thoughts than positive. Why? Because it is our fleshly nature to look for the bad in every person, ourselves and in every situation. We refuse to put on the mind of God and rest in a positive attitude. Today's Scripture text says, "A good man out of the good treasure of the heart bringeth forth good things: and an evil man out of the evil treasure bringeth forth evil things."

Negative thoughts are not pleasing to God. Being positive pleases God, for then we look for the good in all things. God made us to be positive and confident people.

Positivity is the key to an effective Christian life. The world is looking for salvation and hope through a positive, on-fire-for-God Christian. Christians are the only light in this world. I challenge you to examine yourself to determine whether you are a positive or negative Christian. God is not negative, and He doesn't want you to be either.

"Being positive pleases God."

Questions and Answers

SCRIPTURE READING: James 4:2–3

People have a tendency to teach that we should never question God about the circumstances in our lives. Questioning God is often treated as a cardinal sin. If we refuse to question God about life's problems and uncertainties, how can we ever expect to receive His blessings? We reject God's love when we refuse to question Him.

Today's Scripture text teaches us that we can be delivered from the battles that seem to destroy us if we will only seek God regarding the situation. It says, "Ye lust, and have not: ye kill, and desire to have, and cannot obtain: ye fight and war, yet ye have not, because ye ask not. Ye ask, and receive not, because ye ask amiss, that ye may consume it upon your lusts." Refusing to ask means refusing to get an answer. We choose to listen to our own reason rather than the voice of God, therefore, we close the door to truth and communication.

Satan wants you to believe that you shouldn't question God. The longer we go without "asking" God about our lives, the greater the battle becomes. We can't fix things without God's help. If we never ask Him for help, how can we know His will for our lives?

Today's Scripture also teaches us that we fail to receive because we ask amiss. This means we ask for worthless reasons. If you ask God for answers about your life, you should ask because you want to better understand Him and draw closer to Him, not for your own reasons.

I challenge you to take all of your questions to God and allow Him to answer you according to His will for your life. It's okay to question God as long as you allow Him to answer. Seek Him in your circumstances and listen for His voice.

"Take all of your questions to God and allow Him to answer you."

Walking in God's Presence

SCRIPTURE READING: Hebrews 13:6

When we face fear, adversities and rejection, we often go into a shell of hurt and denial toward God. We don't understand what is going on, and we wonder where God is in the midst of all the turmoil. There seems to be no hope for our situation, and our faith in God seems to crumble. Friend, you are always in the presence of God. He is your helper in every situation, and nothing can overcome Him and His presence in your life.

If you walk with God, having faith in Him for all areas of your life, God will deliver you from all harm. Today's Scripture text says, "So that we may boldly say, The Lord is my helper, and I will not fear what man shall do unto me." He wants to show you His presence in your life by delivering you from what you think are hopeless situations.

To walk in God's presence means you have to humble yourself before Him. Confess your sin, thoughts and needs to Him and leave them at His feet, expecting Him to take care of them according to His will for your life.

Walking in God's presence is a privilege for all born again believers. Practice this privilege and let it become a permanent source of survival in your life.

"To walk in God's presence means you have to humble yourself before Him."

A Cheerful Countenance

SCRIPTURE READING: Proverbs 15:13

Do you ever find that you can determine the state of someone's mind just by the countenance on their faces? We, by nature, sum up a person's attitude by the way they respond to us with facial gestures. If someone looks at me with a smile, I automatically have nice thoughts of that person. On the other hand, a person who has a frown or lines on their forehead will usually not respond at all, or if he does, it will not be a kind or gentle response. I avoid this type of countenance because these people already look offended, and I don't want to be the one they retaliate on! However, true Christ-likeness would go out of its way to be kind to this person in particular.

Today's Scripture text says, "A merry heart maketh a cheerful countenance: but by sorrow of the heart the spirit is broken." Our countenance says a lot for us as Christians. I always look for the joy of Christ in a person's countenance. If I don't see a smile or cheerful countenance, then I begin to wonder if they know Jesus Christ as their Savior.

I have met people who are saved and have a lot to be positive about, but still they wore a broken countenance. These people choose to dwell in sorrow.

Begin today working on your countenance. Make everyday a day of cheerfulness in Christ, cheerfulness in your heart and a merry countenance on your face.

"Our countenance says a lot for us as Christians."

A NEW DESIRE

The Crowns of Christians

Scripture Reading: 2 Timothy 4:7–8

How many times in life have we so excitedly set out to do something to only find ourselves defeated and discouraged in the end? Due to the discouragement and challenges of this life, we often give up on our goals too easily. Today's Scripture text says, "I have fought a good fight, I have finished my course, I have kept the faith: Henceforth there is laid up for me a crown of righteousness, which the Lord, the righteous judge, shall give me at that day: and not to me only, but unto all them also that love his appearing."

We live with very fragile emotions. We allow ourselves to be overtaken with doubt, fear, insecurities and shattered dreams. Satan is the author of these doubts and insecurities. He detects and uses our every weakness, and he uses them to deceive and defeat us in our Christian walks. Don't let Satan hinder you from your work for the Lord. God didn't select someone else for your job. He wanted you to do it. Jesus never quit on the task God gave Him, and we must not give up on ours. What we do for God should not be taken lightly; in fact, it should have priority over everything else.

As we run the race of Christianity, we are laying up treasures in Heaven. We have access to five crowns through Jesus' death, burial and resurrection. Those five crowns are the treasures we're building. They are the crown of life, the crown of righteousness, the crown of joy, the crown of glory and the incorruptible crown.

Let's take the next few days to study these crowns in detail, and then let's strive to stand fast in our faith and proudly serve for our rewards.

"As we run the race of Christianity, we are laying up treasures in Heaven."

Corruptible and Incorruptible Crowns

SCRIPTURE READING: 1 Corinthians 9:24–27

Today's Scripture text reminds us of the difference between corruptible crowns and incorruptible crowns. It says, "Know ye not that they which run in a race run all, but one receiveth the prize? So run, that ye may obtain. And every man that striveth for the mastery is temperate in all things. Now they do it to obtain a corruptible crown; but we an incorruptible. I therefore so run, not as uncertainly; so fight I, not as one that beateth the air: But I keep under my body, and bring it into subjection: lest that by any means, when I have preached to others, I myself should be a castaway."

Paul presents the Christian life as running a race so we will understand that serving God requires discipline from us. Serving Him takes hard work, self-denial and planning to receive Heavenly awards. Christianity is not a spectator sport; it is race we must run.

We will forfeit our rewards if we let the things of this world stand in the way of our service. Our will is often misconstrued as God's will, leaving us deceived and defeated. God doesn't change His mind about things like we do. He is certainty and stability in all things. When He calls us to do a service, He expects us to be as certain and stable in that work as He is.

Sure, you will be tested, tried and tired at times, but these are not reasons to let the task go unfinished. You will catch slack from others, and probably even be talked about by those you love, but you must remember that they are not the ones you must please. Your rewards come from God alone, and His rewards are greater than any you could receive from this world.

"Your rewards come from God alone, and His rewards are greater than any."

A NEW DESIRE

The Principles of Obtaining Crowns

SCRIPTURE READING: 2 Timothy 4:5

Today's Scripture text says, "But watch thou in all things, endure afflictions, do the work of an evangelist, make full proof of thy ministry." If we will determine to finish what God has started, He will finish it through us. By making ourselves available to Him, we can be used of Him.

You can't fail in your service if God is directing you. You may make a few mistakes as you grow in your service, but mistakes should not be taken as failures. They are lessons. We can complete our tasks successfully and obtain our crowns by following these five principles.

1) Always make sure God has led you into a service before undertaking it. Don't be led by others or by your own desires. You won't receive rewards if God isn't first and foremost in your service.

2) Seek the Lord's direction on how He'd have you to do your job, and do it exactly as He says. There will always be a voice of discouragement, but close your ears to the negative and follow only the positive voice of God.

3) Never become idle in your service. There are new avenues of approach and exposure for your work if you'll seek and want them.

4) Pray consistently for God's blessings on your work. If God is in your work, you will be attacked, but God will bless your efforts if you'll stay true to Him.

5) Never depend upon your own strength. God is your source of strength, and His grace will be sufficient in all things. Zecharaiah 4:6 says, "Then he answered and spake unto me, saying, This is the word of the LORD unto Zerubbabel, saying, Not by might, nor by power, but by my spirit, saith the LORD of hosts."

> *"You can't fail in your service
> if God is directing you."*

The Crown of Life

SCRIPTURE READING: James 1:12

Obtaining the crown of life is as simple as following the instructions laid down in today's Scripture text. It says, "Blessed is the man that endureth temptation: for when he is tried, he shall receive the crown of life, which the Lord hath promised to them that love him." We must endure temptation and trials to receive the crown.

What does it mean to endure temptation? It means "to be put to proof; to experience, by implication, adversity." The word tried means "to be acceptable, approved, or tried." In other words, we must remain in Christ, regardless of what we must go through, in order to obtain the crown of life.

The only way we can complete an acceptable work for the Lord is to stand strong even when life doesn't seem fair. We must prove our faith, not to God, but to ourselves and others. God already knows how we will respond to life's experiences. It is how the world sees us respond that makes us acceptable servants. God's concern is not what we receive praise for here on earth. His crown of life is the reward of eternal life in Heaven.

As Christians taking a stand for God, we will face adversity, but we must remember that we are bought with a price. Jesus bought us with His own life. He endured temptation, and when He was tried, He was found faithful. He never gave up under the pressure. He never let the opinions of others sway Him. He was given a job to do, and He completed it with love. If He had folded under the pressure, you and I would not have access to the crown of life, but Jesus is the crown of life. If you know without a doubt that you are saved, then you have received this crown. Your reward is in Heaven. The crown of life is a free gift to all who have been born again. Let's work toward the other crowns as we study the following pages.

> *"As Christians taking a stand for God,*
> *we will face adversity."*

The Crown of Righteousness

SCRIPTURE READING: 2 Corinthians 5:17

The crown of righteousness is a crown of justification. When Jesus died on Calvary's cross, you were justified by His blood. As His child, you must now strive to live righteously. Today's Scripture text says, "Therefore if any man be in Christ, he is a new creature: old things are passed away; behold, all things are become new."

Jesus laid the foundation for righteousness; now we must build upon that foundation. Second Timothy 2:19 says, "Nevertheless the foundation of God standeth sure, having this seal, The Lord knoweth them that are his. And, Let every one that nameth the name of Christ depart from iniquity." You must have a desire to turn from your sins, hindrances and selfish habits and live wholly for the Gospel's sake in order to win the crown of righteousness.

The crowns of life and righteousness go together in obtaining a personal relationship with Christ. Jesus is life, and He is righteousness. If He lives in you, then you, too, can live pleasing to Him.

There are seven principles to obtaining the crown of righteousness once you've been born again. We'll devote the next few days to these principles and this crown. Focus your heart on this crown, and let's strive toward receiving it.

"Jesus laid the foundation for righteousness;
now we must build upon that foundation."

Obtaining the Crown of Righteousness, Part One

SCRIPTURE READING: 2 Timothy 2:20–21

There are seven principles to obtaining the crown of righteousness. Let's study them one by one.

1) You must endure hardness as a good soldier. We must separate ourselves from this world. We can't straddle the fence between worldliness and godliness. You must be honest with God, yourself and others to endure hardness. Fight the battle by God's rules; cheating doesn't work with God.

2) You must die to your old ways and partake of the new life in Christ. You must be willing to suffer as Christ did. Taking a stand for God means denying yourself the things that feed your flesh. You must set an example of righteousness for all to see.

3) Study the Word of God. Righteousness is the Word of God, and we'll be defeated if we fail to study it. The enemy will steal the truth right out of our hearts.

4) We must choose God's will over our own. Today's Scripture text says, "But in a great house there are not only vessels of gold and of silver, but also of wood and of earth; and some to honour, and some to dishonour. If a man therefore purge himself from these, he shall be a vessel unto honour, sanctified, and meet for the master's use, and prepared unto every good work." If we don't use the things in our lives to uplift the name of Jesus and for His honor and glory, then it becomes a vessel of dishonor. However, we can purge ourselves from these things and become vessels of honor instead.

Have you applied these first four principles to your life? If not, pray that God will help you to start applying them today. Work toward applying these principles now, and tomorrow we'll study the remaining three.

"We must choose God's will over our own."

Obtaining the Crown of Righteousness, Part Two

SCRIPTURE READING: Philippians 3:13–14

Yesterday, we learned the first four principles to obtaining the crown of righteousness. Today, we'll study the remaining three. Let's seek to apply all seven to our lives.

5) Do not allow yourself to be tempted. This will require you to avoid the things that lead you into temptation, lust and sin. Second Timothy 2:22 says, "Flee also youthful lusts: but follow righteousness, faith, charity, peace, with them that call on the Lord out of a pure heart." To flee temptation, you must have a desire to do so, and you must run with the righteous instead of the worldly.

6) Righteousness requires us to set examples. We must discipline ourselves to represent the characteristics of Christ. We must be gentle to those who we feel don't deserve gentleness. We must show God's unconditional love to a lost and dying world, and we must instruct others in the ways of God.

7) Finally, we must have a disciplined prayer life. We must seek God's will in all things. The key to achieving all of our goals is getting His permission. Failure to pray means doing things our own way and in our own strength. We forfeit God's rewards when we do this.

Jesus Christ is the crown of life and righteousness. Are you striving to receive your crowns? Are you completing your task righteously, or are you backing down from your responsibilities more every day? Today's Scripture text says, "Brethren, I count not myself to have apprehended: but this one thing I do, forgetting those things which are behind, and reaching forth unto those things which are before, I press toward the mark for the prize of the high calling of God in Christ Jesus."

Let's press toward the mark and obtain the crowns.

"Jesus Christ is the crown of life and righteousness."

Crowns of Joy and Glory

SCRIPTURE READING: 1 Thessalonians 2:19–20

Salvation gives us instant joy unspeakable and full of glory. We have this joy because we no longer have to fear death, evil or hell. We stand in the promises of God as His children, and everyone around us is blessed by the light that shines within us. This light is the glory of God manifested in our lives through His indwelling in our hearts.

Many of us feel unworthy of joy. Others allow their joy to be stolen by inner voices of doubt and fear. We fall prey to our insecurities and past defeats. Satan uses these things to distract us from the true reason for our joy. Today's Scripture text reveals the source of our joy. It says, "For what is our hope, or joy, or crown of rejoicing? Are not even ye in the presence of our Lord Jesus Christ at his coming? For ye are our glory and joy."

Paul explains the sufferings of God's servants throughout the second chapter of 1 Thessalonians. They were mistreated and rejected for standing for the Gospel. They were falsely accused and punished as liars and deceivers. Still, they continued to teach and preach the Gospel in a manner pleasing to God. This was their joy and glory.

Our joy and glory should also be in acceptable service to God. We should glory in the cross because through it we have been made free from sin and shame. Our joy should stand in the fact that nothing can ever separate us from the love of God. We can go to Him with everything, and He will be faithful to provide for our needs.

We must strive for the crowns of joy and glory by praising God for all things, good and bad. We have a responsibility to be content in whatever state we are in. The Christian life is not an easy one, but we can still reflect a Christ-like attitude of joy even in our heartaches if we'll put our faith and trust in God.

"We must strive for the crowns of joy and glory by praising God."

A NEW DESIRE

The Incorruptible Crown

SCRIPTURE READING: 1 Corinthians 9:24–27

Today's Scripture text says, "Know ye not that they which run in a race run all, but one receiveth the prize? So run, that ye may obtain. And every man that striveth for the mastery is temperate in all things. Now they do it to obtain a corruptible crown; but we an incorruptible. I therefore so run, not as uncertainly; so fight I, not as one that beateth the air: But I keep under my body, and bring it into subjection: lest that by any means, when I have preached to others, I myself should be a castaway."

Paul persuades us in today's Scripture text to keep running and training for the prize of Heaven. We strive for worldly crowns everyday, but these crowns will never get us into Heaven. They will burn up when the Lord returns. The incorruptible crown we receive as we enter Heaven's gates will never be destroyed. This crown is the one that says you have died to self, lived to Christ and served righteously and joyously.

The incorruptible crown signifies a perfect, completed new person. We will have a new body that doesn't decay. There will be no more depression, death or failures. We will not have to worry about tomorrow or its temptations.

The incorruptible crown is the center of all the other crowns. This is why we should put God first in our lives and strive to be the best we can for Him. We must run to obtain His attention and serve with joy and glory as we strive to live in righteousness. We must be stable in our service and not give up the fight.

Run your race with dignity and self-control. Be willing to sacrifice, suffer and endure until the end. God will honor your efforts regardless of how inadequate they seem. He will use you as long as you're willing to be used. Are you running the race with endurance?

*"The incorruptible crown signifies
a completed new person."*

I Can Do All Things

Scripture Reading: Philippians 4:13

You can receive the crowns we've been studying. There is no need for you to feel less worthy than others or unfit for the job. Today's Scripture text says, "I can do all things through Christ which strengtheneth me."

We will all fall short and make mistakes as we strive to serve God. This is part of our growth in Him. If we were perfect, we'd have already been taken to Heaven. As long as we remain on this earth, we're growing in Him.

If you want to receive your crowns, apply a few simple techniques to your life.

1) Serve because you love God, not because you want to impress someone else.
2) Turn from ALL your sinful ways. Don't leave any of them out. Confess them daily.
3) Don't quit every time you get your feelings hurt. Be strong in your faith.
4) Strive to know God's Word so the Holy Spirit can bring it to your remembrance when you need to use it.
5) Pray about everything.
6) Do all things in the Spirit.
7) Never be ashamed of the Gospel of Jesus Christ. Romans 1:16 says, "For I am not ashamed of the Gospel of Christ: for it is the power of God unto salvation to every one that believeth; to the Jew first, and also to the Greek."

Remember, you can do all things through Christ. Yes, even you. You can receive the five crowns of the Christian. Apply these techniques to your life and start growing in Him today.

"There is no need for you to feel less worthy than others or unfit for the job."

Words of Encouragement

SCRIPTURE READING: Isaiah 26:3–4

We never know what tomorrow holds. In fact, we don't even know what the next moment holds. We can plan out our days and anticipate life's next move, but that doesn't mean things will happen as planned. Life holds many surprises and uncertainties. It holds many heartaches and responsibilities. How can we cope with life's menu? How do we survive when we feel we can't go another mile, think another thought, or breathe another breath?

Today's Scripture text says, "Thou wilt keep him in perfect peace, whose mind is stayed on thee: because he trusteth in thee. Trust ye in the LORD for ever: for in the LORD JEHOVAH is everlasting strength." God gives us the peace to go on. We must place our trust in Him and meditate upon His Word. God will give us strength and comfort when we need it most if we'll only let Him.

Life is as complicated as we make it. When we choose to handle things ourselves, without God's consent, our lives become difficult. We worry when we choose not to trust God. Hurt, worry and panic are allowed in our lives as tools of growth, not as places to dwell. God wants us to care about life's happenings, but He doesn't want us to put so much emphasis on our circumstances that we forget to depend on Him and His power to sustain us.

The greatest encouragement of all must be found in the fact that God will give us peace regardless of the circumstances in our lives. We can survive whatever life sends our way if we'll depend on Him.

Keep your mind on Him, and He will fill you with His peace. He is the Lord Jehovah, and in Him is everlasting strength. He understands all your weakness, frustration and pain. Lay it all at the feet of Jesus. God will use it for His gain.

"When we choose to handle things ourselves, without God's consent, our lives become difficult."

An Instrument of Peace and Encouragement

SCRIPTURE READING: Galatians 6:2

God uses us to minister to one another. We are His instruments of peace and encouragement in each other's lives. God will let us know He cares when we're in our lowest valleys by laying us on someone else's heart. Kind words, phone calls and pretty cards are God's way of loving us through others.

We are God's vessels of love, strength and comfort if we'll allow ourselves to be used of Him. Many ask the question, "How can I comfort or encourage others when my own life is such a mess?" We can still be used if we'll let God work through us. When we decide to use our messes for the honor and glory of God, we can effectively help others. Our experiences can be used to help others in the same circumstances. Today's Scripture text says, "Bear ye one another's burdens, and so fulfil the law of Christ."

Whatever you may be experiencing, someone else out there is having the same or a similar experience. People long to know that they are not the only ones with problems. The world is crumbling due to lack of communication. We all paint a perfect, problem free exterior picture of our lives, but inside we're full of problems and chaos. Friend, the greatest words of encouragement are, "I have been where you are. I really care about your problems, and I truly understand how you feel." This is the fulfillment of our Scripture text.

The law of Christ is love; bearing one another's burdens fulfills that law. Matthew 22:37–40 says, "Jesus said unto him, Thou shalt love the Lord thy God with all thy heart, and with all thy soul, and with all thy mind. This is the first and great commandment. And the second is like unto it, Thou shalt love thy neighbour as thyself. On these two commandments hang all the law and the prophets." Bear one another's burdens. It will make your load lighter and give you hope for tomorrow.

"We are God's vessels of love, strength and comfort."

A NEW DESIRE

Dare to Be Different

SCRIPTURE READING: 2 Corinthians 6:17–18

The Bible teaches us to come out from this world and be a separate people. Today's Scripture text says, "Wherefore come out from among them, and be ye separate, saith the Lord, and touch not the unclean thing; and I will receive you, And will be a Father unto you, and ye shall be my sons and daughters, saith the Lord Almighty." We should dare to be different so we can have a relationship with God as our Father. We should reject compromise and popularity for the truth of God's Word.

Being different requires a sacrifice, calls for independence and produces intimacy with our Lord and Savior Jesus Christ. God always honors our efforts to reject the yearnings of our flesh and the peer pressures from other people. Daring to be different demands the study of God's Word and a willingness to talk about Jesus in private and in public.

God is always the same. He never changes. He is the same in the aisle of the supermarket as He is when we are on our knees at the altar. Being different requires us to care more about what God thinks about us than what others think about us. God is the one we must answer to when this life is said and done.

Daring to be different is being a Christian seven days a week, twenty four hours a day. We should be praying about all things, praising God and learning more about Him everyday. When we hunger to know more about God, we leave ourselves open to make a difference in someone else's life and in this world.

God can make you a different person if you'll allow Him full control of your life. He will teach you His ways and His will for your life. When we give Him control, He can reveal Himself to us in a much more personal realm. We will draw closer to Him, and we'll "dare to be different."

"Being different requires a sacrifice, calls for independence and produces intimacy with our Lord and Savior Jesus Christ."

Calvary's Miracle

SCRIPTURE READING: John 10:10

We are walking, talking miracles if we have accepted Jesus Christ as our personal Savior. The greatest miracle ever performed was the one Jesus Christ handed to us at Calvary. The miracle at Calvary for you and me was a way to escape eternal hell.

Before Christ went to the cross our destination was hell with no way out. Nothing could have ever saved us from a literal fire if Jesus had not gone to the cross and paid our sin debt. This, my friend, is the greatest miracle ever performed.

When God saves someone, the effects of salvation make them change their lifestyle, habits and sins. These are the results of the miracle at Calvary. Another part of the miracle at Calvary is that Jesus provided protection for us while we were still sinners and undeserving of such provisions. There was no other man who could or would have died for the sins of the world. Jesus, the name above all others, has truly worked miracles in our lives. Why did He do it? John 10:10 tells us why: "I am come that they might have life, and that they might have it more abundantly." We truly can have life more abundantly.

How long has it been since you told someone that Jesus performed a miracle in your life by saving you?

"Jesus provided protection for us while we were still sinners."

A NEW DESIRE

God Still Loves Me

SCRIPTURE READING: Luke 23:34

Today's Scripture text says, "Then said Jesus, Father, forgive them; for they know not what they do." I wrote the following poem, titled "God Still Loves Me", after experiencing the reality of these words in my own life.

God's love is like a rapid river,
Rushing out of control.
Not even the largest rocks or reefs
Can stop its constant flow.
I know that when I dam His love
With walls of rejection and pain
That God still loves me through it all,
And that fact will never change.
He loves me when I hate myself,
And when others couldn't care less.
Yes, God still loves me in my weakest hour,
Even when I fail His tests.
So, even though I've failed His tests,
One thing from them I've learned:
God still loves me, no matter what,
And His love doesn't have to be earned.

John 3:16, 17 says, "For God so loved the world, that he gave his only begotten Son, that whosoever believeth in him should not perish, but have everlasting life. For God sent not his Son into the world to condemn the world; but that the world through him might be saved."

Take time today to thank God for His unconditional love.

"God's love doesn't have to be earned."

JULY   217

An Avenue of Escape

SCRIPTURE READING: Colossians 3:1–3

Today's Scripture text says, "If ye then be risen with Christ, seek those things which are above, where Christ sitteth on the right hand of God. Set your affection on things above, not on things on the earth. For ye are dead, and your life is hid with Christ in God."

When we are defeated, persecuted and weary, when life seems hopeless, when our thoughts seem cold and dry and our hearts are empty, we have an avenue of escape. When sin is controlling your life and Satan is tempting and enticing you with His lies and evil thoughts, you have an avenue of escape. The escape is Jesus Christ and His righteousness.

If you are truly saved, then you have an eternal position with Christ, and the Holy Spirit is your power to overcome. The flesh must be forsaken so the Spirit can minister to our hearts. We must think on spiritual things if we want an avenue of escape. This is confirmed in today's Scripture text. Hiding in Christ, seeking things eternal while rejecting things of this world, is your only avenue of escape.

If you find yourself smothering in your weariness and you feel that life is closing in on you, remember that your life is hid in Christ. He is there to show you the way of escape. He is the way.

> *"We must think on spiritual things*
> *if we want an avenue of escape."*

An Old Account Settled

SCRIPTURE READING: John 16:33

We all have sinned and come short of the glory of God. None of us are perfect in this life, but if Jesus is our Savior, we have hope. Jesus lives in our hearts through the Holy Spirit. His blood has washed our sins away, and we are made holy, unblameable and unaccused.

At the cross of Calvary, our old accounts were settled. Our slates were cleaned. Our sins are remembered no more. We can start over in Jesus, trusting Him for all things.

The blood of Jesus has made us free from the destruction of sin, trials, persecutions and rejections which we battle every day in this life. In the flesh, we face these things, but through our new life in Christ we have power to deal with and overcome them. The Bible says in today's Scripture text, "These things I have spoken unto you, that in me ye might have peace. In the world ye shall have tribulation: but be of good cheer; I have overcome the world."

All we have to do is die to self and lay everything at Jesus' feet. It is time we become the children of God who claim, accept and demonstrate our new lives in Christ. It is time we let old things pass away and allow God to bless us with the new things that life in Him contains.

God doesn't remember our sins and iniquities, so why can't we forget them? He is the one we must answer to, and through Him we have overcome the world. Through salvation, our old account was settled with Him; therefore, we should settle our old account in our own hearts.

Be of good cheer. Through Christ you have overcome the past.

"At the cross of Calvary,
our old accounts were settled."

The Forgiveness of Sins

SCRIPTURE READING: Colossians 1:12–14

Today's Scripture text says, "Giving thanks unto the Father, which hath made us meet to be partakers of the inheritance of the saints in light: Who hath delivered us from the power of darkness, and hath translated us into the kingdom of his dear Son: In whom we have redemption through his blood, even the forgiveness of sins."

This Scripture should be enough to transform our minds and rebuild our hope to go on in our lives. Why doesn't it have the effect on us that it should? Why can't we accept what it says and move on? The answer is simple; we still live in the flesh, and the flesh battles the Spirit everyday.

For most of us, we are not studied enough or strong enough in the Lord to understand and accept God's unconditional love. Therefore, we let our flesh control our thoughts and actions, rejecting the new life Christ bestows upon us.

The flesh feels unworthy of God's forgiveness. We live life knowing that Jesus is our Savior, yet we are unwilling to accept His forgiveness. We are even unwilling to forgive ourselves. This leaves room for Satan to deceive us into believing that God would never use someone as sinful and unworthy as we are. Insecurity and inadequacy leave an open door for Satan's deceptions.

It is time we learn to reject the lies of the devil and accept the forgiveness Jesus offered on Calvary's cross. Let's start right now "Giving thanks unto the Father, which hath made us meet to be partakers of the inheritance of the saints in light: Who hath delivered us from the power of darkness, and hath translated us into the kingdom of his dear Son: In whom we have redemption through his blood, even the forgiveness of sins."

"Reject the lies of the devil and accept the forgiveness Jesus offered on Calvary's cross."

A NEW DESIRE

A Source of Encouragement

SCRIPTURE READING: John 16:7

Encouragement is something rare these days. Our own supply of encouragement is so limited that it can't reach beyond self. We run out of encouragement before our own reserve is completely full. There's no possible way we could spare some for anyone else.

When times are hard and we are so heavily burdened, we find it extremely difficult to give words of encouragement to others. Perhaps you just don't have any words of encouragement in you, or maybe you're just not in the mood to be an encouragement to someone else. It could be that you need encouragement so badly yourself, you don't see the need for it in others. The pressures of life have us so bound down that we often can't see our lack of encouragement.

Jesus encouraged the believers while He walked on this earth, and He still encourages us everyday through His Word and His Holy Spirit. John 14:1 says, "Let not your heart be troubled: ye believe in God, believe also in me." John 16:7 says, "Nevertheless I tell you the truth; It is expedient for you that I go away: for if I go not away, the comforter will not come unto you; but if I depart, I will send him unto you." The Holy Spirit is our comforter, and the Word of God is our encouragement, for in it we see the blessed promises of Jesus Christ.

Once we've been encouraged through God's Word, we can share our excitement with others. Through our sharing, they can be encouraged, too. Jesus Christ is glorified when we share excitement with others. Get in the Word so you can be a source of encouragement for someone else.

"Get in the Word so you can be a source of encouragement for someone else."

Dare to Discipline

SCRIPTURE READING: Job 36:10

One of our greatest setbacks in life is losing sight of the goals and desires we set out to achieve. We are easily sidetracked by spontaneous whims. We are hindered by daily routines or pleasurable desires and misled by enemy forces. Something always throws us off balance.

Our Christian growth also falls under this category. We allow our walk and relationship with the Lord to be on the bottom of our list of priorities. It seems to be our nature to put jobs, homes and families at the top of the priority list. It has been said by most everyone that God holds us responsible and expects us to provide for our homes and loved ones. I completely agree, but I must add to this. God gave us our homes, jobs and families. He blesses us with these things, but He expects us to use them for His honor and glory. The Scriptures tell us in Hebrews 3:4 that, "Every house is builded by some man; but he that built all things is God." Therefore, pleasing God should be the first thing on our lists of priorities. Without Him we wouldn't have these earthly possessions and blessings.

Discipline is something we all battle. Most of us stay so preoccupied with life that discipline has become totally impossible. We get so caught up in day to day circumstances that we are more troubled than anything. We allow everyday life to control our thoughts, take up all of our time and hinder us from fellowship with the one and only true God of our lives. To most people, discipline is getting up and going to work everyday, paying the bills and fulfilling their role as a member of church, family and society. However, the discipline that I'm speaking of is a constant and dedicated relationship with God. Discipline is the daily practice of spending time with God.

God is the path to setting our priorities. As we dare to discipline ourselves into an effective and powerful relationship with Him, we must first examine ourselves. God is faithful to show us our ways. Our Scripture text says, "He openeth also their ear to discipline, and commandeth that they return from iniquity." Dare to discipline yourself so God won't have to.

"Discipline is the daily practice of spending time with God."

The Discipline Battle

SCRIPTURE READING: Romans 7:18

Paul had been hindered in his service. Like you and me, he had to regroup from time to time to keep himself disciplined and pleasing to God in the work of the ministry. Paul tells us in Romans 7:18–22 that he battled daily with discipline. He said, "For I know that in me (that is, in my flesh,) dwelleth no good thing: for to will is present with me; but how to perform that which is good I find not. For the good that I would I do not: but the evil which I would not, that I do. Now if I do that I would not, it is no more I that do it, but sin that dwelleth in me. I find then a law, that, when I would do good, evil is present with me. For I delight in the law of God after the inward man."

Paul had taken time to examine himself. He found his flesh in battle with the Spirit. This had often put Paul in a troubled state of mind. He wanted to do good in the sight of God, but his flesh constantly hindered him. However, Paul never fell prey to the flesh; instead, he disciplined himself to seeking the Lord in these times. He always states that his "delight" is the law of God after the inward man. Once again Paul had searched his heart, and in spite of the lusts of the flesh and its temptation, his heart's desire to please God overpowered his fleshly lusts. In other words, Paul examined himself, found the source of his hindrance, sin, etc . . ., and overcame by walking in the Spirit.

Born again believers can overcome anything as long as we let God be our power. We do not have to live such uncontrollable lives. We do not have to get mentally, physically, emotionally and spiritually drained and defeated. We have the power and permission to rebuke these unwanted enemies. Romans 8 teaches that the Spirit overpowers and delivers from the flesh. As God's children, we are no longer under that condemnation.

*"Born again believers can overcome anything
as long as we let God be our power."*

Flesh or Spirit?

SCRIPTURE READING: Romans 8:5

Romans 8:4–5 says, "That the righteousness of the law might be fulfilled in us, who walk not after the flesh, but after the Spirit. For they that are after the flesh do mind the things of the flesh; but they that are after the Spirit the things of the Spirit." We must examine ourselves to see if we are in the flesh or the Spirit. Before we can determine exactly why we need renewal we must determine what has put us in the situation we are facing. The key verse for making our determination is the first part of 2 Corinthians 4:8. It says, "We are troubled ("to crowd, suffer, tribulation, trouble, throng, afflict.") on every side, yet not distressed." If we feel like we need renewal, then there is something in our lives making us feel troubled or bothered, but maybe not totally destroyed. Perhaps you long to have an answer about a personal problem or maybe you long to feel the presence of God and have some time alone with Him. Many things could be causing you to feel so stale and distant from God.

Often the things that cause our tribulations and crowd our lives also make us feel unfit. This allows negative thoughts to build within us, leading to feelings of unworthiness. Therefore, we feel we shouldn't cling to the Lord and His power. We allow our minds to overtake us, and we cheat ourselves out of freedom.

If you are troubled, you do not have to be distressed. Distress goes one step farther than trouble. Distress means "to hem in closely or cramp." If you feel distressed, then you haven't relied on the Lord in your troubled times. The Bible teaches that we will face trouble as long as we put Christ and His ministry first in our lives. However, we don't have to faint at this trouble by becoming distressed. If we have allowed ourselves to become distressed then we have rejected God's power and become undisciplined in our walk with Him. We have put ourselves in an unfit condition. The Lord is our power for becoming disciplined not only in a day by day walk with Him, but for our whole life. If you depend on Him for all things, you will not feel hemmed in when your trouble comes. You will have a life of peace.

"The Lord is our power for becoming disciplined not only in a day by day walk with Him, but for our whole life."

A NEW DESIRE

Get Fit

SCRIPTURE READING: 1 Corinthians 15:58

Daily practice of walking with God keeps us from spiritual, mental, physical and emotional destruction. Examining ourselves on a daily basis will protect us from becoming unfit Christians. Let's see how we measure up in our walk with God. This will let us know the areas we are disciplined in and those weaker, less disciplined areas that we might need to work on.

A Spiritual Fitness Program
Measuring Up:
What is the problem? What is most important in your life? Are you happy with yourself? What uplifts the flesh? What magnifies God? Is your life leading you to who or what you want to become?
Getting Motivated:
How do we get motivated? Decide what you want to become. Look in the mirror. Set yourself goals. Weigh the balance. Set your priorities.
Becoming Fit—Starting To Exercise:
Maintain a plan. Pray, study, sacrifice. Pace yourself by running with patience. Walk in the Spirit. Increase; become stronger through personal activation.
Becoming Presentable—Reaching The Finish Line:
Learn it. Activate it. Appreciate it. Receive the reward (crown).
Presenting It—Public Proclamation Of Christ:
Wear it. Share it. Promote it.

   Once we have completed the program we must discipline ourselves to continuous exercise. We must never be content to the point where we stop exercising. We should never reach the point where we no longer need exercise. We progress in the plan by setting higher goals once we have fulfilled the original plan. By doing this we continuously grow in Christ.

"Examining ourselves on a daily basis will protect us from becoming unfit Christians."

Burden Bearers

SCRIPTURE READING: Galatians 6:1

Jesus Christ is the greatest burden bearer you will ever know. He not only bears your burden; He gets rid of it. In Matthew 11:28 Jesus says, "Come unto me, all ye that labour and are heavy laden, and I will give you rest." Who else do you know who would give you rest from your burdens? No one will ever care for you like Jesus. However, the Lord will put people in our lives who love and care about us, people who will pray with us and listen to us without condemnation or judgement, people who will not break our confidence. These people are true burden bearers, and we must learn to let them be. Galatians 6:1 says, "Brethren, if a man be overtaken in a fault, ye which are spiritual, restore such an one in the spirit of meekness; considering thyself, lest thou also be tempted."

People everyday are carrying burdens they will not share with anyone else. They allow these burdens to become weights and hindrances while Satan uses them to make them feel ashamed, unworthy, confused and unstable. That is why it is so important for us to have a burden bearer, someone whom we can go to and share any problem with.

A qualified burden bearer is someone who has accepted Jesus Christ as their Savior, truly loves Him and manifests His person in their daily walk. A burden bearer is a prayer warrior who has a longing to help and love others right where they are, just as they are. Burden bearers never gossip or spread the burdens of others with anyone else. They pray fervently for direction from God in order to help the troubled one. Burden bearers stop at nothing to be there when needed. They have an unconditional love without boundaries. When the burdened cries, so does the bearer; when the burdened prays, so does the bearer; when the burdened is relieved, the bearer rejoices. These are the qualifications of a God-called burden bearer.

This is the example that the great burden bearer, Jesus Christ, has given us to follow. If we follow His example, it will be Him in us bearing the burden.

"A qualified burden bearer is someone who has accepted Jesus Christ as their Savior."

A NEW DESIRE

Bear Another's Burden

SCRIPTURE READING: Galatians 6:2

Are you a pleasing burden bearer? We must please the Lord in every thing we do, especially when it comes to leading others in the path of righteousness. Does your life reflect godliness to the point that others can feel free to share their problems and cares with you, knowing they won't go any farther? Can others trust you to pray?

We should take more time to care about one another. We must value each other's burdens so much so that we carry them around with us in our hearts. Have you ever thought of letting your heart be a pillow for someone to rest on? Allow others to place their burdens on that pillow and leave them there. The Bible says in Galatians 6:1–2, "Brethren, if a man be overtaken is a fault, ye which are spiritual, restore such an one in the spirit of meekness; considering thyself, lest thou also be tempted. Bear ye one another's burdens, and so fulfill the law of Christ."

My friend, I challenge you to become a burden bearer for Jesus. People are hurting and longing for help and hope in their troublesome times. If you will lay aside your cares for the cares of others, you will see the mighty working power of God in both your life and theirs. The only hope you can give anyone is Jesus Christ, Lord of all. If people are not willing to let God help them, then there is no hope for their lives. You will not be an effective burden bearer unless you let God bear the burden through you. Without God we can do nothing.

Everybody needs somebody to whom they can go for help, prayer, love and understanding. We can't survive our problems alone. Ecclesiastes 4:9 says, "Two are better than one; because they have a good reward for their labour. For if they fall, the one will lift up his fellow: but woe to him that is alone when he falleth; for he hath not another to help him up." Are you helping someone up today, or are you so burdened down that you need help? God loves you, and He is there for you. The Lord wants to bear your burdens so you will know that you are not alone, and He wants to bear others' burdens through you.

"We, as Christians, should take more time to care about one another."
AUGUST

Praying for Others

SCRIPTURE READING: James 5:16b

Do you ever wonder if your prayers for others are effective and correct? Do you wonder if God honors your prayers for others? I can assure you that God will always honor your sincere prayer from the heart. Whether they are prayers for someone else or for you, God will honor them.

How many times have you asked the Lord to teach you how to pray? There is neither a proper way to pray nor any selected words God expects us to say. All He asks is for us to be genuine in our prayer life. If someone asks you to pray for them, God expects you to do so. That is being genuine. Even if others don't tell you exactly what their problem is, it is still your responsibility to lift them up to God in prayer. We don't need to know their problem to pray for them. We don't even need to know their name. Praying for someone because you told them you would makes your prayers effective and correct. James 5:16b, today's Scripture text, says, "The effectual fervent prayer of a righteous man availeth much."

There have been many occasions in my own prayer life when my prayers for others seemed very shallow and unimportant, but God answered them and He showed me that He honored my efforts. The reason I felt this way is because sometimes all I knew to pray was: "Lord, I lift this person up to you. I don't know what they need or who they really are, but I know I'm supposed to pray for them. Lord, supply their needs and deal with their circumstances according to your will for their life." As time passed I began to see changes in their life, and God would remind me of that "shallow, unimportant" prayer that I thought wouldn't do any good. As you pray for others, remember your prayers are very important.

"If you pray from the heart with sincerity, God will always honor your prayers."

A NEW DESIRE

Pray Without Ceasing

SCRIPTURE READING: 1 Thessalonians 5:17

The secret to an effective and correct prayer life is to keep yourself right with the Lord. There are several reasons you may not see changes in the people you are praying for. Perhaps you are not where God wants you to be, or maybe the person you're praying for is just not ready for the changes God must make in their life. It could be you are praying selfishly, or that it's just not time for that specific prayer to be answered. You can know which one of these is your problem simply by asking the Lord to show you. He is faithful to reveal these things to you. All you have to do is go to the Word of God, and your answer will be there. Don't stop praying for someone just because there might be sin in your life. Confess your sin, turn from it and continue praying. I have seen this happen in my own life. Once I got the sin out of my life, my prayers for others were answered.

I find so much joy in praying for others. I love to see the Lord work in people's lives. I no longer worry if I am praying correctly or effectively. I just believe the Lord's words: "Ask and ye shall receive." I now go to the throne boldly, believing that He hears my prayers for those for whom my heart is heavy, those whom I love and care for dearly, those who are strangers but have asked me to pray. When they come into my thoughts, I immediately pray wherever I am, knowing that God hears and cares. I praise the Lord that I have truly come to understand what today's Scripture text means. It says, "Pray without ceasing."

God will hear and answer your prayers for others. Don't give up in prayer.

"I pray wherever I am, knowing that God hears and cares."

Interceding for Others

SCRIPTURE READING: James 5:16a

I recall one night between 1:30 and 2:00 AM, the Lord woke me out of a deep sleep. I suddenly sat straight up in the bed. My heart was beating rapidly, and I could sense fear and evil all about me. I woke my husband. He got up, went outside and looked around only to find nothing. As he returned to bed, I still sensed danger for someone somewhere. I asked the Lord to put His protective hedge about everyone who might be in danger, and I began to call out the names of people who came to mind. When no more names came to mind, I began to feel safety and God's presence about me, and peace followed.

I knew that God had heard my prayer. I knew that He had woke me up just to pray for someone who was in danger at that very moment. I believe that whoever it was did not even know they were in danger, but God knew! I have no idea who was in danger, and I may never know, but I know God intervened, and I praise Him for allowing me to pray for others.

Today's Scripture text says, "Confess your faults one to another, and pray one for another, that ye may be healed." We never know who needs what, but I can assure you of one thing: everyone needs prayer. Who is on your heart today?

Interceding for others may make a difference in their lives that neither you nor that person will ever know. Don't dismiss that burden on your heart. Make intercession for that person now, and make a difference in their life. Jude 22 says, "And of some have compassion, making a difference."

"We never know who needs what, but I can assure you of one thing: everyone needs prayer."

A NEW DESIRE

The Altar of Prayer

SCRIPTURE READING: Mark 6:31

The toils of life come and go. While some days don't seem as toilsome as others, each day leaves its mark of weariness. After a few battles, a broken heart or a day of discouragement we grow tired. We begin to wonder if there will ever be a place or moment of rest for our burdened hearts, weary souls and scattered minds. We fight to survive the effects that our busy, troubled, crowded lives have brought upon us. Nothing brings us rest; we finally end up discouraged and defeated with all of life.

We go to church only to leave with no hope; we read the Word only to hear nothing. We pray only to feel that our prayers are of none effect. What is it going to take to find relief? What must we do to find rest? We must do what Jesus did when He experienced this. Jesus is the example we must follow. He was human just like we are. He grew tired, weary and discouraged, and He experienced feelings of defeat just like we do. Do you remember when He was tired and hungry from fasting forty days and nights? Do you remember when He suffered the loss of friends and wept at the death of a loved one? Do you remember when He was angry and discouraged at the acts of the people when they turned His house of prayer into a den of thieves? Do you remember His cry as He hung on the cross of Calvary: "Father, forgive them, for they know not what they do."?

Jesus called on the Father in prayer as He struggled with the things we struggle with. Jesus always made His requests to the Father. He asked God for guidance, strength and power. He prayed daily as He sought to do the Father's will.

We can receive instruction through learning or by following an example; the latter is the most effective. Jesus is our example in prayer. We should do as He did in His prayer life. Prayer was the resting place for Jesus. He loved to pray, and for Him prayer was a regular habit. It was His remedy in every circumstance. Mark 6:31 says, "And he said unto them, Come ye yourselves apart into a desert place, and rest a while: for there were many coming and going, and they had no leisure so much as to eat."

"Prayer was the resting place for Jesus."

He Was Praying

SCRIPTURE READING: Luke 11:1

Today's Scripture text says, "And it came to pass, that, as He was praying in a certain place, when He ceased, one of His disciples said unto Him, Lord, teach us to pray, as John also taught his disciples." In just a few short minutes, we could quote all of Jesus' prayers set forth in the gospels. However, we know that sometimes He prayed all night. We know He prayed for Himself and for others. He prayed when He was tired, when He was troubled and when He was grieving. He prayed for backsliders, for sinners, for the children and for the hurting. We also see that He prayed alone, with His disciples and in crowds. He prayed out loud, and He prayed silently within Himself. He prayed at the altar, on a mountain and in the garden; He prayed in the water at His baptism and at the grave of a loved one. He prayed on the cross. He used the deserts, mountains and solitary places as His altar of prayer. This is perfect proof that God hears us wherever we are.

Christ lived in a spirit of prayer. He learned that prayer was a way of being alone with God even in great crowds. His inner thoughts were always in and with God. He never experienced broken fellowship with God because He always prayed. Prayer was His power.

Prayer should be our resting place after a trying day. Mark 6:30–31 says, "And the apostles gathered themselves together unto Jesus, and told him all things, both what they had done, and what they had taught. And he said unto them, come ye yourselves apart in to a desert place, and rest awhile: for there were many coming and going, and they had no leisure so much as to eat." The altar of prayer can refresh, strengthen and build our faith for the journey of life.

"God hears us wherever we are."

The Pattern of Prayer

Scripture Reading: Matthew 6:9–13

Jesus gave us a pattern of prayer in Matthew 6:9–13. Although He used the Disciple's prayer as the example, He did not mean for us to have to pray with form, fancy words or impressive language. The Disciple's prayer implies the attitude and condition of our hearts toward Christ.

"Our Father who art in Heaven."—Prayer begins with the recognition that God is your Father and He has the resources to meet your needs.

"Hallowed be thy name"—Prayer should always exalt God. God is to be reverenced in authority and power.

"Thy kingdom come"—When you pray "Thy kingdom come" you are praying for Christ to reign on earth as He already does in Heaven.

"Thy will be done, In earth as it is in Heaven"—Your prayers make a difference. Praying for God's will to be done on earth is an aggressive prayer. We must want God's will done regardless of the circumstances.

"Give us this day our daily bread"—God is the source of all our provisions. This teaches us that we are to approach God as our great provider.

"And forgive us our debts as we forgive our debtors"—This implies confession of our sins. This is the believer's prayer for the Father's forgiveness. It also implies that we receive God's forgiveness only when we forgive others who have wronged us. It's possible to confess our sins and still not know the joy of forgiveness. How? Failure to forgive others!

"And lead us not into temptation but deliver us from evil"—We are to pray, "Lord, protect us from any future sin and protect us in our future trials." Trials are for our good, but God will never allow us to be tempted beyond our endurance.

"For thine is the kingdom and the power and the glory forever. Amen."—Recognizing the almighty power, person and presence of God is the key to an effective prayer life. We must approach Him with this understanding, knowing that all things are His.

"God will never allow us to be tempted beyond our endurance."

Ask

SCRIPTURE READING: Luke 11:9

Today's Scripture text says, "And I say unto you, Ask, and it shall be given you; seek, and ye shall find; knock, and it shall be opened unto you." The Lord gives us three steps into the very heart of God: ask, seek and knock. When we pray, we are making request to God for our most earnest needs and desires as we approach Him with our troubles and burdened hearts for others and ourselves.

Asking is the first step toward the resting place of prayer. The Greek word here means "to beg, call for, crave, desire, require, to ask; it is strictly a demand for something due." With this definition, prayer must take a whole new perspective in our lives. If asking is a demand for something due, then Jesus wants us to ask, beg and demand from Him our hearts desire, and He will give it to us. Aren't there conditions to this? Doesn't God require us to ask things according to His will? Yes, the asking is conditioned by sympathy with God's will and purpose. There are many who admit that they have asked, but because they asked outside of God's will, certain requests in prayer were not received. James 4:3 says, "Ye ask, and receive not, because ye ask amiss, that ye may consume it upon your lusts." What is the correct way to ask and receive? How do we know if we are asking according to God's will?

First of all, we must understand that asking implies dependence upon God. To ask for something that we know is going to turn us from our attention to and dependence upon God is only going to result in a non-receiving prayer. The principle to asking and receiving is to live in righteousness. The Lord honors our prayers when we pray in righteousness, reality and reverence: in righteousness because He is righteous; in reality because He doesn't play mind games, and He doesn't appreciate or respect selfish prayers; in reverence because we are commanded to ask in His name.

Ask in righteousness and watch God answer.

"The Lord honors our prayers when we pray in righteousness, reality and reverence."

A NEW DESIRE

Pray, in Jesus' Name

SCRIPTURE READING: John 14:12–14

Praying in Jesus' name doesn't mean to phrase it in Jesus' name only. It means to ask in His authority with His character. When we pray in Jesus' name, it signifies being in His nature, having His mind. We need to remember we serve a jealous God, and anything that doesn't give Him the honor and glory is not pleasing to Him. If the request is not of God it will not be granted.

John 14:12–14 says, "Verily verily, I say unto you, He that believeth on me, the works that I do shall he do also; and greater works than these shall he do; because I go unto my Father. And whatsoever ye shall ask in my name, that will I do, That the Father may be glorified in the Son. If ye shall ask any thing in my name, I will do it." Jesus is speaking of works of righteousness here, things done and asked for in His name. He is righteousness. I pray that you understand the words "in Jesus name." When we ask in Jesus name, we are supposed to be asking for righteousness sake with His character in the reality that all things should glorify Him. The use of the divine name implies a frame of mind rather than a form of speech.

If a wife has been praying for years for her lost husband to be saved but he has not yet received salvation, what could the problem be? It is very possible that she is not praying in God's will and in Jesus' name. She may be saying the words "in Jesus name," but she may not have His character in her heart as she asks. She may want Him saved so her life will be easier, especially if she is married to a drunkard, a drug addict or a jealous, abusive man. It would be any woman's nature to pray for salvation for this kind of husband. However, the real reason to pray for that lost loved one would be to glorify God. Christ is the only one who can impart salvation to our loved ones. He will not save the husband for his wife's sake. He will save him for the sake of Jesus. He will save him to keep him out of hell and for righteousness' sake. The wife just reaps the benefits of God's blessings. When we pray for lost loved ones, we need to make sure we pray in God's will, not ours. Let's not pray for our benefit, but for God's benefit.

"Let's not pray for our benefit, but for God's benefit."

Ask and Receive

SCRIPTURE READING: John 16:24

We are given permission to ask for things in prayer through Jesus Christ's death, burial and resurrection. When we receive Christ as our Savior, He permits us to ask Him for whatever we need. Salvation is our permission. Through being born again, we are permitted to go to the throne of grace boldly. Hebrews 4:14–16 says, "Seeing then that we have a great high priest, that is passed into the heavens, Jesus the Son of God, let us hold fast our profession. For we have not an high priest which cannot be touched with the feeling of our infirmities: but was in all points tempted like as we are, yet without sin. Let us therefore come boldly unto the throne of grace, that we may obtain mercy, and find grace to help in time of need."

Salvation makes us children of the King. He promised us we will receive whatever we ask according to His will and in His name. When we become God's children we are set apart and made holy. Being sanctified gives us permission to ask and receive. Prayer is God's way for Christians to have fullness of joy. Jesus said in John 16:24, "Hitherto have ye asked nothing in my name: ask, and ye shall receive, that your joy may be full." We are His dear children. He longs to give us what we ask for. If He supplies for the fowls of the air and the lilies of the field, He will be faithful to hear and answer your prayers. Because of who we are in Him, we are given permission to have our prayers answered.

Come boldly to the throne of grace in prayer.

"Prayer is God's way for Christians to have fulness of joy."

A NEW DESIRE

"He That Seeketh Findeth"

SCRIPTURE READING: Luke 11:10

S eeking, in Luke 11:9, implies urgency, constraining us to search until we find. In the very next verse, Jesus tells us that "he that seeketh findeth." Today's Scripture text says, "For every one that asketh receiveth; and he that seeketh findeth; and to him that knocketh it shall be opened." What are we supposed to seek after? How do we seek?

Seeking follows asking. Therefore, knowing that asking implies making our request known, seeking requires us to know God's will so our request can be granted and received. It is very important to seek God's will in everything. We should be so in tune with God and so anxious to serve Him that we stop at nothing to find, know and activate His will in our lives. God expects us to seek after His will.

We seek by searching and studying the Word of God. The very first thing that Jesus tells us to seek is the "kingdom of God (Matthew 6:33)." God wants us to let Christ rule and reign in our hearts and lives. We must seek with urgency Christ's rule and reign in our lives. He should be first, and He should have control of everything about us. When we seek first the kingdom of God, we seek after righteousness. Christ will be magnified through our walk, talk and actions. When this happens, we have found God's will.

The Word of God is the Holy Book where we seek to know the will and mind of God. As we seek it, we are taught what He allows us to ask for. He tells us that living righteously is the will of God. Therefore, we can ask for righteousness and receive it. The Word of God is God's plan for every Christian's life. As you seek it, you will see your sins and your problems. You will see how all-knowing God is; we can't hide anything from Him. You will see remedies for sicknesses, answers to your questions, solutions to your problems and comfort for your troubled soul. The Word of God will convict us, strengthen us and guide our steps. It is our resting place, and we can rest in it for all eternity.

"The Word of God will convict us, strengthen us and guide our steps."

The Word of God

SCRIPTURE READING: Hebrews 4:12

We find the power of God's Word in Hebrews 4:12, "For the word of God is quick, and powerful, and sharper than any two-edged sword, piercing even to the dividing asunder of soul and spirit, and of the joints and marrow, and is a discerner of the thoughts and intents of the heart."

It says that the Word is quick. This means it is alive or lively. In other words, God's Word is real, true and alive today. Whatever it says, you can believe it.

God's Word is powerful. This means it is active, operative and effectual. It is effective and in action today. If it says something will happen, it will. It is sharper than any two-edged sword. The word sharper means it cuts with a single stroke. It is decisive and keen. This means that all it takes to know who you really are in God is in one single glance at the Word of God. It will immediately give you truth. It cuts through all of your sin, deception and doubt and very keenly shows you your position and condition in Him. God's Word is piercing even to the dividing asunder of soul and spirit. The word piercing means it penetrates through all the sin, deception, etc., and reaches through to the heart, the seat of our affections. God's Word cuts through all of our hidden frailties. It separates sin from righteousness, wrong from right. The Word of God, when sought, gets down deep. It separates the heart and the mind, the flesh and the Spirit. It is so keen, sharp and powerful that it is the only thing that can make these distinctions.

Finally, the Word of God discerns, decides and discriminates the right in your life, the sin in your life and the true intentions behind the actions you take. The Word of God shows you your sincerity. It teaches you your true thoughts, feelings and emotions.

Get in God's Word and experience its power.

"The Word of God shows you your sincerity."

If Ye Abide in Me

SCRIPTURE READING: John 15:7

Seeking the Word of God is exactly what we are commanded to do if we want answers to prayer, power from God, and rest for our weary souls. We are allowed to know God's will if we seek it, to receive God's will if we want it and to ask God for our needs, desires and major and minute possessions and receive them if they are of and for God and received with thanksgiving.

John 4:23 says, "But the hour cometh, and now is, when the true worshippers shall worship the Father in spirit and in truth; For the Father seeketh such to worship him." The word seek also means to worship and desire. The Lord seeks for Christians who are willing to live according to His will in righteousness and sincerity. As long as we are seeking God's Word we can rest patiently, confidently and joyfully in the presence and power of God. We can have our hearts' desires because they will be righteousness and holy desires instead of worldly and fleshly desires.

The key to seeking and finding is abiding in the Word of God. Today's Scripture says, "If ye abide in me, and my words abide in you, ye shall ask what ye will, and it shall be done unto you." What does Jesus mean when He says to abide in Him, abide in His Words? He means for you to stay attached to Him without doubt, without wavering. Endure, continue, remain, stand in Him, His truths and His principles, and you will receive whatever you ask. The condition for seeking and finding lies in the believing, studying and living of the Word of God. The results are given to us in the next verse. Jesus said in John 15:8, "Herein is my Father glorified, that ye may bear much fruit; so shall ye be my disciples." In this you have found and received.

Attach yourself to God's Word and stand on it at all times.

> *"Attach yourself to God's Word and stand on it at all times."*

Coming Together

SCRIPTURE READING: Ecclesiastes 4:12

Nehemiah, a man with a heavy burden, was granted permission from the king to return to his homeland to rebuild the walls of Jerusalem. To do this successfully, Nehemiah needed help. He first asked the king to send letters to the governors and the keeper of the forest to let him pass through. He also asked if timber may be given to him to build the beams for the gates of the palace (Nehemiah 2:7–8). The king supplied him with the letters and supplies as well as men to help.

We all have burdens we need help carrying. Everyone has trying times, devastating circumstances, weaknesses, attacks, sin and personal and spiritual problems. These are the reasons we should come together. We can't survive these things without the love, support, fellowship and help of others. When we have each other to depend on we can make it with the power of God strengthening us. Today's Scripture text says, "And if one prevail against him, two shall withstand him; and a threefold cord is not quickly broken."

Nehemiah is a great example of the importance of coming together. He went out with a few men to inspect the damage and the task of rebuilding the walls. He then went back and gathered the people together and urged his people to rise up and build (2:17–18). Nehemiah knew he couldn't rebuild the wall by himself. He told the people that God's hand was good upon him and that he had already been granted permission from the king. The people quickly came together and started building and working to relieve the burden of Nehemiah. They knew this was a good work, and they, too, had the desire to see their homeland rebuilt.

Our burdens should be for the work of the Lord. We should come together for the strengthening, companionship, support and counsel of our brothers and sisters in Christ. Help those who are struggling to overcome. Come together to help those who are trying to do a good work or further the Gospel.

"When we have each other to depend on we can make it with the power of God strengthening us."

A NEW DESIRE

$\mathscr{A}$ Mind to Work

Scripture Reading: Nehemiah 4:6

There have been many times in my Christian service that I would have given up and quit had it not been for the encouragement and help of others who believed in what I was doing for the Lord. Galatians 6:1–2 says, "Brethren if a man be overtaken in a fault, ye which are spiritual, restore such an one in the spirit of meekness; considering thyself, lest thou also be tempted. Bear ye one another's burdens, and so fulfill the law of Christ."

My friend, I don't know about you, but I always need someone to help bear my burdens, pray for or with me or to just be there while I walk through my circumstances. God put us together to help each other, to spread His Gospel and to get His work done.

Nehemiah's people joined together for one great cause, and God strengthened and provided them with the means to accomplish their task. You see, God knew the rebuilding of the wall would glorify Him. Therefore, He gave them the permission, power and provisions they needed.

The third chapter of Nehemiah starts the building of the walls. Each person was assigned a specific job, and they performed their jobs faithfully. Some jobs were more demanding than others, but no one complained; they just did what they were assigned to do. If you read the whole book you will see in chapter four that their tasks weren't easy. They faced opposition from the enemy. They were mocked, criticized, troubled, discouraged and they wanted to quit at times. They even had conflict among themselves, but they worked out their differences and stayed together to finish the task.

When God is in control of our lives, great and wonderful things happen. The Bible tells us why these people were able to accomplish their task. Nehemiah 4:6 says, "So built we the wall; and all the wall was joined together unto the half thereof: for the people had a mind to work."

Coming together with a mind to work is what it takes to see things happen for the Lord.

"When God is in control of our lives, great and wonderful things happen."

Labor Together

SCRIPTURE READING: Philippians 1:5–6

Having the determination to overcome our circumstances by depending on God is what it takes to be closer to and live more for Him. We will face conflict, trouble and criticism as we take a stand for truth and righteousness, but there is power beyond our comprehension when we come together with God and His people.

When we come together in His name for His honor and glory, great things happen. We see the presence of God; we receive the wisdom of God; we receive answers to our prayers. We have victory, renewal and revival. We see results as we take action in areas of our lives that once paralyzed us with fear and anxiety.

We must come together with Christ first. Without Him we can do nothing; through Him we can do all things. Once we have come together with Him, then we can labor together with others. Just like in Nehemiah, we need to protect each other from the enemy's attacks. We must work together with one hand while we fight the demons of Satan with the Word of God in the other. We must labor together night and day for the Gospel's sake. When we see one hindered, we must help them remove the hindrance. We must fight for God's will to be done in each other's lives. We must endure together in the work of the Lord until He returns to take us home. Philippians 1:3–6 says, "I thank my God upon every remembrance of you. Always in every prayer of mine for you all making request with joy, for your fellowship in the Gospel from the first day until; Being confident of this very thing, that he which hath begun a good work in you will perform it until the day of Jesus Christ."

Do you see someone struggling, hurting, discouraged or defeated? Then come together with a brother or sister whom you have confidence in and share, pray and work together for victory. God is always there to see you through and to send someone to minister to your needs.

"God is always there to see you through and to send someone to minister to you in your needs."

Vessels of Honor

SCRIPTURE READING: 2 Timothy 2:19–21

Today's Scripture text says, "Nevertheless the foundation of God standeth sure, having this seal, The Lord knoweth them that are his. And, Let every one that nameth the name of Christ depart from iniquity. But in a great house there are not only vessels of gold and of silver, but also of wood and of earth; and some to honour, and some to dishonour. If a man therefore purge himself from these, he shall be a vessel unto honour, sanctified, and meet for the master's use, and prepared unto every good work."

A "vessel" is simply something that can be used. It could be anything from a utensil to an apparatus; it could even be a person. The Bible uses the word vessel approximately 146 times. It symbolizes something of use such a cooking utensil, a container for holding fluids or a person used for God's kingdom. The latter point is the one the above Scripture is speaking of.

We are the vessels of God. He created us as containers or holding tanks for His Holy Spirit to dwell in. It is through the Holy Spirit that we are identified as sanctified vessels of God. When we receive Christ, we are set apart and made holy; we are sealed by the presence and power of the Holy Spirit. Ephesians 1:13 says, "In whom ye also trusted, after that ye heard the word of truth, the Gospel of your salvation: in whom also after that ye believed, ye were sealed with that holy Spirit of promise." Through the Holy Spirit, we are identified as Christ's work.

We are held accountable for how we present ourselves because we belong to God. We should want to appear pleasing and acceptable before Him since He purchased us and made us what we are through the body and blood of Jesus Christ, His only begotten Son. This is why we are strongly urged by Paul in today's Scripture text to depart from iniquity.

"Through the Holy Spirit, we are identified as Christ's work."

"The Work of Thy Hand"

SCRIPTURE READING: Isaiah 64:8

As we all know, a vessel was marred or crushed in the hand of the potter if it was found with flaws or blemishes. The potter would very carefully crush the clay and rework it on the wheel until he was pleased with his work. The potter always has a plan, purpose and presentation already envisioned for his piece of clay. He may crush it numerous times before he molds it according to his vision. Therefore, the finished product is always something pleasing to the potter and able to be used for its purpose.

God intends for us to be effective and useful for Him. He is the potter; we are the clay. Isaiah 64:8 says, "But now, O LORD, thou art our father; we are the clay, and thou our potter; and we all are the work of thy hand." God will crush us in His hand until we become vessels of honor. He will work out flaws and impurities and rework us to His specifications. He will then use us to further His kingdom and to magnify His Son. This is why we are told in 2 Timothy 2:19 that at the name of Christ we must depart from iniquity. Jesus Christ became sin for us, and all who call upon His name for salvation should turn from sin and evil. Jesus died at Calvary so we could escape such impurities. If we remain in sin, we become dishonorable vessels.

In the name of Jesus Christ, it is His will for us to live and shine as honorable vessels.

"God intends for us to be effective and useful for Him."

A NEW DESIRE

Becoming a Vessel of Honor, Part One

SCRIPTURE READING: 2 Timothy 2:19–25

Paul gives us the requirements for becoming vessels of honor in the sight of God in today's Scripture text. There are seven of these requirements, and we can apply and live them through the power of the Holy Spirit.

First of all, we must flee youthful lusts by "following after righteousness (2 Timothy 2:22)." Following after righteousness demands a sacrifice. We must turn from the things of this world if we ever want to be someone God can use. This is why Paul says in 2 Timothy 2:20–21 that we should purge ourselves from gold, silver, etc . . . so we can be meet (useful) for the Master's use. Silver, gold, wood and earth are things that easily distract us from following and living in righteousness. This should make all of us want to examine our lives and clean the impurities out of our vessels. Putting God first and foremost in our lives is the key to living as a righteous vessel.

The second requirement is living by faith. An honorable vessel always lives by hope and faith in Jesus Christ, resting in the promises of God's Word rather than on what we see with the eye and what we produce by our own efforts. Living by faith requires us to totally trust in and depend upon God for all things. As long as we live life depending on ourselves, we will be flawed vessels. When we're depending on our own efforts, we are not allowing God to work in our lives.

The third requirement is charity. Love is the very essence of an honorable vessel. We are required to love the Lord our God with all of our heart, soul and mind and to love our neighbor as ourselves. This means that honorable vessels live one hundred percent for God because they love Him with all of their being. Because they love God, they also love others, for He is love. The love of God within us allows us to love those we don't even know, those who are hurting, those who are in sin, those who are our enemies and even those who don't want to be loved.

"Love is the very essence of an honorable vessel."

Becoming a Vessel of Honor, Part Two

SCRIPTURE READING: 2 Timothy 2:19–25

The fourth requirement for becoming a vessel of honor is peace. A vessel meet for the Master's use is so in tune with God's Word that, regardless of his circumstances, he can live peacefully knowing that God is in control of all things. Peace is something we all battle with because we can't understand why some things happen in our lives. We must always remember that God is working in our lives for good. Romans 8:28 says, "And we know that all things work together for good to them that love God, to them who are the called according to his purpose." Trusting Him to work out the circumstances even though our flesh may be in turmoil is the peace that passes all understanding. If there is no peace in your life, be still and know that God is God. This concept will truly make you an honorable vessel.

The next requirement of an honorable vessel is being gentle unto all. When we can be kind, loving and understanding in circumstances and situations we don't want to be gentle in, then we can count ourselves as fitting vessels. Jesus often had to be strict and to the point, but anger and lack of self–control were not problems for Him. He always prayed and kept Himself under the control of the Holy Spirit. As we live in the flesh, we, too, must pray, study God's Word and strive to be more under the influence of the Spirit so we can be presented as vessels pleasing to the Lord. Being gentle to others is an attribute we long to possess.

"We must always remember that
God is working in our lives for good."

A NEW DESIRE

Becoming a Vessel of Honor, Part Three

SCRIPTURE READING: 2 Timothy 2:19–25

The sixth requirement of an honorable vessel is being apt to teach. Every born again child of God is a teacher of some kind to someone. We are teachers of Christianity to people we are not aware of. We should not only be teachers of action and lifestyle, but we should also be teachers of the Word of God. We have the liberty to share whatever we learn from the Bible. Whatever God performs in our lives should be shared with others, teaching them that God can perform the same in their lives as He does in ours. This, my friend, is being apt to teach.

The seventh and final requirement for becoming an honorable vessel is "in meekness instructing." This seems to many to mean the same thing as teaching, but instructing means that we walk them through the teaching by demonstrating the principles of the lesson taught. For example, Jesus teaches us to be righteous, but then He instructed us how to do so by walking with us and showing us our strengths and weaknesses. He also instructs us on how we can better ourselves for His use through the reading and studying of the Word of God. The Bible is the instruction manual for making every person a vessel of honor.

We can become vessels pleasing to the Lord if we have a desire to. God loves each and every one of us in a very special and intimate way. He will work and rework us until we are vessels of honor for His kingdom, prepared unto every good work. Examine your vessel; let God show you if you are honorable in your service to Him. Remember, if you are born again, you are already a chosen vessel; allow Him to clean you up, fill you up and prepare you to be even more for His honor and glory.

"You are already a chosen vessel."

An Unfeigned Love

Scripture Reading: Matthew 22:37–40

What is unfeigned love? Unfeigned love is a genuine or sincere love. It is an eternal love that holds no boundaries. This love is found in the Bible only twice, and in both Scriptures it urges us to have unfeigned love toward others. Second Corinthians 6:3–6 says, "Giving no offence in any thing, that the ministry be not blamed: But in all things approving ourselves as the ministers of God, in much patience, in afflictions, in necessities, in distresses, In stripes, in imprisionments, in tumults, in labours, in watchings, in fastings; By pureness, by knowledge, by longsuffering, by kindness, by the Holy Ghost, by love unfeigned." Regardless of the circumstances around us, we are to prove ourselves godly by demonstrating sincere love.

God is love; He is the author and giver of love. Love is the key to life. Jesus tells us in Matthew 22:37–40, "Jesus said unto him, Thou shalt love the Lord thy God with all thy heart, and with all thy soul, and with all thy mind. This is the first and great commandment. And the second is like unto it, Thou shalt love thy neighbour as thyself. On these two commandments hang all the law and the prophets."

Jesus loved us enough to give His life for us. Therefore, His example of unfeigned love is the example we should follow as we live each day. Jesus didn't die just for the wealthy or some other special group of people. He died for everyone; His love is for everyone. Jesus loves the sinners just as much as He loves the saints. He even loves those who deny, mock and abuse Him. He never rejects anyone who comes to Him. This is an unfeigned love.

Do you have an unfeigned love for others?

"Love is the key to life."

A NEW DESIRE

The Source of Unfeigned Love

SCRIPTURE READING: 1 John 4:7–8

We are commanded to love others with Jesus' love. The only way we can do that is to be born again. First John 4:7–8 says, "Beloved, let us love one another: for love is of God; and every one that loveth is born of God, and knoweth God. He that loveth not knoweth not God; for God is love." If we are saved, we can love others with the love of God because His Spirit lives in us. It is through His love that others are able to see Him in our daily walk.

If we love others as Jesus loves them, we will not be able to shun, reject or belittle them. First Peter 1:22–23, says, "Seeing ye have purified your souls in obeying the truth through the Spirit unto unfeigned love of the brethren, see that ye love one another with a pure heart fervently: Being born again, not of corruptible seed, but of incorruptible, by the word of God, which liveth and abideth for ever." Salvation is the key to an unfeigned love with and from Jesus Christ and toward those around us.

It is our nature to choose those we want to love. We walk through life loving people for what they have to offer us. If something goes wrong, feelings get hurt or the relationship goes sour, we have a tendency to shut off our love for this person. We refuse to forgive and forget. This, my friend, is not the unfeigned love of God. God always forgives and forgets. He doesn't love us because of what we have to offer Him. The Bible says in 1 John 4:10–11, "Herein is love, not that we loved God, but that he loved us, and sent his Son to be the propitiation for our sins. Beloved, if God so loved us, we ought also to love one another." God's love is so genuine that He loved us before we ever thought of loving Him. That's right; while we were sinning and enjoying it, Jesus died for us. While we were rejecting His love, His blood was being shed at Calvary for our sins. No greater love hath man than this, my friend. Jesus is the only source of true, unfeigned love.

"God always forgives and forgets."

Loving God First and Foremost

SCRIPTURE READING: 1 John 4:19–21

Most of us only love God when we need Him. When life dishes out a bad day, we are quick to call on Him; on the good days, He never enters our minds. In church and around Christian friends, we lift Him up. In the street and on our jobs, He is never mentioned. Before we can fulfill the commandment to love one another, we must first love God sincerely. First John 4:19–21 says, "We love him, because he first loved us. If a man say, I love God, and hateth his brother, he is a liar: for he that loveth not his brother whom he hath seen, how can he love God whom he hath not seen? And this commandment have we from him, That he who loveth God love his brother also." Until we can genuinely love God with all of our being, we will always have a problem demonstrating unfeigned love toward others.

We may think that we love God sincerely, but when our love for Him is tested we find ourselves less committed to Him than we thought. A good example of this is Peter, the disciple who said he would never deny God. Jesus told him that before the cock crowed twice, Peter would deny Him three times. Peter said, "No Lord, I will never deny you." Shortly after this statement, Peter denied the Savior.

How many times have we professed to love God, but at a time when our profession should have been exposed we denied our sincere feelings? I have to confess my guilt of this. There was a time when I was straddling the fence. To a Christian I would profess God, but in the world I would profess worldliness. The amazing thing to me is that God knew all about it, yet He continued to love me sincerely. Peter really thought he would never deny Jesus, but the Lord knew Peter's heart better than Peter himself did. He knows our hearts better than we do, too. He knows how genuinely in love with Him we are, and this tells Him how sincerely we love others also.

Love God first and foremost, then love others with His love.

"God knew all about it, yet He continued to love me sincerely."

A NEW DESIRE

Unfeigned Love in Action

SCRIPTURE READING: 1 Corinthians 13:4–7

The unfeigned love of God is demonstrated once again after Jesus' resurrection. The young man in the sepulchre gave the women the message that Jesus had risen, and he told them to go tell the disciples and Peter that He would see them in Galilee (Mark 16:4–7). When he spoke the words, "and Peter," forgiveness and unfeigned love were demonstrated. Peter's denial did not kill God's love. Peter had to be tested and taught by the Lord what genuine love is, and He will also have to test and teach us about this love. Our love for others often comes with conditions. Therefore, God has to teach us in His way how to unconditionally love others.

Unfeigned love is God's love, and we are given the responsibility of seeking and serving others with His love. We can be the greatest Christians in the world, but if we don't show love to others then our Christianity is null and void in the eyes of God. Paul expounds on the importance of serving and living in love in 1 Corinthians 13. Throughout the whole chapter, we find that love is the method for everything we do. Verses 4–7 say, "Charity suffereth long, and is kind; charity envieth not; charity vaunteth not itself, is not puffed up, Doth not behave itself unseemly, seeketh not her own, is not easily provoked, thinketh no evil; Rejoiceth not in iniquity, but rejoiceth in the truth; Beareth all things, believeth all things, hopeth all things, endureth all things." When we read this we should not be surprised at the fact that most of our actions of love are just the opposite of Paul's definition of genuine love.

The bottom line is this: when we love others through our flesh we present love opposite of that defined by Paul. When we love others with God's love, then we love through our hearts, and we see and demonstrate love the way Paul describes it in today's Scripture text. This is the kind of love Jesus demonstrated to Peter when He forgave and forgot Peter's denial.

Is your love in action fulfilling Paul's definition of unfeigned love?

"Peter's denial did not kill God's love."

The Nine Principles of Unfeigned Love

SCRIPTURE READING: 1 Corinthians 13

People are always looking for love. Whether if be from our spouse, our parents, our family, our friends or strangers, love is what we long for. Everyone needs comfort, encouragement or a simple smile. Many people stop at nothing to find this love; some even turn to drugs, alcohol and other sinful avenues searching for it. We must reach out to them and offer them God's love by sincerely helping them to change their lives. We do this by teaching them Jesus, the source of genuine love.

As the source of genuine love, Jesus demonstrated to us the nine principles of love. These principles are given to us in 1 Corinthians 13. Love is patient, or as Paul says, "suffers long." Love is kind. Love is approving, or "envieth not." Love is modest, or "vaunteth not itself." Love is humility, or "is not puffed up." Love is discretion, or "doth not behave itself unseemly." Love is sharing, or "seeketh not her own." Love is calm, or "is not easily provoked," and love is righteousness ("thinketh no evil"). This is the kind of love that Jesus unselfishly displayed for us on the cross of Calvary even while we were demonstrating the nine things that love is not.

Love is not envy. James 3:16 says, "For where envying and strife is, there is confusion and every evil work." Love is not arrogant, or, as Paul says in 1 Corinthians 13, "puffed up." Love is not selfish, it is not provoked or easily angered, and it is not evil. Love is not unrighteousness, sin and iniquity. Most of all, love is not failing. All of these things are contrary to the love that Jesus demonstrated toward us from Calvary's cross.

Find someone who needs a heart of love and give them Jesus by letting them see Him in your life. Love forgives, love heals, love helps and love is eternal. Won't you give your heart to someone? Jesus gave His heart for you.

> *"We must reach out to them and offer them God's love."*

The Power of Influence

SCRIPTURE READING: Proverbs 15:21–22

When we think of influence, we think of other people and their opinions in a specific situation. Many decisions are made based upon the influence of others. Is this good or bad? Is this lack of confidence in ourselves? How does this effect our lives, and what does the Lord think about the influence of others?

Allowing others to influence our lives and our final decisions can be both good and bad. Influence is often misused and causes great difficulty for many people. When someone chooses to make a decision based on the influence of others, it can be bad for them if they don't carefully examine the whole situation. Some people's opinions are based on their personal views or their positions in the situation. Therefore, their influence will be based upon how it will affect them personally or how it will make them appear to you. Some people will deceive us by telling us things they know we want to hear. The bad part of influence is when we take a person's opinion as truth. We can be easily deceived and our minds will run wild with us if we allow this to happen.

On the other hand, the influence of others can be good if it is sought after correctly. The proper way to seek influence is to use it as insight for discernment, not as truth to act on. We should always seek counsel when we are in doubt or confusion. This counsel should be carefully selected and based upon the person's knowledge, wisdom, experience and, most of all, their relationship with God. Proverbs 15:21–22 says, "Folly is joy to him that is destitute of wisdom: but a man of understanding walketh uprightly. Without counsel purposes are disappointed: but in the multitude of counsellors they are established." When we seek the influence of others it should be for helping us to view the situation from all directions, not to use as a final decision.

Seek godly influence, but don't let the opinions of others make your decisions for you.

*"The influence of others can be good
if it is sought after correctly."*

The Right Way to Go?

SCRIPTURE READING: Proverbs 16:25

Allowing others to influence us is not a sign of weakness. It is okay to share your problems and circumstances with others. The Lord teaches us to bear one another's burdens. We should never look down on ourselves because we can't make a decision alone. The problem begins when we choose to rely solely on a person's influence instead of God's. Today's Scripture text says, "There is a way that seemeth right unto a man, but the end thereof are the ways of death."

God is the great counselor, and His counsel will always be truth. His counsel will always lead us in the right path. When others influence us, it effects our lives according to how we respond. If we let their influence impress us to the point of having impulses and uncontrollable thoughts, negative feelings and improper actions then we have allowed our flesh and Satan room to deceive us into the wrong attitude. However, when we put the influence of others together with the overall picture while seeking the Lord, then influence can be a positive, helpful tool for reaching a decision.

Jesus was the perfect influence for our lives. He never allowed Himself to be negatively influenced by others. When the people brought the adulterous woman to Jesus they wanted her stoned. He could have been influenced by them, but He stood firm and sent her away forgiven. When the thief hung on the cross, Jesus wasn't influenced by his past life. Instead, He promised him paradise. While you were still a sinner, Jesus died for you.

How do others influence you? Do you let their gossip and opinions effect your feelings toward others? Do you allow them to plant negative feelings in your mind about certain things and people? Do you base your life on the influence of others? How long has it been since you have asked the Lord what He thought about your circumstances? How long has it been since you did what God told you to do? Which way is the right way to go?

It is time to stop being ruled by the world and its influence and let God have complete control of our thoughts, feelings and decisions. With God's influence you can never be misled.

"God is the great counselor, and His counsel will always be truth."

A NEW DESIRE

So Also Do Ye

SCRIPTURE READING: Colossians 3:12–15

Today's Scripture text says, "Put on therefore, as the elect of God, holy and beloved, bowels of mercies, kindness, humbleness of mind, meekness, longsuffering; Forbearing one another, and forgiving one another, if any man have a quarrel against any: even as Christ forgave you, so also do ye. And above all these things put on charity, which is the bond of perfectness. And let the peace of God rule in your hearts, to the which also ye are called in one body; and be ye thankful."

These verses give us the characteristics of walking in the Spirit. This is our new man in Christ Jesus. He lives in us, and He will manifest these attributes through us if we will humbly bow ourselves before Him. We are made more than conquerors, and nothing in life can separate us from God.

When we walk in the Spirit of God, we will not dwell on the things of our flesh or the things of this world. We will dwell on heavenly and holy things. We will be kind because Jesus is kind. We will love and forgive because that's what Jesus would do. We will be patient and trust God for our provisions because we know that He is faithful to provide. Most of all, we will be able to handle all that life dishes out because we will be resting in the peace of God.

You no longer have to doubt your salvation, battle with addictions, worry, fear or live in weakness. Christ has given you a route to power; all you have to do is want it.

> *"Christ has given you a route to power;*
> *all you have to do is want it."*

All in the Name of Jesus

SCRIPTURE READING: Colossians 3:16–17

Today's Scripture text says, "Let the word of Christ dwell in you richly in all wisdom; teaching and admonishing one another in psalms and hymns and spiritual songs, singing with grace in your hearts to the Lord. And whatsoever ye do in word or deed, do all in the name of the Lord Jesus, giving thanks to God and the Father by him."

God's Word is our map to walking in the Spirit and being able to stand fast regardless of life's little detours. We, as Christians, should strive to know God in a more personal relationship. We should strive to be more for God and a greater help to others. When we focus on Jesus, we find ourselves spending more of our time caring for others' needs rather than our own, doing it all in the name of Jesus for His glory.

Our Scripture text should be used as a litmus test for sincere, spirit-filled Christians. How would you answer these questions:
• Are you able to teach and help others bear their burdens?
• Are you mature enough in God's Word that you can be an example to others even when God has selected you for a battle?
• Can you praise the Lord when persecutions come?
• Can you truly thank Him for the hard times as well as the good times?
• Have you learned to be content, regardless of the state you're in?

Consider the answers to these questions today. Tomorrow we'll learn what to do with them.

> "We should strive to be more for God and a greater help to others."

Applying the Scriptures

SCRIPTURE READING: Colossians 3:16–17

How did you answer yesterday's questions? If you answered yes to these questions, then you are doing all in the name of Jesus! You are pleasing to Him, and He will use you for His honor and glory. If you answered no to some of them, then it's possible you are in a state of defeat.

What must you do to overcome defeat? Apply today's Scripture text. It is the same as yesterday's. It says, "Let the word of Christ dwell in you richly in all wisdom; teaching and admonishing one another in psalms and hymns and spiritual songs, singing with grace in your hearts to the Lord. And whatsoever ye do in word or deed, do all in the name of the Lord Jesus, giving thanks to God and the Father by him."

Let the Word of Christ dwell in you.

Apply the Word of God to your situation.

Turn knowledge of God into wisdom by obeying what He says.

Sing with grace in your heart to the Lord.

Use your defeat for the sake of Jesus by thanking Him for the battle.

My friend, find the problem and take it to Jesus. Don't try to fix it yourself. Trust Him to get you through it. He is faithful to deliver you.

"Turn knowledge of God into wisdom
by obeying what it says."

To Seek the Lord

SCRIPTURE READING: 2 Chronicles 20:3

Life comes with battles everyday. Each battle is difficult, but some are more damaging than others. Every battle leaves scars, but some leave deep wounds that take a lifetime to heal. Have you ever wondered why some battles are so hard to overcome, or why some just seem to last forever?

Jehoshaphat answers this for us quite understandably through his own personal battles. We can learn from his example if we'll do as he did. We can fight our battles and win every time by following his example.

In 2 Chronicles 20, Judah was being plotted against. Judah was facing many problems, and Jehoshaphat was afraid for his people. He knew they didn't have the forces to defend themselves against such powerful enemies. From the evidence, their situation appeared hopeless. They were defeated before the battle ever took place.

What was the king to do? Our Scripture text gives us the answer. It says, "And Jehoshaphat feared, and set himself to seek the LORD, and proclaimed a fast throughout all Judah." Jehoshaphat ran to God for help.

Some battles seem hard to overcome, and it seems like they last forever because we forget to seek the Lord. When we fear the enemy, we must flee him and run to God. God is the only one who can protect us.

Do as Jehoshaphat did. Run to God and set yourself to seek the Lord in the battle.

"When we fear the enemy, we must flee him and run to God."

A NEW DESIRE

Holy Women

SCRIPTURE READING: 1 Peter 3:4–5

The Bible teaches us of the righteous behavior of a godly woman in 1 Peter 3:1–6. First, it tells us to be in subjection to our own husbands so that if our husbands are not Christians, they may be won to Christ by our behavior. We are then instructed not to place our emphasis on our outward appearance.

The makeup, hairdos and pretty clothing we wear are all appealing and helpful for gaining our husband's attention, but the inward apparel will catch their attention much faster and more effectively. Our hearts and our sincerity are more important than our outward appearance. Today's Scripture text says, "But let it be the hidden man of the heart, in that which is not corruptible, even the ornament of a meek and quiet spirit, which is in the sight of God of great price. For after this manner in the old time the holy women also, who trusted in God, adorned themselves, being in subjection unto their own husbands."

The hidden man is the heart. Our spirit, the drive within us, should come from our heart. If we live according to the thoughts and intents of our minds, we will possess a spirit of lust, dissatisfaction and sin. We will not be godly examples to our companions or anyone else.

When we walk in the spirit of our minds, we manifest an attitude of self-centeredness, greed and worldly prosperity. This is not the kind of woman God is pleased with (verse five of the Scripture text).

It is okay to make ourselves attractive for our husbands. It is okay to want to please them, but we must do it with sincerity and godliness as holy women of God.

> *"We must make ourselves attractive*
> *with sincerity and godliness."*

The Spirit of a Woman

SCRIPTURE READING: 1 Peter 3:4

What kind of spirit are you possessing? Do others see a spirit of satisfaction, pleasure and godliness in you? Are you sharing what God has done in your life? Are you giving God the honor and glory for all things?

Maybe you have become a quiet, withdrawn, preoccupied Christian? Maybe you have a spirit of rebellion. Don't allow yourself to be defeated. Put on a spirit of determination, and let God use you.

We should always let others see Christ's Spirit within us. We should be careful to guard our approach toward and actions before others. If we are constantly complaining, moaning and gossiping, we are not in the right spirit. Our Scripture text says, "But let it be the hidden man of the heart, in that which is not corruptible, even the ornament of a meek and quiet spirit, which is in the sight of God of great price." Moaning and complaining is not what God considers meek and quiet.

The word quiet means to be a woman content and satisfied with God and life. This kind of woman is one who praises the Lord for her life continuously. Regardless of her circumstances, she always trusts God. She reflects a life of control and balance, and she sets her priorities according to God's will for her life. She puts God first as she faces her daily challenges.

Becoming women with meek and quiet spirits does not mean that we are to become women who never share, speak or conversate with others. It simply means we are to be women who find pleasure and satisfaction in the Lord. This is the spirit of a woman who is of great price in God's sight.

*"Put on a spirit of determination,
and let God use you."*

Men or God?

SCRIPTURE READING: Galatians 1:10

I am very strict when it comes to the place of a woman in Scripture. I have studied for many years the scriptural role of a woman. Trust me when I tell you I know my place. I respect my place in Scripture, and I respect man and God's authority in my life. I know when to shut up and when to speak up. I long to be a woman with a meek and quiet spirit, but not a woman with a meek and silent spirit. If we are silent women, how are we going to help other women, younger women and especially our children?

The Lord does not intend for us to be silent Christians. It is time to get past the traditions of men and in tune with the truth of the Scriptures.

Galatians 1:10 says, "For do I now persuade men, or God? or do I seek to please men? for if I yet pleased men, I should not be the servant of Christ."

Esther was a submissive woman to the king, but she was brave enough to follow the leadership of the Lord. She put herself in danger to man in order to save the lives of her people. She broke a few man-made rules to do God's will. Esther had a spirit of courage, and she did what she had to do.

Ruth may have been humble and compassionate, but she had a determined spirit to win the heart of Boaz and provide for Naomi. Ruth went beyond the limit to be accepted by Boaz. In the end, she was blessed and received because of her determination.

My friend, in the sight of God, you are of great price. You, too, are blessed and honored. Stand for the truth and righteousness and reject the traditions of men.

> ## "The Lord does not intend for us to be silent Christians."

Great Is Thy Faithfulness

SCRIPTURE READING: Lamentations 3:22–23

There are many examples in the Bible that prove God's love in all situations. Naomi is a perfect example of a comfortable life gone bitter. She had all a woman could ever want, but in a short period of time her whole life was shattered. She even changed her name to Mara, meaning bitter, to reflect the spirit she had taken about life. In the end of her story, however, God refreshes her hope and restores her family, and Naomi overcomes.

David is another example of God's steadfast love. He was a man after God's own heart. He was the king of Israel, yet he decided to walk in the flesh because of his overwhelming desire for a beautiful woman. However, in spite of his sin and the effects it brought upon him and others, God was faithful to forgive and restore David. David went on to be a fearless and faithful servant, just as God had planned him to be.

Then there was Noah and the seven other members of his family who were spared from the flood because of Noah's righteousness. The whole earth was destroyed by flood because of sin and rebellion, but God spared Noah and his family because of Noah's obedience to build the ark.

God gave Noah, David and Ruth a new start. There is a new start for you also. Every morning, God's mercy is new in your life. His love is strong and enduring in your life, just as it was in Naomi's bitterness, David's lust and Noah's flood. Nothing is too great for God.

Today's Scripture text reminds us of God's faithfulness as we face bitterness, lust and storms. It says, "It is of the LORD'S mercies that we are not consumed, because his compassions fail not. They are new every morning: great is thy faithfulness."

"Nothing is too great for God."

A NEW DESIRE

Life More Abundantly

SCRIPTURE READING: John 10:10

Rahab, the harlot of Joshua 2, is a perfect example of someone who decided to make drastic changes in her life. Rahab had the reputation of being a proud, independent, idolatrous woman who had indiscriminately yielded herself to every man approaching her. It is easy to assume in studying Rahab that she had her own home apart from her family and that she entertained local men and passing travelers. Rahab, like everyone else, had a self-will.

Self-will and independence brought Rahab much heartache and strife. She was known as a harlot, and her home was a place of disrespect. Her family was still alive at this time, so there were probably some strained relationships within her family because of the life she had chosen. Perhaps she had been disowned and rejected by her family, thus reaping the consequences of her decisions in life.

God used Rahab and her sinful life as a place of protection and covering for His people to spy out the land. Rahab's knowledge of what was about to take place opened her eyes to the only One who could help her.

Rahab had a sudden change of heart, and she was ready to make changes in her life. She began to examine her heart, and she began to fear God. She realized that the God of the spies was the only true God.

Rahab showed kindness and offered protection to the spies. She told them which way to flee and instructed them in their exit out of Jericho. Her decision to show kindness to the spies gave Rahab and her family a pardon from death. On her own free will, Rahab made the decision to change her way of life.

We, too, must make changes in our lives. The first step to change and live more abundant is a reverence of the one and only true God, Jesus Christ our Savior. Remember the words of our Scripture text: "The thief cometh not, but for to steal, and to kill, and to destroy: I am come that they might have life, and that they might have it more abundantly."

"Life more abundant is a reverence of the one and only true God."

Time of Decision

SCRIPTURE READING: Titus 2:11–12

We must be the one to make the decision to be a Christian. No one can make that decision for us. Only God can save us from a life of sin and unrighteousness. We must be willing to live for God, whatever the cost. We must rest in the blessed assurance that God will give us the strength to stand.

With the decision to be a Christian, you will also be making the decision to change other areas of your life. Christianity is not a life of being saved and then living like the world. Christianity is a decision to be totally different from the world. The Bible teaches this in today's Scripture verse. Titus 2:11–12 says, "For the grace of God that bringeth salvation hath appeared to all men, Teaching us that denying ungodliness and worldly lusts, we should live soberly, righteously, and godly, in this present world."

As Christians, we must let the world see the changes that God has performed in our lives. We must be prepared to lose friends, forsake sinful habits and flee our old ways. We must be ready for the challenge of transformation. Titus 2:13–14 defines the purpose of such transformation. It says, "Looking for that blessed hope, and the glorious appearing of the great God and our Saviour Jesus Christ; who gave Himself for us, that he might redeem us from all iniquity and purify unto himself a peculiar people, zealous of good works."

It is a time of decision for all of us. It is time to decide who and what we are going to follow. Who will you choose today? Transform your life into the likeness of Jesus Christ.

"Christianity is not a life of being saved and then living like the world."

A NEW DESIRE

Dreams

Scripture Reading: Colossians 3:1–2

Each of us have lifelong dreams. Those dreams or goals become such a longing within us that we can't seem to focus on anything else. We build our lives around achieving those dreams, and sometimes we don't build on the solid foundation of Jesus Christ.

The effects of building on our own hopes and dreams often cause us to experience some uncomfortable situations. God is the only foundation upon which we must build our dreams and goals. If we set our affections on things above instead of on the things of this world, then we are building on the one and only firm foundation. God is the power to make our dreams come true. We may go through some things that try us and discourage us, but if we keep hoping and trusting in God our foundation for building will always be strong. We can overcome the hurdles by trusting in God.

Everyday, life hands us another difficult situation or slaps us in the face with unexpected challenges. Regardless of what your situation or challenge may be today, or throughout your life, God can and will see you through it. God can make your dreams come true, turn your hope into reality and turn your weakness to strength if you build and plan your dreams around His will for your life. The secret to dreams coming true is found in today's verse. Colossians 3:1–2 says, "If ye then be risen with Christ, seek those things which are above, where Christ sitteth on the right hand of God. Set your affection on things above, not on things on the earth. For ye are dead, and your life is hid with Christ in God."

"God is the power to make our dreams come true."

Christian Companions

SCRIPTURE READING: Philippians 2:25

What is a Christian companion? Why should we strive to have them or to be one?

Christian companions are people who are saved by the grace of God through faith in Jesus Christ. These people have purposed in their life to be an example and a friend. A great example of a Christian companion is found in today's Scripture text. Paul labels Epaphroditus as such a person. It says, "Yet I supposed it necessary to send to you Epaphroditus, my brother and companion in labour and fellow soldier but your messenger and he that ministered to my wants."

Paul explains here that to be someone's companion, you must be their friend, servant and fellow soldier. Paul and Epaphroditus were soldiers for the cause of Christ. Through their laboring together, it is evident that these two men had become "PALS."

Paul and Epaphroditus had grown to truly love and care for one another. They both had the same desires and purpose in life. These two men had gone beyond normal human limits to set an example of Christian companionship that we should strive to follow. We should put forth an effort to become companions for Christ.

Who needs your companionship today? Take the challenge to be to them what our Scripture verse teaches. God is sending you by someone who needs to see Him through you. They will then say this about you: "Yet I supposed it necessary to send to you Epaphroditus, my brother and companion in labour and fellow soldier but your messenger and he that ministered to my wants."

"We should put forth an effort to become companions for Christ."

A NEW DESIRE

PALS

SCRIPTURE READING: Ecclesiastes 4: 9

There is an effective pattern for developing relationships to obtain Christian companionship. This pattern lies in a small, four-letter word called "PALS."

In my heart, I believe Paul and Epaphroditus were true "PALS." I also see "PALS" in Ruth and Naomi and Mary and Elizabeth. We can definitely see companionship between Moses and Aaron. The Bible is full of examples of people who stuck together and became "PALS" for the sake of the Gospel.

The importance of being Christian companions and "PALS" lies in today's Scripture text. It says, "Two are better than one; because they have a good reward for their labor." If we stand together as Ruth and Naomi and the others in the Bible did, we will have a good reward for our labor, too.

I would like to teach you for the next four days what it takes to become PALS for Christ's sake. Search your heart. Determine who needs you to be their companion. Find someone who is battling sin or depression in their life or someone who is struggling spiritually and purpose in your heart to become these four things:

P artners
A greeing
L aboring
S erving

For the next four days, we will study each one of these.

"Purpose in your heart to be someone's friend."

Partners

SCRIPTURE READING: Ruth 1:12–14

Becoming partners means partaking in an activity with another or others. As Webster defines it, partners are players on the same team.

Ruth and Naomi are a true example of partners. They joined together to get through life. Naomi, angry, bitter and tired from the severe hardships of life, had forgotten the love and comfort she could receive in Ruth and God if only she would let her guard down. Ruth was so determined to be there for Naomi that she didn't fold under the pressure of Naomi's rejection. She purposed in her heart to stay with, love, follow and take care of her mother-in-law.

Ruth 1:12–14 says, "Turn again my daughters, go your way; for I am too old to have a husband. If I should say I have hope, if I should have an husband also tonight, and should also bear sons, would ye tarry for them till they were grown? Would ye stay for them from having husbands? Nay, my daughters; for it grieveth me much for your sakes that the Lord is gone out against me. And they lifted up their voice, and wept again; and Orpah kissed her Mother-in-law; but Ruth clave unto her." Nothing Naomi said or did could move Ruth's determination to share her life.

There is not a more beautiful example of true partnership than these two ladies. Naomi, old and tired, was still young Ruth's friend and fellow soldier. This is so sweetly revealed to us in the words of this Scripture that say, "Ruth clave unto her." "Clave" means Ruth attached herself to Naomi. Nothing could prevent Ruth from clinging to her beloved partner and friend. Every woman in the world should challenge herself to be a Christian companion in the life of someone older and younger. Joining together as sisters in Christ makes us players and partners on the same team, hence fulfilling the definition for partners.

> *"Every woman should challenge herself to be a Christian companion."*

Becoming Partners, Part One

SCRIPTURE READING: 2 Corinthians 8:16–22

There are five requirements for becoming a partner and companion for Jesus' sake. These requirements are found in today's Scripture text. Paul uses Titus as the example of a Christian partner.

Second Corinthians 8:16–17 gives us the first requirement. It says, "But thanks be to God, which put the same earnest care into the heart of Titus for you. For indeed he accepted the exhortation; but being more forward, of his own accord he went unto you." Requirement number one is "accepting the exhortation." This means that in order to be a partner for Christ you must accept the invitation. This word "exhortation" comes from the Greek root *parakaleo* which means "to call near, bid invite, call for, desire." Titus accepted the call to Christ and became a partner in the Gospel with Paul. We must accept partnership with the Lord unto salvation before we can become partners and companions like Paul and Titus.

The second requirement is also found in Verse 17: "But being more forward, of his own accord he went." The second requirement is being ready, willing and full of zeal. Titus didn't sit around and wait to become a companion for Christ. He got up and made things happen for the cause of Christ. The word "own accord" means that Titus voluntarily chose to be a partner with Paul.

What could you make happen for the cause of Christ? Are you ready, willing and full of zeal as Titus was? When others see your willingness and excitement they will want what you have. They will want to become your partner in spreading the Gospel of Jesus Christ.

The remaining requirements are found in tomorrow's devotion. Be sure you finish these requirements so you can become a faithful partner for Christ.

"When others see your willingness and excitement they will want what you have."

Becoming Partners, Part Two

SCRIPTURE READING: 2 Corinthians 8:16–22

Yesterday we studied the first two requirements for becoming effective Christians in the lives of others. Today, we will conclude this subject by studying the three remaining requirements.

Second Corinthians 8:21 reveals the third requirement. It says, "Providing for honest things, not only in the sight of the Lord, but also in the sight of men." This Scripture calls for us to be "honest in all things." Partners and companions are always truthful and trusting with one another. Titus was known for his honesty not only in the sight of God, but men also recognized his truthfulness. True Christian companions are those who will be honest with themselves, with others and most of all with God.

The fourth requirement found in Titus' life is in verse 22 of today's Scripture text. Being diligent requires us to be strong, to study and to carry the Gospel with eagerness and confidence. It says, "and we have sent with them our brother, whom we have often times proved diligent in many things, but now much more diligent, upon the great confidence which I have in you."

The fifth and final requirement is found in 2 Corinthians 8:24. It is the key to the prior requirements. This requirement is to be loving. Titus was so loving in his walk with God and his ministry. Second Corinthians 8:24 says, "Wherefore show ye to them, and before the churches, the proof of your love, and of our boasting on your behalf." If we are going to be effective partners, we must first be loving.

These requirements are in the Word of God for our benefit and instruction. To be partners we must act on these and allow God to use us in the lives of others.

"Partners and companions are always truthful and trusting with one another."

A NEW DESIRE

Agreeing

SCRIPTURE READING: Matthew 18:19–20

Once we have made the decision to become partners for Christ, the next step to effectiveness is agreeing. People who avoid each other because of social, personal or religious differences are never in agreement. They are always standing alone, cheating themselves out of companionship. Ecclesiastes 4:9 says, "Two are better than one; because they have a good reward for their labour." Notice the Hebrew definition for the word labour in this verse. It means "to toil, a wearing effort; hence worry, grievance, travail."

We cannot fight the battle alone. It is so important for us to lean on each other for survival. The enemy seeks to destroy and separate God's people. He doesn't want people helping and befriending one another. Satan thrives on keeping conflicts going among the body of believers, the Church.

We must agree together in Christ. This life is full of toil and grief. If we stand together, we can uplift one another. Matthew 18:19–20 says, "Again I say unto you, that if two of you shall agree on earth as touching anything that they shall ask, it shall be done for them of my Father which is in heaven. For where two or three are gathered together in my name, there am I in the midst of them." The word agree here means "to be harmonious, agree together with." This means we must put aside childish things, petty feelings, social preferences and just love one another as Christ loves.

When we agree together it must be based on Scriptural truth, not on personal opinion or preference. God has never honored social, worldly or fleshly agreements. He honors truth agreements only.

> "We cannot fight the battle alone.
> We must agree together in Christ."

Laboring

SCRIPTURE READING: 1 Corinthians 16:13–17

The key to laboring together as partners is found in today's Scripture text. It says, "Watch ye, stand fast in the faith, quit you like men, be strong. Let all your things be done with charity. I beseech you brethren, (ye know the house of Stephenas, that it is the first fruits of Achaia, and that they have addicted themselves to the ministry of the saints.) That ye submit yourselves unto such, and to everyone that helpeth with us, and laboureth, I am glad of the coming of Stephanas and Fortunatus and Achaicus: for that which was lacking on your part they have supplies. To they have refreshed my spirit and yours: therefore acknowledge ye them that are such."

These Scriptures expound on the principles for laboring together as Christians. They start out telling us that to be laborers we must be strong people of courage. Laboring requires us to be in love with Jesus Christ and with people. Laboring in Christ means we become addicted to Jesus and His divine will for our lives. We must set aside our ways and willingly supply others with God's truths.

Paul gives us a word of counsel on this subject in Colossians 4:12. He says, "Epaphras, who is one of you, a servant of Christ, saluteth you, always labouring fervently for you in prayers, that ye may stand perfect and complete in all the will of God." The word "labouring" here means, "to literally struggle, to contend with an adversary, to endeavor to accomplish something, fight, labor fervently, strive."

To be companions in Christ, we must labor under these same conditions. We must forsake the desires of our flesh when it would be so easy to feed our flesh. We must rebuke Satan constantly. This is laboring. Are you laboring?

"Laboring in Christ means we become addicted to Jesus."

A NEW DESIRE

Serving

SCRIPTURE READING: Romans 12: 9–10

The Bible tells us in Acts 20:19 to serve the Lord with all humility, with many tears and temptations. The word serving in this verse means "to be in bondage, to be in service, a slave in, to be in subjection to or be a servant." When we serve in this manner, we can say we have truly forsaken ourselves for others.

Serving means giving ourselves over to the requests and needs of something or someone else. Our Scripture verse also teaches us our purpose in serving. It says, "Let love be without dissimulation. Abhor that which is evil: Cleave to that which is good. Be kindly affectionate one to another with brotherly love; in honor preferring one another; not slothful in business; fervent in spirit; serving the Lord; Rejoicing in hope; patient in tribulation; continuing instant in prayer; Distributing to the necessity of the saints; given to hospitality."

All of these Scriptures give us simple, uncomplicated principles for becoming effective Christian companions in serving. When we can apply these to our lives and then act upon them, we will be putting on Christ's nature, and we will make a difference in the lives of others for His sake.

Christ is the reason we serve. If we don't walk as He walked, then we can't serve productively as Christians. We will never be the partners or pals that Paul and Titus were. We will never understand the Christ-centered relationship of Ruth and Naomi. Life will continue to be full of generational conflicts, denominational confusion and spiritual ineffectiveness.

It is never too late to be a light in someone's life. I challenge you once again to find someone younger than you and someone older than you to serve with. It will change your life, challenge your walk with God and encourage you to be more like Jesus.

"It is never too late to be a light in someone's life."

Just Believe

SCRIPTURE READING: Mark 10:26–27

Today's Scripture says, "Who then can be saved? And Jesus looking upon them saith, with men it is impossible, but not with God: for with God all things are possible." When Jesus made this statement from our Scripture text He was addressing the questions of the rich young ruler. This man wanted to know what he must do to enter the kingdom of God. When Jesus told him to sell all he had, give it to the poor and take up his cross, the man was speechless. The Bible states in Mark 10:22 that "he was sad at the saying and went away grieved, for he had great possessions." This man chose his great wealth and possessions over salvation and God's great love.

I'm amazed at the love of God. I'm amazed that He would heal me and perform miracles in my life. I have learned many things through these miracles but the greatest, most important principle I have learned is that I don't have to understand. I do not have to try to figure God out; all I have to do is believe Him for all things. I have learned that nothing here on earth is more valuable than God's power. Nothing or no one can provide for our lives like Jesus.

So often, we are like the rich ruler. We don't want to do what it takes for God to perform miracles. Jesus tells us that riches or possessions cannot save us or work miracles in our lives. Refuse to be like the rich young ruler. Give all you have, take up your cross and watch God perform miracles for you.

Remember, you don't have to understand. Just believe God for all things.

> ## *"Nothing or no one can provide for our lives like Jesus."*

Miracle Made Possible

Scripture Reading: Matthew 19:26

The word miracle means "to be of power, a force or specifically miraculous power." Webster's defines a miracle as "an event that apparently contradicts known scientific laws or a remarkable thing." In other words, a miracle is anything that God chooses it to be for the simple fact that man has absolutely no power to perform them or to comprehend God's power or reasoning.

I will never forget the words my doctor spoke to me one day. He said, "Brenda, I don't know what else to tell you except we have your seizures as controlled as they will ever be. The medications do not seem to be working well and I don't have anymore suggestions or answers." I walked out of there with a feeling of hopelessness. I was having nine to twelve seizures a month when he told me this. He was basically telling me I was going to have to accept this way of life.

I knew it would take a miracle from God for me to live. Four years later God performed a miracle and healed me of the seizures. God did what man thought was impossible. When I tell them God healed me they look at me very strangely. All I can say is what Jesus said in today's Scripture text. "But Jesus beheld them, and said unto them, With men this is impossible; but with God all things are possible."

Only God can make miracles possible. Trust Him today for your miracle. Allow God to do a remarkable thing in your life today.

*"Allow God to do a remarkable thing
in your life today."*

The Hand of Power

S<small>CRIPTURE</small> R<small>EADING</small>: Psalms 139:5

Today's Scripture text says, "Thou hast beset me behind and before, and laid thine hand upon me." Psalm 139 is one of the most beautiful chapters in the Bible. It describes the power of God in our lives. It is the echo of God's voice that the Holy Spirit leads me to hear when I feel unworthy, ashamed or defeated. My greatest comfort is in knowing that God has searched me. He knows me, yet He is still with me, in spite of my actions, words or thoughts.

God's children are never separated from Him. The Bible tells us that God will never leave or forsake us. God knows our faults, failures and sins, yet He understands. In verse two of Psalms 139 He says, "Thou knowest my downsitting and mine uprising." Yes, God knows everything we deal with in our lives. Our thoughts are before Him long before we take them to Him. That's the kind of all-knowing God He is. In the last part of Psalm 139:2 God says He knows our uprising. Just as He sees the negative in us, He also sees our accomplishments.

There are things we can't control about our lives no matter how hard we try. In Psalms 139:5 David tells us that God has confined our lives to His control. In other words, God has power over everything about us. We must rest in Him and wait upon Him to free us. "Thou has beset me behind and before, and laid thine hand upon me." God's hand is the one that we should want to be upon our every circumstance. His hand is surely the hand of power.

> *"God's hand is the one that we should want to be upon our every circumstance."*

A NEW DESIRE

Never Separated

SCRIPTURE READING: Psalms 139: 6

We find in today's Scripture text a picture of God's omniscience. "Such knowledge is too wonderful for me; it is high, I cannot attain unto it." God has full knowledge about us; therefore, we shouldn't even try to figure out or fix things that only God can handle. You see, God knows so much about our every circumstance that He already knows the end result even though we don't. This is exactly why the Psalmist states in the verse above that he cannot attain unto such wonderful knowledge. The next few verses goes on to explain how God's presence is ever with us. They say, "Whither shall I go from they Spirit? or whither shall I flee from thy presence? If I ascend up into heaven, thou art there: If I make my bed in hell, behold, thou art there. If I take the wings of the morning and dwell in the uttermost parts of the sea; Even there shall thy hand lead me, and thy right hand shall hold me." These verses can be summed up in two simple words: never separated!

David explains God's love for His children in these Scriptures. Wherever you go, He Goes. Whatever you think, He already knows. Whatever you say, He hears it before you can speak it. These Scriptures prove to us that God is constantly with us. We are always on His heart.

Such knowledge is too wonderful for our minds to comprehend, but oh what joy it is to never be separated from God's love.

> *"Wherever you go, He Goes. Whatever you think, He already knows. Whatever you say, He hears it before you can speak it."*

The Evidence of Love

SCRIPTURE READING: 1 John 4:10

What is love? For most of us it is a four-letter word used loosely to get what we want and to justify our behavior of jealously, envy and strife. How many times have you justified your improper behavior by saying, "I reacted like this because I love you so much?" We even blame much of our ill behavior on love, but 1 Corinthians 13 tells us that love is not puffed up.

Man's definition of love has always been based on merit, social standing and personal profit. Man's love is conditional and limited. We measure our love for someone according to what they do for us. If they please us a lot, then we love them a lot. If they seem inattentive and distant, then we don't regard them as much. They are not as beneficial to us. Therefore, we tend to avoid them. These facts are sad, but they are so true. We have all been guilty of this at one time or another.

Our love for God is pretty much based on this same system. The more God does for us, the more we do for Him. Our walk with God is based on how good we think He is to us. Our love for Him is just like our love for one another; it is conditional and limited. The evidence of our love does not reflect God's love.

God's love is evident in the giving of His only begotten Son. He gave Him up to death for you and me. This is why the verse says, "Herein is love, not that we loved God, but that He loved us, and sent His Son to be the propitiation for our sins." What greater evidence of love is there to be seen? Jesus' love toward us is that He freely gave His life to die for our sins. He loved us so much that He took our place at Calvary. We really should take a hard look at our love for Him.

"God's love is evident in the giving of His only begotten Son."

Righteous Rahab

SCRIPTURE READING: Romans 3:23

Rahab surrendered her life to righteousness. She presented her body to God, and He transformed her life. She hid the spies and put those who sought them on a fake trail as she helped the spies escape. She courageously protected her nation's enemies. Her daring faith and willingness to sacrifice for a cause she knew to be of God was a perfect example of her salvation.

In Rahab's decision of salvation, she left a beautiful example for us to follow. Through her life, we know the blood of Jesus can make the vilest clean and change the hardest heart. We learn that the grace of God reaches to the most despised life and lifts it up to a life of honor and beauty.

God has a plan for everyone. We, like Rahab, are well worth saving from an evil, sinful life for the sake of Jesus Christ. If Rehab the harlot can make the decision to live for God, we, too, must make the decision to be a Christian. Rahab's life was no more sinful than our own. God showed her mercy and kindness, and He does the same for us. Romans 3:23 says, "For all have sinned, and come short of the glory of God."

Righteous Rahab was not perfect, but her heart was in pleasing God. Her whole family was delivered from a pagan and idolatrous nation through her righteousness. Maybe we should start today following in the footsteps of Rahab.

*"The blood of Jesus can make the vilest clean
and change the hardest heart."*

She Made a Difference

SCRIPTURE READING: Jude 21–22

Today's Scripture text says, "Keep yourselves in the love of God looking for the mercy of the Lord Jesus Christ unto eternal life. And of some have compassion, making a difference."

Rahab set us another example to follow through her concern for the salvation of others. She not only asked for pardon and safety for herself, but she asked for salvation for the rest of her family as well. Her changed heart lifted her from a life of selfishness and disgrace to one of love and concern for others whom she cared deeply for. She made a difference in the lives of others.

Rahab's transformation from harlot to holy brought peace in her heart for the safety of her whole household. We, too, should have the same yearning intercession for our own families.

Rahab's decision for salvation also teaches us that faith and works go hand in hand. Rahab was an example of faith in the New Testament while James says she was justified by works. Works is simply faith in action. When we make the decision to be devout Christians, we will make changes that raise questions in the minds of others. However, our decision must be one of complete surrender and absolutely no compromise.

It's time to examine our lives and make decisions that please the Lord. We were created by God, for God and anything we decide to live for outside of Christ and His righteousness is of none effect. What pattern of life are you walking in today? Is your life in shambles or are you standing strong in the Lord? Whatever the case, make a difference in someone's life.

"It's time to examine our lives and make decisions that please the Lord."

The Pattern for Living

SCRIPTURE READING: Ephesians 1:4

As we examine the world we live in, we find many different types of people: different religions, personalities and opinions. Most people pattern their lives by someone else's theory of successful living. God patterned the whole world. His pattern is truth, and it will stand throughout eternity. His theory is based on truth and righteousness, but few will follow or surrender to His standard of living.

God's pattern will not require you to have social drinks, tell ugly jokes or pass the time with gossip. God's pattern will catapult you into self-judgement, confession, repentance and a drastic change in your way of life. God set the successful pattern for living before the foundations of the world. He intended for us to live confidently in Him by grace through faith in Jesus Christ. Ephesians 1:4 sets up the pattern according to God's call upon our lives. It says, "According as He hath chosen us in Him before the foundation of the world, that we should be holy and without blame before Him in love." "Holy" is the pattern for our living.

Like everything else in life, holy living is a decision. God created everyone with a self-will. We all make decisions about our lives daily. With every decision we make we are looking out for ourselves more than anyone else. When Jesus went to the cross, His intentions were not to do what was in His best interest. He went to the cross with your best interest in mind. Jesus set the pattern for living when He made the decision to die for you.

*"He went to the cross with your best interest
in mind."*

The Origin of Love

SCRIPTURE READING: 1 John 4:7–8

Our Scripture text says, "Beloved, let us love one another for love is of God; and everyone that loveth is born of God, and knoweth God. He that loveth not knoweth not God; for God is love." We, in the flesh, put so many boundaries on love, we fail to make love unconditional and eternal. I am so thankful that God doesn't react toward us in this way. I praise Him for teaching me how to love with His love. I am so thankful that He has taught me how far love must go.

Love is of God. In order to love, we must have God within us. The evidence of our love is manifested in our position with God. If we are born again, then we have God's love. As God's children, we have power to love anyone regardless of who they are or what they have done.

We have power to love our enemy and to forgive any wrong done to us. God's love in us is our power for all things. God's love is so merciful and forgiving. Every time you activate forgiveness, concern or comfort toward someone you are experiencing God. God is all the love any person needs for all of life's circumstances.

Every time you find yourself harboring hatred, bitterness and anger remember that these things are not of God. God's love can change your heart, and you, too, can love like God loves. Empty yourself in God's love today.

"God's love in us is our power for all things."

Characteristics of God's Love

SCRIPTURE READING: 1 John 4:12

God's love in us is our power for all things. How many of the characteristics of God's love do you possess? God's love is demonstrated when we fulfill today's Scripture text: "No man hath seen God at any time. If we love one another, God dwelleth in us, and his love is perfected in us." The characteristics of God's love are listed below:

Limitless: God's love is limitless and life-giving. He loves the drunkard and murderer just as much as He loves the saint. His love is light as it reflects hope and kindness, and it makes us lively in Him. Our liveliness stems from our knowledge of His almighty presence within us.

Omnipotent: God is all powerful and His love is omnipotent. This means that the power of God's love can heal the deepest hurt, forgive the greatest sin and build bridges that only His love can build. When we let God's omnipotent love control our lives we will forgive when we don't want to forgive. We will love those we don't want to love.

Valuable: God's love also makes us valuable for the Lord. As a matter of fact, we were so valuable to God that He gave Jesus for our sins. In God's eyes we are precious and worth dying for. I pray that you recognize your worth as a child of God. You are very valuable to His kingdom work.

Eternal: God's love for us is eternal. He will never stop loving us. We never need to fear the day that God says, "My love for you ends today." Eternal is time with no end. Can you say you possess this eternal love for others?

God's love is truly limitless (no boundaries), all powerful (omnipotent), valuable and eternal in all of our lives today.

> *"The power of God's love can heal the deepest hurt."*

The Fruits of God's Orchard

SCRIPTURE READING: Galatians 5:22–23

October is a month of harvest celebration, so let's take the opportunity this month to study the fruits of God's orchard. We find those fruits in today's Scripture text. "But the fruit of the Spirit is love, joy, peace, longsuffering, gentleness, goodness, faith, Meekness, temperance: against such there is no law."

Throughout the month, we will expound on these fruits, one at a time. We will not devote a great deal of time to the fruit of love because we studied love in detail in February. It is very important that we know how to obtain, apply and demonstrate each of these fruits for effective Christian living. Without these fruits, we are unproductive in our work for the Lord. We may profess being a child of God, but unless we possess the qualities of being His child we only fool ourselves and others.

As we study the Fruit of the Spirit, we will learn a lot about ourselves, about God and about our relationship with Him. We will see that we already own and exercise some of these fruits while we see that we need to work toward producing some of the others. We will learn how to gain the fruits we lack as we watch the Holy Spirit reveal Himself to us in a very personal way.

I pray that you will take this spiritual walk with me. I challenge you to study along in Galatians 5 and determine in your own heart to possess all of the fruit the Spirit wants to manifest in you. Remember, the fruit of the Spirit is your influence in a lost and dying world. If you don't take these fruits seriously (not these devotions, but the fruits we're studying through them), you stand the chance of destroying your witness for Christ. Determine to let Christ come to life in your heart and in the lives of those you come in contact with by allowing the Spirit to manifest His fruit in your life.

> *"Remember, the fruit of the Spirit is your influence in a lost and dying world."*

The Fruit of the Spirit

SCRIPTURE READING: Galatians 5:22–23

The nine fruits of the Spirit are listed in today's Scripture text. Reviewing what we learned yesterday, we see that it says, "But the fruit of the Spirit is love, joy, peace, longsuffering, gentleness, goodness, faith, Meekness, temperance: against such there is no law."

We must maintain all nine of these fruits in order to be completely effective in the work of the Lord. Unless we can claim all of the them, we are walking in the flesh rather than walking in the Spirit. Nine, in Scripture, is the number of completion. When we possess these nine fruits there is nothing else needed as wrought by the Holy Spirit's presence in our hearts.

The Holy Spirit, through these fruits, demonstrates a Christ-like character through us. As we apply and exercise these fruits, we become a greater light to others and we grow closer to the Lord. Activating these fruits in our lives means abiding in Christ because it is His power that performs through us.

The nine fruits of the Spirit are God's nature, personality and attitude. God is love, joy, peace, longsuffering, gentleness, goodness, faith, meekness and temperance. These are characteristics that we, in the flesh, have no ownership of. Rather, in the flesh we are just the opposite: hate, sorrow, turmoil, impatience, unkindness, evil, faithless, rebellious and uncontrollable. Therefore, in order to manifest His fruit, we must abide in Him.

John 15:4–5 says, "Abide in me, and I in you. As the branch cannot bear fruit of itself, except it abide in the vine; no more can ye, except ye abide in me. I am the vine, ye are the branches: He that abideth in me, and I in him, the same bringeth forth much fruit: for without me ye can do nothing."

"The nine fruits of the Spirit are God's nature, personality and attitude."

Flesh Vs. Spirit

SCRIPTURE READING: Galatians 5:17

We can never take credit for anything fruitful in our lives. Jesus is our power and resource for all things. Anything outside of Him, for a child of God, is unfruitful and taken away. John 15:2 says, "Every branch in me that beareth not fruit he taketh away: and every branch that beareth fruit, he purgeth it, that it may bring forth more fruit." We must be careful of the intention with which we do things. Wrong fruit is rotten fruit.

Remember, we were not born with a nature of love. Some may have the fruit of joy while others have the fruit of longsuffering (patience), but to proclaim all nine means to proclaim trials, sacrifices, persecution and years of knowledge and wisdom through God's Word. The fruits of the Spirit cannot be produced by our own self-effort. They are the reflections of Christ character produced within us by the Holy Spirit. We hold a title to them at the moment of salvation, but they will be manifested only as we strive to become more Christ-like.

Due to the warfare between the flesh and the Spirit, we must strive to attain our goals of manifesting our spiritual fruit. Today's Scripture text says, "For the flesh lusteth against the Spirit, and the Spirit against the flesh: and these are contrary the one to the other: so that ye cannot do the things that ye would." Peer pressure, lusts of the flesh and our rebellious self-will hinder the outworking of the fruits of the Spirit. Prayer, studying and love for God, on the other hand, help us to lay hold on the fruit given by the Spirit.

We must want to be like Christ and willing to give up old sinful habits for newness of life. We must want Christ to be seen outwardly through our lifestyle and actions (Galatians 2:20). What is more important to you, the flesh or God? Your closeness to Him will be determined by your answer.

> *"We must want to be like Christ and willing to give up old sinful habits for newness of life."*

The Fruit of Love

SCRIPTURE READING: 1 Corinthians 13:1–3

As we studied in February, love is the superior fruit of the Spirit. As we read in our Scripture text for today, anything we perform or pursue motivated by anything but love is invalid, and it profits nothing. It says, "Though I speak with the tongues of men and of angels, and have not charity, I am become as sounding brass, or a tinkling cymbal. And though I have the gift of prophecy, and understand all mysteries, and all knowledge; and though I have all faith, so that I could remove mountains, and have not charity, I am nothing. And though I bestow all my goods to feed the poor, and though I give my body to be burned, and have not charity, it profiteth me nothing." All of the other gifts are nothing without love.

Without Christ in our lives we can't obtain this true, agape love that 1 Corinthians 13 speaks of. God is love. He is the Giver and Creator of love. You can't experience God's love until you have received His love through Christ.

Our prayer every day should be, "Lord, fill me with your love and teach me how to magnify this love in the lives of others. Lord, teach me to look beyond my opinions and attitudes and love others with your never-ending love."

God's love for us and for others is unconditional. Our love should be the same. First John 4:20 says, "If a man say, I love God, and hateth his brother, he is a liar: for he that loveth not his brother whom he hath seen, how can he love God whom he hath not seen?"

True love is a fruit of the Spirit. We can neither know nor share true love with others outside of God. Study 1 Corinthians 13 to see the contrast, character and consistency of God's love. Does your love for yourself and for others match this definition of love? If not, allow the Spirit to cultivate His love in your heart.

"Anything we perform or pursue motivated by anything but love is invalid, and it profits nothing."

The Fruit of Joy

SCRIPTURE READING: John 15:9–11

The fruit of joy, along with love and peace, relates to God. God is the giver of these attributes, and they can only be obtained through salvation. As we see in today's Scripture text, the key to joy is loving God. "As the Father hath loved me, so have I loved you: continue ye in my love. If ye keep my commandments, ye shall abide in my love; even as I have kept my Father's commandments, and abide in his love. These things have I spoken unto you, that my joy might remain in you, and that your joy might be full."

In order to understand joy, we must understand what joy is not. Satan has many of us deceived about what true joy really is. We look for joy in material possessions, prosperity, relationships and worldly pleasures. We think that joy is in success and popularity, and we live our lives searching for this joy. This is not joy at all. It is simply a temporary satisfaction of the flesh.

True joy does not come from the flesh. It comes from deep within our souls, and it is produced through the leadership of the Holy Spirit. Jesus revealed its source in John 15:10: "If ye keep my commandments, ye shall abide in my love; even as I have kept my Father's commandments, and abide in his love." Abiding in God's love is the source of joy, and we abide there by keeping His commandments to love Him above all else and to love others as we love ourselves.

True joy comes from trusting in a God we've never seen. It comes from knowing that we have eternal life through the blood Jesus shed on Calvary. True joy doesn't tear us down, disappoint us or give us sudden urges to satisfy our flesh. Instead, it builds our faith, strengthens our hearts and satisfies our souls with things eternal. Is yours a temporary satisfaction or an eternal joy?

"Abiding in God's love is the source of joy."

A NEW DESIRE

Joy Defined

SCRIPTURE READING: Matthew 5:3–11

The Beatitudes give us the perfect definition and explanation of true joy. As we study Matthew, chapters five through seven, we find that Jesus taught that we will not find His joy in the things of this world.

In today's Scripture text we are given the principles for obtaining true joy. It says, "Blessed are the poor in spirit: for theirs is the kingdom of heaven. Blessed are they that mourn: for they shall be comforted. Blessed are the meek: for they shall inherit the earth. Blessed are they which do hunger and thirst after righteousness: for they shall be filled. Blessed are the merciful: for they shall obtain mercy. Blessed are the pure in heart: for they shall see God. Blessed are the peacemakers: for they shall be called the children of God. Blessed are they which are persecuted for righteousness' sake: for theirs is the kingdom of heaven. Blessed are ye, when men shall revile you, and persecute you, and shall say all manner of evil against you falsely, for my sake."

These principles for attaining true joy surely clash with our way of life. According to this text, we must be willing to come humbly to Christ for true joy. Verse four says that we can find joy in mourning. That sounds difficult, but it is in times of mourning that we find the precious comfort of our Savior. Our nature is not one of meekness, but we find that meekness is a key to having joy. Meekness requires us to give control of our lives to God. True joy comes when we rest in the power of God to control the circumstances of our lives. We learn that seeking righteousness brings joy, but instead we seek to satisfy the lust of our flesh and settle for temporary satisfaction instead of abiding joy. True joy is an activation of the Spirit of God living within us. Joy is obtained through obedience to God. Are you willing to deny self for the joy of the Lord?

"True joy comes when we rest in the power of God."

A Joyous Example

SCRIPTURE READING: John 15:5

Joy is not always seen and felt. We often have to battle Satan and the flesh, but we still have the joy of the Lord within us if we are truly born again. God is always for us. At those times when you can't feel joy, it is very possible that you are not completely depending upon God in your circumstances.

Joy is a fruit of the Spirit. Therefore, we are responsible for manifesting that fruit in our lives daily. Without joy, we are not very good examples of Christianity to this world. The best example a troubled, hurting or lost person can see is a child of God who is always trusting in the Lord regardless of her circumstances.

The joy of the Lord is not necessarily a feeling of excitement that is reflected outwardly. Many times, God's joy is simply the inner security of knowing that God knows all about us, that He will always be our strength and that it is His power that gets us through every situation. When others see this security in us, they are seeing the joy of the Lord surfacing in our Christian life.

Joy is one of the key fruits of the Spirit, and we can't share or exercise it unless we allow Him to do it through us. Regardless of your life's circumstances, you must abide in the Lord and bear the fruit of joy. However, you can't do that outside of Him. Today's Scripture text says, "I am the vine, ye are the branches: He that abideth in me, and I in him, the same bringeth forth much fruit: for without me ye can do nothing."

Are you abiding in Him? Do you have joy in spite of your circumstances? Are you a joyous example to others who are troubled, hurting or lost? Challenge yourself to manifest the fruit of joy in your life so that you might be a joyous example and a witness for Christ to others.

"God's joy is simply the inner security of knowing that God knows all about us."

A NEW DESIRE

The Fruit of Peace

SCRIPTURE READING: Philippians 4:5–7

Peace is the final fruit that relates to God and reveals His attributes within us when we are born again. It seems that peace is the hardest fruit to obtain and understand. Circumstances rob us of our peace and control our every thought.

Peace comes from knowing who God really is. You can say that you have the fruit of peace when your life is falling apart yet you still trust in God for the outcome. When our lives reflect Christ-likeness in our most critical circumstances, then God can uncover His peace in our day to day walk.

Peace is shadowed by perplexity when we question God and rely on our own resources for survival. In order to overcome this perplexity we must apply the principles taught in today's Scripture text. "Let your moderation be known unto all men. The Lord is at hand. Be careful for nothing; but in every thing by prayer and supplication with thanksgiving let your requests be made known unto God. And the peace of God, which passeth all understanding, shall keep your hearts and minds through Christ Jesus."

Verse five says that we should let our moderation be known to all. We must be gentle and patient as an example to others even in times of tribulation. Verse six reminds us that we can cast our cares upon the Lord. Giving the situation to Him releases us from anxiety and allows us to have His peace. Verse seven reassures us that peace is the result of trusting God with our circumstances and turning them over to Him.

Let's learn to produce the fruit of peace by giving God full control of our lives. Let's love Him and rest in Him. Let's allow Him to use us even when peace seems distant and almost forgotten. We can claim peace by completely depending on God. Let's follow the command of Colossians 3:15: "Let the peace of God rule in your hearts."

"Peace comes from knowing who God really is."

The God of Peace

SCRIPTURE READING: 1 Thessalonians 5:22–23

The key to obtaining peace is to detect what strips us of it. We must realize that finances, materialism, worry, fear and anxiety are all thieves of our peace. These are things we have no control over, and we allow that to rob us of our peace.

Our peace can be restored if we will search our hearts and minds, study God's Word, pray, have faith in and depend on God. Today's Scripture text reminds us that God is also the God of peace. "Abstain from all appearance of evil. And the very God of peace sanctify you wholly; and I pray God your whole spirit and soul and body be preserved blameless unto the coming of our Lord Jesus Christ." We must seek God in everything in order to maintain peace regardless of our circumstances.

If God is the God of peace, we must realize that the devil seeks to destroy our peace. He seeks to deceive us with thoughts of personal power. He tells us that we can handle our circumstances on our own when in fact we are powerless, and certainly peaceless, without God. If we allow Satan to control our thoughts, we give him access to control our actions.

We must recognize Satan's tactics and abstain from them. Remember, our Scripture text tells us to "Abstain from all appearance of evil." Refuse to be brought under Satan's forces. Instead, allow God to sanctify you by leaning on Him for all things, including power and peace.

God is the only one who can turn us from evil, present us blameless before Him and preserve us until His coming. He is the only one who can make peace come alive in us. He can truly give you peace when your life seems to have no place for it. Philippians 4:9 says, "Those things, which ye have both learned, and received, and heard, and seen in me, do: and the God of peace shall be with you." He is the God of peace.

"Allow God to sanctify you by leaning on Him for all things."

The Fruit of Longsuffering

SCRIPTURE READING: Ephesians 4:1–3

We've covered the fruits of love, joy and peace which relate to God. The next three fruits we will cover relate to man. The first of these is longsuffering. Paul said in today's Scripture text, "I therefore, the prisoner of the Lord, beseech you that ye walk worthy of the vocation wherewith ye are called, With all lowliness and meekness, with longsuffering, forbearing one another in love; Endeavouring to keep the unity of the Spirit in the bond of peace."

The Greek definition of the word translated longsuffering has a threefold meaning. The first translation is long-animity, meaning to have patience in times of provocation. The second definition given is forbearance. This means refraining from doing or saying the things we know we shouldn't. The third definition found is fortitude. Fortitude means patient endurance of trouble and pain, to have courage.

Obviously, based on these definitions, we will never acquire these fruits through our own self efforts. We must rely on the Holy Spirit to be longsuffering. As human beings, it is easy to be patient and courageous when the hard times are on someone else, but when we're facing our own hard times we become impatient and uncontrollable.

Longsuffering requires a willingness to be patient, self-controlled people rather than being demanding and impatient. Patience and self-control will bring honor and glory to God. If we can do this through someone else's tragedies, then we should be able to do it under our own circumstances. Many times we scar our Christian character because of our impatience and misinterpretation of day to day life.

Let the Holy Spirit produce longsuffering in your life, during your trials and tribulations, so you can bring honor and glory to God.

"Longsuffering requires a willingness to be patient, self-controlled people rather than being demanding and impatient."

The Spirit of Longsuffering

SCRIPTURE READING: Ephesians 4:29–32

We are all aware that life is not always fair, and it is very hard to be self-controlled when it seems as if our life is falling apart. It is our human nature to defend ourselves when we feel attacked by those around us. It is difficult to refrain from taking revenge. Our flesh thrives off of such actions, but our Spirit is grieved at such behavior, for it is contrary to the Spirit of longsuffering.

Today's Scripture text defines the Spirit of longsuffering for us. "Let no corrupt communication proceed out of your mouth, but that which is good to the use of edifying, that it may minister grace unto the hearers. And grieve not the holy Spirit of God, whereby ye are sealed unto the day of redemption. Let all bitterness, and wrath, and anger, and clamour, and evil speaking, be put away from you, with all malice: And be ye kind one to another, tenderhearted, forgiving one another, even as God for Christ's sake hath forgiven you."

In order to apply these Scriptures to our own lives, we must give the weaknesses of our flesh which cause such reactions to the Lord and ask for His help in turning from them. Then, we must seek His guidance in pinpointing and eliminating the things which cause our unjust reactions. For instance, anything that we are too possessive of will cause us to be impatient and unforbearing. These feelings are brought on by anything that makes us feel threatened or challenged.

The Spirit of longsuffering, on the other hand, is patient, forbearing and self-controlled. God is not selfish or greedy, and He has no evil or vengeance in His heart. He doesn't retaliate with evil when attacked. He is eternal, and He doesn't place His attention and love on things temporal like you and I do. Let's strive to have the Spirit of longsuffering by focusing on things eternal.

*"The Spirit of longsuffering is patient,
forbearing and self-controlled."*

Cultivating Longsuffering

SCRIPTURE READING: Philippians 4:13

What must we do to cultivate longsuffering in our lives? First, we must examine our lives and find out where we stand both spiritually and in the flesh. If you have anger or bitterness in your heart toward God or anyone else, you must repent of this and put forth the effort to make amends with this person. Next, you must identify those things in your life which separate you from God. In any situation where you are tense and stressed out, longsuffering is not in action. Lay these things, whether they are related to your job, your home, your finances, your marriage or material possessions, at the feet of Jesus and realize that you do not have the power to handle them.

Today's Scripture text gives us the secret for cultivating longsuffering. "I can do all things through Christ which strengtheneth me." You must give yourself completely to God and depend on Him in every situation and circumstance. Longsuffering requires serving and loving the Lord at all times, not just in the hard times. You must pray daily without ceasing, serve without swaying, study God's Word and then apply what you've learned to your own life. As you do these things your impatience will turn into peace as you become more mature and stable in your walk with Christ. When everything around you seems hopeless, you will be standing strong and putting your faith in God instead of trying to handle the situation yourself and growing frustrated with it.

God wants you to be an effective vessel for His use. If you aren't letting His characteristics shine forth in you, then it is very possible that you're not bearing the fruit of the Spirit. Put forth an effort to be more patient and understanding in all circumstances. Give them all to Jesus and let Him produce the fruit of longsuffering in your life.

> ## "God wants you to be an effective vessel for His use."

OCTOBER   295

The Fruit of Gentleness

SCRIPTURE READING: 2 Corinthians 10:1

Gentleness is the second of the three fruits which relate to man. Paul says in today's Scripture text, "Now I Paul myself beseech you by the meekness and gentleness of Christ, who in presence am base among you, but being absent am bold toward you." Gentleness is a character of our inward nature which we can all demonstrate if we'll only allow the Holy Spirit to produce this fruit within us. Our gentleness is the gentleness of Christ. It is a gift of God displayed within us as we walk in the Spirit.

Often our flesh wants to reject gentleness because gentleness requires humility in situations where our flesh wants to lash out. When we lash out in revenge against others, we have rejected the Spirit's guidance into gentleness.

What does having gentleness mean? Gentleness, in the original Greek, means "to be useful or to have moral excellence (in character or demeanor)." It's hard to comprehend that being gentle means being useful. How can being gentle make us useful? Christ is seen in our lives through our acts of gentleness, spreading the Gospel through our very actions. Therefore, the person who walks in gentleness will always be useful, kind and good.

The key to obtaining the fruit of gentleness is having a desire to be like Jesus. Jesus displayed gentleness throughout His time on this earth. Even in the most tempting and difficult situations, Jesus relied on the power of the Holy Spirit to produce gentleness within Him. Jesus' desire and determination to please the Father and complete His will kept His attitudes and priorities in proper perspective. We must apply this same principle to our lives as well.

We should all want to share gentleness. It produces love and gives understanding in situations where love and understanding seem impossible. Let's be gentle toward others!

"The fruit of gentleness is having a desire to be like Jesus."

A NEW DESIRE

Gentleness in Action

SCRIPTURE READING: Luke 23:34

The words of today's Scripture text are words of gentleness in action. "Then said Jesus, Father, forgive them; for they know not what they do. And they parted his raiment, and cast lots." Jesus left us many examples throughout the Gospels where He demonstrated gentleness in situations where you and I might have reacted judgmentally in the flesh.

The adulterous woman whom the Jews brought before Jesus to be stoned was one example of gentleness in action. Man displayed heartlessness, but Jesus showed true tender-heartedness. He said in John 8:11, "Neither do I condemn thee: go, and sin no more."

Again, as He hung on the cross, Jesus gave us an example of gentleness in action. Both of the thieves who hung with Him had mocked our Lord earlier in the day. However, one thief had a change of heart and said, "Lord, remember me when thou comest into thy kingdom. And Jesus said unto him, Verily I say unto thee, To day shalt thou be with me in paradise" (Luke 23:42–43).

Jesus showed the same gentleness toward those who had crucified Him and those whose sins had sent Him to Calvary, including you and me. As He hung dying, He uttered the words of today's Scripture text, "Father, forgive them; for they know not what they do."

Our goal in our Christian life should be to bestow upon others the element of gentleness. The Holy Spirit longs to speak and act through you with words of kindness and understanding to all whom you may come into contact with. We determine how much of Jesus others see in us. When we seek the Lord, follow the leadership of the Holy Spirit and lay aside our fleshly thoughts for the thoughts of God, then we can see gentleness in action in our own lives.

"Our goal in our Christian life should be to bestow upon others the element of gentleness."

The Fruit of Goodness

SCRIPTURE READING: Ephesians 5:9

Goodness, in the original Greek, means "virtue and beneficience." We can demonstrate goodness without bearing the fruit of the Spirit. The flesh can portray an act of goodness in moral conduct, but the goodness of God comes only for the Spirit.

The word virtue in Webster's dictionary means "a general moral excellence, a specific moral quality regarded as good, or a good quality." In general, it is our desire to be good and to have good qualities, yet in spite of this our flesh still has a tendency to compromise to do evil and wrong acts. The only way to overcome this natural reaction of our flesh is to rely on the Spirit of God to produce the character of God within us.

The word beneficience in Webster's dictionary means "being kind; it is a charitable act or gift." In order for this to be active in our lives, we must rely on the power of the Spirit. Now every charitable act doesn't necessarily come from God, but God can use even boastful acts of goodness to reveal His presence and power in someone's life. Often we boast when we help others or give to those in need. We can't wait to tell others about the good deed we've done so we'll look good in front of them. This, my friend, is not the goodness of the Holy Spirit. This is the moral acts of our flesh, and they are absolutely useless in the eyes of God.

Today's Scripture text says, "For the fruit of the Spirit is in all goodness and righteousness and truth." The goodness of God is demonstrated in those things you do in silence, not requiring any credit or recognition. The Holy Spirit demands no recognition or pats on the back for the good deeds that He does through us.

Are you expecting recognition for your good deeds toward others? God longs to fill you with His goodness. Lay aside your glory and let God work through you.

"The goodness of God is demonstrated in those things you do in silence."

A NEW DESIRE

Sowing in Goodness

SCRIPTURE READING: Romans 2:4

When we've cultivated the goodness of God which is the fruit of the Spirit, we enjoy the simple things of life. We enjoy helping others. It thrills our hearts to see our goodness effect the lives of others in a positive and spiritual manner.

The goodness of God that we express through the Spirit will always be effective for the sake of the Gospel. A deed that you perform through the Spirit in someone's life, whether it be a friend or a stranger, will be effective spiritually in that person's life. It may not appear to be effective at that very moment, but God will bring your good deed back to that person's mind at the moment it is needed the most.

Your deeds of goodness, if they are led by the Spirit, can lead someone to the Lord, be the words that provoke rededication or comfort the heart of someone who is hurting. You should never take the goodness of God lightly when it comes to sharing it in a dark and evil world. Today's Scripture text says, "Or despisest thou the riches of his goodness and forbearance and longsuffering; not knowing that the goodness of God leadeth thee to repentance?"

We don't always like to do good, especially in certain circumstances, but if we will endure and reflect the goodness of God in these times then our goodness will be used in a positive and powerful way. God's goodness toward us and through us represents grace, love and mercy. Deeds of goodness are from the Holy Spirit, and they are done through us by the Holy Spirit in order to make God manifest in our lives.

In order to demonstrate the goodness of God, we must separate ourselves from acts that feed our flesh and give ourselves instead to the leadership of the Spirit. Sow in goodness under His leadership and watch the harvest that you reap.

"The goodness of God that we express through the Spirit will always be effective for the sake of the Gospel."

Activating the Goodness of God

SCRIPTURE READING: John 8:34–36

How do we learn to live in and activate the goodness of God through the Holy Spirit? We learn this by living in truth and righteousness just as we learned in Ephesians 5:9: "For the fruit of the Spirit is in all goodness and righteousness and truth." We must look back on our lives and separate fleshly acts of goodness from Spirit-filled acts of goodness.

You must get to know the truth. The truth is Jesus Christ and Him crucified, buried and alive again today so that we could be made free and have eternal life and righteousness. Our Scripture text for today says, "Jesus answered them, Verily, verily, I say unto you, Whosoever committeth sin is the servant of sin. And the servant abideth not in the house for ever: but the Son abideth ever. If the Son therefore shall make you free, ye shall be free indeed."

This is the goodness of God. The good acts of the flesh make us servants of sin. We must live in righteousness by allowing ourselves to be servants of righteousness instead. With every demonstration of righteousness there is also a deed of goodness.

Matthew 12:33–36 says, "Either make the tree good, and his fruit good; or else make the tree corrupt, and his fruit corrupt: for the tree is known by his fruit. O generation of vipers, how can ye, being evil, speak good things? for out of the abundance of the heart the mouth speaketh. A good man out of the good treasure of the heart bringeth forth good things: and an evil man out of the evil treasure bringeth forth evil things. But I say unto you, That every idle word that men shall speak, they shall give account thereof in the day of judgment."

Is your tree good or evil? Evaluate your actions toward others to determine whether you possess the fruit of goodness or if you're still green and bitter.

"With every demonstration of righteousness there is also a deed of goodness."

A NEW DESIRE

The Fruit of Faith

SCRIPTURE READING: Romans 10:17

The word faith is mentioned 246 times in the Bible. Where does faith come from? Our Scripture text says, "So then faith cometh by hearing, and hearing by the word of God." God wants us to have faith in our lives by reading, listening and heeding to His Word.

Faith is the first of the final three fruits that make up the fruit of the Spirit. As we have already learned, love, joy and peace are the elements of the fruit of the Spirit in relation to God. Longsuffering, gentleness and goodness are in relation to man. Faith, meekness and temperance relate to our inner life, that personal relationship we form with God.

We must have faith to be born again. Ephesians 2:8 says, "For by grace are ye saved through faith; and that not of yourselves: it is the gift of God." Faith is essential for salvation and vital in Christian growth. Hebrews 11:6 says, "But without faith it is impossible to please him: for he that cometh to God must believe that he is, and that he is a rewarder of them that diligently seek him."

Of the 246 times faith is mentioned in the Bible, only two are in the Old Testament. On average, the word faith appears nine times in each book of the New Testament. Jesus Himself mentions the word, or some form of it, 46 times in the New Testament. With these figures, we can rest assured that God wants us to apply and demonstrate what His Word teaches us about faith.

As we study faith, seek your heart to find what God wants you to apply to your life. Remember, "without faith it is impossible to please him: for he that cometh to God must believe that he is, and that he is a rewarder of them that diligently seek him."

"We must have faith to be born again."

Saving Faith and Living Faith

SCRIPTURE READING: Philippians 1:6

We are taught to apply two types of faith throughout the Scriptures. They are saving faith and living faith.

The first of course, is saving faith. Saving faith requires us to believe in someone whom we have never seen. Saving faith gives us an eternal position with God. Jesus is our access to salvation. It is through faith in Him that we are saved.

Saving faith is instantaneous. It is ours at the moment we receive Christ as our Savior. Romans 10:9 says, "That if thou shalt confess with thy mouth the Lord Jesus, and shalt believe in thine heart that God hath raised him from the dead, thou shalt be saved." To believe in and trust the risen Savior is to have saving faith.

Once we've been born again, we need to apply living faith to our lives. Applying living faith is a process that we go through as we experience situations which force us to depend on God. Living faith is demonstrated through the heroes of faith we read about in Hebrews 11.

To have living faith, we must have confidence in our risen Savior. We must put our faith to work, being confident that God is in control of our lives. Today's Scripture text says, "Being confident of this very thing, that he which hath begun a good work in you will perform it until the day of Jesus Christ."

Hebrews 11:1 defines faith for us: "Now faith is the substance of things hoped for, the evidence of things not seen." This is where faith becomes living faith, when we trust God in situations we can't control. This type of faith is often more difficult for our flesh than simply worrying, but when we put our hope in God our faith becomes a living reality.

Faith allows God's presence and power to become evident in our lives. Trust in God and allow your trying times to become learning times instead.

"Faith allows God's presence and power to become evident in our lives."

How Much Faith Do You Have?

SCRIPTURE READING: Ephesians 3:17–19

The amount of faith you have in God is based upon your love for and knowledge of God. The more time you spend in the Word of God, the more you will learn about Him. Remember, we have learned that faith comes by hearing the Word of God (Romans 10:17). The more of God's Word you adhere to, the greater your faith in God will be. God will become so real to you that having faith in Him will come naturally and easily for you.

Faith is so rewarding for those who demonstrate it. God is so faithful to show Himself to us if we will trust in Him. Faith is the element of our Christianity that determines our closeness with God. It is a hard lesson to learn, but faith will become a part of our lives if we'll only pray for our faith to increase. However, we must also have a willingness to be tried, tested and tempted. God will be faithful to show Himself to us in every situation, and we will become more mature, stable Christians who are pleasing to God.

The Holy Spirit produces faith in our lives. We must let Him produce this faith by yielding to His leadership. If we lack the element of faith in our own personal lives, we have no one to blame other than ourselves. We have the power of God within us to obtain faith through His Spirit.

Paul prayed in today's Scripture text, "That Christ may dwell in your hearts by faith; that ye, being rooted and grounded in love, May be able to comprehend with all saints what is the breadth, and length, and depth, and height; And to know the love of Christ, which passeth knowledge, that ye might be filled with all the fulness of God." Whether or not this faith blossoms in your life is up to you.

Get in God's Word and learn of His truths. Let Him speak to you, and open your heart to hearing Him so that your faith may increase.

"Faith is so rewarding for those who demonstrate it."

The Fruit of Meekness

SCRIPTURE READING: Matthew 11:29

Meekness is the second element of the fruit of the Spirit relating to our inner life. This life, and the fruit that pertains to it, determines the depth of our relationship with God. Ephesians 3:16 reveals this to us. It says, "That he would grant you, according to the riches of his glory, to be strengthened with might by his Spirit in the inner man." The inner man is the heart, the seat of God's Spirit. Meekness, the key to humility, is increased in our inner man through the Holy Spirit.

Meekness means to be gentle, humble and to show humility. These are characteristics of Jesus Christ that can only be produced in our hearts through the Holy Spirit. We can reveal these characteristics in the flesh, but we can't reveal the true characteristics of them outside the Holy Spirit.

Humility must begin in our hearts. In Matthew 11:29, Jesus said, "Take my yoke upon you, and learn of me; for I am meek and lowly in heart: and ye shall find rest unto your souls." Jesus revealed Himself as having a character of meekness. Jesus always made Himself lower in order to reach others. Meekness requires humility and lowliness. This doesn't mean we are to let the world beat us down or destroy our self-esteem, but it does mean we have to love those who despitefully use us.

Meekness will speak for us as Christians. When we put on the character of Christ, we will show kindness, gentleness and love in all situations. We learn to love as Jesus loves. When we learn to love like Jesus loved, then we can understand the humility He showed on the cross of Calvary. Jesus didn't degrade himself at Calvary; He humbled Himself in love.

Allow the Spirit of God to develop a Spirit of meekness in you today.

"Meekness, the key to humility, is increased in our inner man through the Holy Spirit."

Meekness, the Principle of Lowliness

SCRIPTURE READING: Philippians 2:3

Today's Scripture text says, "Let nothing be done through strife or vainglory; but in lowliness of mind let each esteem other better than themselves." Can you give up for Jesus and others what Jesus gave up for you? If you are saved, you have the power within you through the Holy Spirit to do so. True meekness is when we start humbling ourselves before God, realizing that we are nothing without Him. Like Jesus, we must think of others and their condition, especially their eternal destination, before we give up on them.

It is not our nature to forsake ourselves for the sake of others, but we can do it if we truly love God and have a desire to be followers of Jesus. Can you give up things in your life to be made lowly? Can you give them up without expecting anything in return? Can you give to God and others without wanting recognition or a pat on the back for what you've done? Are you willing to do without to see that others do not have to? Jesus never received a pat on the back for the time He left His heavenly abode with the Father to come to earth where people hated and rejected Him. This is not to say that in order to have meekness you must give up every material, pleasurable and prosperous possession you own, but you must be willing to give them to God and to use them for His honor and glory. Lowliness is not being stripped of everything. It is the desire and willingness to be stripped.

Being pleasing to God and having the fruit of meekness should be one of our greatest goals as Christians. Take a survey of your life. Are you gentle, humble and lowly, or are you worldly, greedy and self-centered? God loves you just as you are, but let Him create in you a Spirit of meekness. Take the first step to meekness by saying, "God, I am absolutely nothing without you."

"Lowliness is not being stripped of everything.
It is the desire and willingness to be stripped."

The Fruit of Temperance

Scripture Reading: 1 Corinthians 9:25

Although it is the final of the nine fruits of the Spirit, temperance is the most essential to apply in order to demonstrate the eight before it. Temperance, like meekness and lowliness, relates to our inner man.

Temperance means to control our actions, feelings, thoughts and especially our tongues. In simple definition, it means we are to have self-control in all circumstances. Today's Scripture text says, "And every man that striveth for the mastery is temperate in all things. Now they do it to obtain a corruptible crown; but we an incorruptible." Striving for the mastery means we're competing for a prize.

The secret to winning is staying calm, thinking positively and being confident with ourselves. Achieving these things requires self-control. If we panic, think the worst and allow fear and doubt to enter our minds, we instantly lose control of the situation. The best strategy for victory is self-control.

Our walk with God requires the same strategy for victorious Christian living. Temperance, or self-control, must be exercised in every area of our lives if we are to be pleasing to God.

Don't let circumstances hinder your fellowship with God. Don't break fellowship with Him by losing control in what is truly a minute situation. Rather than handling things with an attitude of rudeness and hostility, do all things through the Holy Spirit and allow Him to manifest the fruit of temperance in you.

> "Don't let circumstances hinder
> your fellowship with God."

A NEW DESIRE

Temperance, Our Way of Escape

SCRIPTURE READING: 1 Corinthians 10:13

Temperance has a tremendous effect in our lives in many ways. Temperance reveals to those around us the type of people we truly are. Rudeness and hostility reveal the flesh; temperance is a characteristic of God's control in our lives. Temperance is revealed in our patience, understanding, compassion and righteousness in all circumstances.

Each of us have things in our lives we lose control over. We must learn to call on God and walk in His Spirit, allowing Him to be the producer of our self-control. This is the fruit of temperance.

Today's Scripture text says, "There hath no temptation taken you but such as is common to man: but God is faithful, who will not suffer you to be tempted above that ye are able; but will with the temptation also make a way to escape, that ye may be able to bear it." Applying this verse to your life is applying temperance to your life.

Temperance means we don't fall apart over everything; we call on God instead. We rest in the protective care of our loving Father. Temperance is resting in the knowledge that God is in control of everything. Temperance is turning from sin's temptation rather than heeding to it.

God can deliver us from all sin and temptation, but we must apply discipline and temperance to our lives. Jesus was tempted just as we are, but the same Spirit who kept Him righteous and under control lives within you if you are born again.

Allow temperance to be demonstrated in your life by rejecting the things that hinder your fellowship with God.

"Temperance is a characteristic of God's control in our lives."

Victory Through Temperance

SCRIPTURE READING: 1 Corinthians 9:27

Discipline and self-control work together for victory in our lives. We must discipline ourselves to study, pray, sacrifice and repent. We must separate ourselves from the flesh and bring our bodies of flesh into subjection to the Spirit. The more we do this, the more self-control we will have.

Today's Scripture text says, "But I keep under my body, and bring it into subjection: lest that by any means, when I have preached to others, I myself should be a castaway." Paul strove to receive a crown for his service by keeping himself under subjection to the Spirit. He resisted the flesh so that his Gospel message would be received by others. Temperance was Paul's key to victory in service to God.

We, too, should run the race of self-control. We can't be effective servants for Him unless we're in subjection to Him. Temperance is not gained overnight. It is a day to day process that will eventually take over as we allow God to teach us to walk in it.

Lack of temperance can hurt our testimony immensely. A Christian with an attitude of greed, selfishness, boastfulness or pettiness is damaging to the reputation of Christians. A mature, stable Christian will quickly identify these as acts of the flesh or Satan. A lost or backslidden person will identify them as childish, poor examples of a Christian.

Search your heart, examine your ways and see if you possess temperance. The fruit of the Spirit can never be completely manifested in your life if you reject this element. Your walk with God will always be unstable or confusing until you humble yourself and allow Him to change you. Allow God to fill you with His temperance today, and get victory over the things that hinder you from fellowship with God.

> "Lack of temperance can hurt our testimony immensely."

A NEW DESIRE

Claiming the Fruit

SCRIPTURE READING: John 15:4

We have completed our study on the Fruit of the Spirit. Did you search your heart sincerely to see if you were demonstrating these characteristics? You must have a desire to manifest this fruit. As our desires grow, we begin to weed out the undergrowth that smothers these qualities. As we weed them out, our communion with the Holy Ghost begins to mature. We begin to rest in and appreciate the grace of Jesus Christ, and we begin to enjoy the love of God.

When we claim the fruit of the Spirit and strive to manifest each element of it in our lives, we are blessed with the benefits of our salvation. As we use and live in this fruit (love, joy, peace, longsuffering, gentleness, goodness, faith, meekness and temperance), we learn to depend on the Holy Spirit instead of our flesh. We realize that these attributes are truly the personality of the Holy Spirit.

The Holy Spirit introduces each element of His fruit into our lives as we allow Him to do so. The more of this fruit we bear, the more righteous we become. We abide in Christ when we bear the fruit of the Spirit. Today's Scripture text says, "Abide in me, and I in you. As the branch cannot bear fruit of itself, except it abide in the vine; no more can ye, except ye abide in me."

There is only one God and only one Spirit. The nine fruits we've studied all work together to make up the character of the one and only Holy Spirit. As we apply each element, we become more whole and holy in Christ.

Give yourself humbly to God and allow Him to control your life. He will produce His fruit in you and use them for His service. Claim the fruit of the Spirit today.

*"We abide in Christ when we bear
the fruit of the Spirit."*

The Gifts of God's Spirit

SCRIPTURE READING: 1 Corinthians 12:1

Today's Scripture text says, "Now concerning spiritual gifts, brethren, I would not have you ignorant." The characteristics of Christ in our lives, which we have studied all month, give us access to the gifts of His Spirit.

One of the things we must not be ignorant of concerning these gifts is the requirements we must meet to manifest them in our lives. The first requirement is to study each gift individually to be sure that we understand and know the gift well enough that we do not take its meaning out of context or attempt to produce it through our own abilities.

There are different gifts, and each person has his or her own gifts. They are given to us according to the grace of God and increased according to our proportion of faith. Romans 12:4–6 says, "For as we have many members in one body, and all members have not the same office: So we, being many, are one body in Christ, and every one members one of another. Having then gifts differing according to the grace that is given to us, whether prophecy, let us prophesy according to the proportion of faith."

Just as their are nine fruits of the Spirit, there are also nine gifts. However, we will not be able to possess all nine of these gifts. The gifts are listed in 1 Corinthians 12:8–11: "For to one is given by the Spirit the word of wisdom; to another the word of knowledge by the same Spirit; To another faith by the same Spirit; to another the gifts of healing by the same Spirit; To another the working of miracles; to another prophecy; to another discerning of spirits; to another divers kinds of tongues; to another the interpretation of tongues: But all these worketh that one and the selfsame Spirit, dividing to every man severally as he will."

Study these gifts in depth as we do a brief study of them.

> **"The characteristics of Christ in our lives give us access to the gifts of His Spirit."**

A NEW DESIRE

The Distribution of Gifts

SCRIPTURE READING: 1 Corinthians 12:18

The gifts of the Spirit are distributed to every man as the Spirit chooses. We don't all need the same gifts. If we all had the same gifts, we'd be stumbling over one another trying to exercise them in Christian service.

God gives us gifts according to our ability to use them. He's not going to give us gifts that we would be unwilling or incapable of using, and He's not going to give each person in a local assembly the same gift. If each person in a church body had the gift of discernment, what good would it be? First Corinthians 12:17 says, "If the whole body were an eye, where were the hearing? If the whole were hearing, where were the smelling?"

Every believer is a member of the body of Christ. They are given gifts for the profit of the whole body and to work with the other members of the body. We do not have a choice about which gifts we are given. That decision is left up to God, and we must accept, use and distribute the gifts that God has so graciously given us. Today's Scripture text says, "But now hath God set the members every one of them in the body, as it hath pleased him."

We should not covet one another's gifts. We should use the gift God has given us to work with those who have other gifts in accomplishing God's work. Remember, God distributes gifts according to His will. Let's be thankful for our own gifts.

"God distributes gifts according to His will."

The Best Gifts

SCRIPTURE READING: 1 Corinthians 12:22–23

All gifts of the Spirit are important. No one gift is more important than another. How many times have you caught yourself using the excuse that your gift is not very important to God or to others? We're so busy coveting others' gifts that we don't realize that God wants to use our gifts. Satan uses this to make us feel unimportant and unnecessary.

Today's Scripture text proves how important even those "unimportant and unnecessary" gifts are. It says, "Nay, much more those members of the body, which seem to be more feeble, are necessary: And those members of the body, which we think to be less honourable, upon these we bestow more abundant honour; and our uncomely parts have more abundant comeliness."

It does not matter if you are sick, poor or feel like the least of all people. God has given you a gift, and He wants you to use it for His honor and glory. God has a purpose for each of our lives, and He has given each of us a gift to accomplish that purpose. If we really love God, we will strive to demonstrate the gifts of the Spirit which He has given us as He gives us the liberty and opportunity to do so.

"It does not matter if you are sick, poor or feel like the least of all people. God has given you a gift."

Differences of Administrations

Scripture Reading: 1 Corinthians 12:5

Just as there are different gifts, there are different administrations. Administration refers to the offices or services in which we use our gifts. Today's Scripture text says, "And there are differences of administrations, but the same Lord." These different services are how the Gospel is spread all over the world. Our gifts are demonstrated and revealed through these administrations.

As we learned yesterday, God distributes gifts according to His will for each person's life. He knows what it will take to prepare you for this office of ministry. For some, it only takes a small gesture on God's part, but for others it takes a lifetime of instruction and chastening from God before they're ready to give in. Administration comes easily and naturally for some, while others seem to build on a foundation of trial and error. Some serve with joy and peace while others make the administration of their gift a chore or obligation.

God never said serving Him would be easy. Second Timothy 4:5 says, "But watch thou in all things, endure afflictions, do the work of an evangelist, make full proof of thy ministry." We will get tired and frustrated in our service for God, but true service reacts as this Scripture defines. Someone in their proper, God-given gift and service will endure in their ministry work.

The key to endurance is staying close to God. The power for endurance is found in following the leadership of the Holy Spirit. Stay close to God, follow the leadership of the Spirit and stay strong in service.

"Administration refers to the offices or services in which we use our gifts."

Letting the Spirit Lead

SCRIPTURE READING: 1 Timothy 4:4–6

Today's Scripture text gives us the requirements for letting the Spirit lead in our lives. It says, "For every creature of God is good, and nothing to be refused, if it be received with thanksgiving: For it is sanctified by the word of God and prayer. If thou put the brethren in remembrance of these things, thou shalt be a good minister of Jesus Christ, nourished up in the words of faith and of good doctrine, whereunto thou hast attained."

We should have a thankful heart for the ministry God has blessed us with. A spirit of thankfulness activates the presence of the Holy Spirit within our lives. The Holy Spirit is gentle in His leadership in our lives. He is ready and willing to lead those whose hearts are open to Him.

The main key to letting the Spirit lead is found in verse five of our Scripture text: "For it is sanctified by the word of God and prayer." The Holy Spirit is kept active in our lives when we feed Him the Word through studying. The Word of God stirs the Spirit within us. When we study, the Holy Spirit reveals to us the meaning, plan and purpose of God's will for our lives. He is able to teach us how to be good ministers.

Prayer is the next step. We feed the Spirit through study, and we humble ourselves before God in prayer. God knows our needs before we do, and prayer allows Him to reveal His love to us. Prayer must come before, during and after study.

The Holy Spirit can take our service and use it effectively while giving us the strength, confidence, desire and right attitude while we do it. Let your gifts be demonstrated with joy and gladness by letting the Spirit lead.

"The Word of God stirs the Spirit within us."

Your Specific Service

SCRIPTURE READING: 1 Timothy 4:12–16

Isn't it a wonderful thought to know that God has a specific service chosen and selected just for you? Even when we don't feel adequate for the service, we should trust in Him for our performance and serve Him with willingness. We should praise Him for being so specific in our lives.

Today's Scripture text says, "Let no man despise thy youth; but be thou an example of the believers, in word, in conversation, in charity, in spirit, in faith, in purity. Till I come, give attendance to reading, to exhortation, to doctrine. Neglect not the gift that is in thee, which was given thee by prophecy, with the laying on of the hands of the presbytery. Meditate upon these things; give thyself wholly to them; that thy profiting may appear to all. Take heed unto thyself, and unto the doctrine; continue in them: for in doing this thou shalt both save thyself, and them that hear thee."

Every time you catch yourself wishing your service was like someone else's, remember that God didn't call you into their administration. He called you into your administration for a purpose. Regardless of the administration you're in or how many different ones there are, God has given them all for the purpose and intent of leading the lost to Jesus Christ, uplifting the believers and spreading the Gospel.

If you seem to be struggling with insecurities, regret or serving through obligation or habit, you need to hear a word from the Lord regarding your service. Sometimes we can be put into service because of man's wants and needs instead of God's will for our lives.

Keep your eyes on God and His will for your life, and leave the lives of others in God's hands.

> *"We should praise Him for being so specific in our lives."*

Uniting the Gifts

Scripture Reading: Ephesians 4:11–12

Today's Scripture text says, "And he gave some, apostles; and some, prophets; and some, evangelists; and some, pastors and teachers; For the perfecting of the saints, for the work of the ministry, for the edifying of the body of Christ." It is important to note that these are not additional gifts. These are types of people to whom God has given specific gifts. All of our gifts should be united for the purpose of edifying the body of Christ.

Romans 12:6 says, "Having then gifts differing according to the grace that is given to us, whether prophecy, let us prophesy according to the proportion of faith." Prophecy here means to predict or be an inspired speaker. It is the same meaning of the word in 1 Corinthians 12. They are the same gift used in different types of service. Anyone can have the gift of prophecy, but what makes them different is the area of service and how it's distributed.

A pastor usually has the gift of prophecy which he demonstrates by preaching the Gospel. I may have the gift of prophecy, but I demonstrate it through singing or teaching God's Word. Anyone who is born again should be able to edify and exhort the body of Christ. My pastor may have a higher calling in prophecy than I do, but as members of the same body, we are members of one another. We must unite our gifts in service to edify and exhort the body. Uniting our gifts will put things in their proper perspective.

> *"We must unite our gifts in service to edify and exhort the body."*

The Purpose of the Gifts

SCRIPTURE READING: Ephesians 4:12–15

Today's Scripture text simply explains to us the purpose of the gifts of the Spirit. It says, "For the perfecting of the saints, for the work of the ministry, for the edifying of the body of Christ: Till we all come in the unity of the faith, and of the knowledge of the Son of God, unto a perfect man, unto the measure of the stature of the fulness of Christ: That we henceforth be no more children, tossed to and fro, and carried about with every wind of doctrine, by the sleight of men, and cunning craftiness, whereby they lie in wait to deceive; But speaking the truth in love, may grow up into him in all things, which is the head, even Christ."

God gives us gifts to help one another to grow in our walk with Him. We are to use our gifts for His honor and glory and for the growing up of the believers. The gifts that God has given you are very important, and they should never be taken lightly. They must be used to build up the kingdom of God.

We must unite our gifts in love. First Corinthians 13:2 says, "And though I have the gift of prophecy, and understand all mysteries, and all knowledge; and though I have all faith, so that I could remove mountains, and have not charity, I am nothing." Love is the key that unites everything that God gives us together. It is the key for obtaining the gifts of the Spirit and the key to effectively demonstrating those gifts.

Use your gifts in love, uniting them with the gifts of others in the body of believers. This is the only way to achieve the purpose God has for you.

> *"God gives us gifts to help one another to grow in our walk with Him."*

True Wisdom

SCRIPTURE READING: 1 Corinthians 2:5

What is the simplest definition for wisdom? True wisdom is possessing and exercising spiritual knowledge of God and His instructions. It is more than knowledge; it is an understanding and application of what you know.

Our Scripture text for today says, "That your faith should not stand in the wisdom of men, but in the power of God." The wisdom that is given to us as a gift of the Spirit is not a fleshly wisdom. It is not wisdom that someone else can give us. It is a spiritual wisdom that comes from God alone.

We can gain lots of earthly wisdom throughout our lives, but this wisdom has no eternal value. Paul verifies the uselessness of this wisdom in 1 Corinthians 2:1–5. He says, "And I, brethren, when I came to you, came not with excellency of speech or of wisdom, declaring unto you the testimony of God. For I determined not to know any thing among you, save Jesus Christ, and him crucified. And I was with you in weakness, and in fear, and in much trembling. And my speech and my preaching was not with enticing words of man's wisdom, but in demonstration of the Spirit and of power: That your faith should not stand in the wisdom of men, but in the power of God."

Don't be deceived into thinking that your education, your social standing or your financial status gives you a superior wisdom. In truth, these things tend to make us ignorant because we let them dominate our lives. Let's heed to the words of Proverbs 23:4: "Labour not to be rich: cease from thine own wisdom."

"Wisdom comes from God alone."

The Consequences of Man's Wisdom

SCRIPTURE READING: Proverbs 23:5–8

The consequences of leaning on our own spiritual wisdom is spiritual dryness and foolishness in the eyes of God. The consequences of man's wisdom are found in today's Scripture text. It says, "Wilt thou set thine eyes upon that which is not? for riches certainly make themselves wings; they fly away as an eagle toward heaven. Eat thou not the bread of him that hath an evil eye, neither desire thou his dainty meats: For as he thinketh in his heart, so is he: Eat and drink, saith he to thee; but his heart is not with thee. The morsel which thou hast eaten shalt thou vomit up, and lose thy sweet words."

Leaning on our own wisdom leads us back to ineffective service. James 3:15–17 compares and contrasts our fleshly wisdom and the wisdom from God. "This wisdom descendeth not from above, but is earthly, sensual, devilish. For where envying and strife is, there is confusion and every evil work. But the wisdom that is from above is first pure, then peaceable, gentle, and easy to be entreated, full of mercy and good fruits, without partiality, and without hypocrisy."

Wisdom is ours for the asking. James 1:5–6 says, "If any of you lack wisdom, let him ask of God, that giveth to all men liberally, and upbraideth not; and it shall be given him. But let him ask in faith, nothing wavering. For he that wavereth is like a wave of the sea driven with the wind and tossed."

Let's take the next few days to learn how to apply this gift of wisdom to our lives.

"Leaning on our own wisdom leads us to ineffective service."

Obtaining Wisdom, Part One

SCRIPTURE READING: Proverbs 4:7

We learned yesterday that wisdom is free for the asking. If you want wisdom, you must first ask God for it, then believe, without doubting, that He will give it to you.

Wisdom is a principle for our Christian growth. Today's Scripture text says, "Wisdom is the principal thing; therefore get wisdom: and with all thy getting get understanding." Wisdom is imparted to us when we ask God for it; however, it is not an instant, overnight process. Wisdom comes through our growth and experiences in our daily walks with God.

Wisdom holds many lessons and trials, but we must be willing to be taught and tested. Job 12:12–13 says, "With the ancient is wisdom; and in length of days understanding. With him is wisdom and strength, he hath counsel and understanding." In order to obtain wisdom, you must be willing to go through what it will take for God to impart it to you.

Wisdom is obtained by knowing who God is and heeding to His authority. Proverbs 9:10 says, "The fear of the LORD is the beginning of wisdom: and the knowledge of the holy is understanding." The word fear in this verse means "to reverence." Godly fear is the reverence of God the Father and respect for His power and authority in our lives. Wisdom begins with fearing God in this manner. God is the Father of wisdom. If we fail to recognize His sovereignty, then we will never obtain His wisdom.

Let's put on the mind of Christ so that we'll be constantly aware of who's in control of our lives.

"Wisdom is a principle for our Christian growth."

A NEW DESIRE

Obtaining Wisdom, Part Two

SCRIPTURE READING: Proverbs 16:16

We must realize the importance of having wisdom. Many times, we mistake knowledge for wisdom. Knowledge is head-understanding; wisdom is heart-understanding. God rules and reigns in our hearts while Satan and the flesh attack our minds. This is why God places so much emphasis and value on wisdom. Today's Scripture text reveals the value of wisdom: "How much better is it to get wisdom than gold! and to get understanding rather to be chosen than silver!" Wisdom is years of knowledge applied to our lives and exercised daily to draw us closer to God.

Wisdom is obtained by those who are teachable. Psalm 119:33–34 says, "Teach me, O LORD, the way of thy statutes; and I shall keep it unto the end. Give me understanding, and I shall keep thy law; yea, I shall observe it with my whole heart." Everything that comes our way becomes an avenue of wisdom if we remain teachable. If we refuse to remain teachable, we'll wander around seeking answers and doubting God in everything that happens in our lives.

Wisdom is essential in overcoming temptation, sin and Satan's tactics. It is evident in those who are spiritually mature. Those who hunger and thirst after righteousness will be open to the things God wants to teach them through their trials and temptations.

I pray that you are willing to go through what it takes to obtain the gift of wisdom. I pray that you love God enough to use what you have and know already for the furtherance of the Gospel. Remember, God honors what you'll use for His honor and glory.

"Wisdom is obtained by those who are teachable."

Filled with Wisdom

SCRIPTURE READING: Colossians 1:9

Our goal should be to obtain spiritual maturity. In order to do this, we must be sincere about living for the Lord. You must discipline yourself to spending precious time with God. You need to develop a personal relationship with Him. Seek His face and hunger to draw closer to Him. Obey God at all times.

Obedience is a key to being filled with wisdom. Think of it like this: Knowledge is knowing God's will; wisdom is doing God's will. When we obey God, we are on the pathway to a life of righteousness, being filled with His wisdom.

Wisdom allows us to be valuable in service to the Lord. We see wisdom in the lives of those who have continued in their service in spite of temptations, battles and persecutions. Wisdom is seen in mothers who have faithfully trusted in the Lord through the devastating times their children have faced. Wisdom is seen in the pastor whose congregation is worldly, back-biting and seeking to get rid of him, yet he still loves them and doesn't compromise the Word of God for an ear-tickling message.

Ephesians 4:11 mentions apostles, prophets, evangelists, pastors and teachers. They all had to be filled with wisdom in order to serve Christ effectively. We, too, must seek after this same wisdom in order to be effective in our service and more educated about God's will for our lives. My prayer for you today is found in today's Scripture text: "For this cause we also, since the day we heard it, do not cease to pray for you, and to desire that ye might be filled with the knowledge of his will in all wisdom and spiritual understanding."

> *"Knowledge is knowing God's will;*
> *wisdom is doing God's will."*

A NEW DESIRE

The Gift of Knowledge

SCRIPTURE READING: 1 Corinthians 12:8

Today's Scripture text speaks of both knowledge and wisdom. It says, "For to one is given by the Spirit the word of wisdom; to another the word of knowledge by the same Spirit." There is definitely a difference in knowledge and wisdom. Knowledge is the understanding or learning of something; wisdom is the applying or actions of the understanding. We can learn everyday, but it does not become knowledge until we use what we've learned. We either use it or lose it.

Part of the value of knowledge is that it strengthens us for handling life's circumstance. Proverbs 24:5 says, "A wise man is strong; yea, a man of knowledge increaseth strength." The more knowledge you get, the stronger you become. Strength, in return, makes us mature and stable when our lives seem to be falling apart. If we are learned in the Scriptures, then our greatest understanding is knowing it is God who strengthens us. Isaiah 33:6 says, "And wisdom and knowledge shall be the stability of the times, and strength of salvation: the fear of the Lord is his treasure."

There are many different kinds of knowledge that we can obtain, but the first and most important knowledge is the saving knowledge of Jesus Christ. John 17:3 says, "And this is life eternal, that they might know thee the only true God, and Jesus Christ, whom thou hast sent." Christ sees to it that everyone hears the Gospel of salvation, but we must decide what to do with this knowledge once we have heard it.

The knowledge that is mentioned in our Scripture text is a spiritual knowledge. We can have all the knowledge of the world our minds can absorb, but if we don't apply it to our spiritual lives it will never amount to anything of value. Worldly wisdom is nothing more than head knowledge in the eyes of God.

"Knowledge is the understanding or learning of something."

Filled with Knowledge

SCRIPTURE READING: Philippians 1:9

Spiritual knowledge is a gift of God. We should all hunger and strive to receive it. It only takes a sincere heart and a righteous attitude to have the knowledge of God. Paul prays for us to be filled with this knowledge in today's Scripture text. He says, "And this I pray, that your love may abound yet more and more in knowledge and in all judgment."

If we are truly saved, then we can all be filled with this knowledge. How much we receive is based on our sincerity and desire to live for God. If we truly love the Lord, we will long to know His will for our lives and this knowledge will automatically put us into obedience. If we obey His will, then our knowledge increases and will eventually turn into wisdom. John 7:17 says, "If any man will do his will, he shall know of the doctrine, whether it be of God, or whether I speak of myself." Doing the will of God is essential for receiving the gift of knowledge.

Spiritual knowledge comes with many rewards. Second Peter 1:5–9 explains some of these rewards to us. It says, "And beside this, giving all diligence, add to your faith virtue; and to virtue knowledge; And to knowledge temperance and to temperance patience; and to patience godliness and to godliness brotherly kindness and to brotherly kindness charity. For if these things be in you, and abound, they make you that ye shall neither be barren nor unfruitful in knowledge of our Lord Jesus Christ. But he that lacketh these things is blind, and cannot see afar off, and hath forgotten that he was purged from his old sins."

If you have the gift of knowledge, make sure that you are using it for God. Examine yourself in what you know to see if you are in the will of God.

"Spiritual knowledge comes with many rewards."

A NEW DESIRE

Knowledge Applied

SCRIPTURE READING: 2 Timothy 3:5–7

Knowledge and wisdom are separate gifts but they also work together for your spiritual maturity. When God let's you know something, you have been given knowledge from God. He has made you aware of what He wants you to do. Therefore, you have been given the understanding of this thing. When you act upon this head knowledge, it becomes heart knowledge. If you choose not to act upon it, then you stand the chance of walking in disobedience.

When God teaches us something, He wants us to acknowledge His authority by doing as He has told us to do. God will not waste His time teaching you something else until you've applied the knowledge He's already given you. The Scriptures speak of this type of person in today's Scripture text: "Having a form of godliness, but denying the power thereof: from such turn away. For of this sort are they which creep into houses, and lead captive silly women laden with sins, led away with divers lust, Ever learning, and never able to come to the knowledge of the truth."

Knowledge is a great and beautiful Christian virtue. We should never abuse it or use it for our own gain or to make others feel intimidated. We are to use it for the glory of God and for the lifting up of His Kingdom. We should be anxious to share God's knowledge with those in our lives as well as the world. We need to be willing to sacrifice whatever it takes to increase it. It is better to get knowledge and give it away than it is to have knowledge and hoard it inside you where it rots away.

What are you doing with your knowledge?

"Knowledge is a great and beautiful Christian virtue."

Growing in Knowledge

SCRIPTURE READING: 2 Peter 3:18

Studying the Scriptures is another key principle for receiving knowledge. The Scriptures will not deceive us. They will teach us truths that will stand for eternity. Second Timothy 3:14–17 teaches us the importance of studying the Scriptures for growing in knowledge. "But continue thou in the things which thou hast learned and hast been assured of, knowing of whom thou hast learned them; And that from a child thou hast known the holy Scriptures, which are able to make thee wise unto salvation through faith which is in Christ Jesus. All Scripture is given by inspiration of God, and is profitable for doctrine, for reproof, for correction, for instruction in righteousness: That the man of God may be perfect, throughly furnished unto all good works." The Scriptures are a vast supply of knowledge for us; all we have to do is want it badly enough to pursue it.

To some it may seem that I'm contradicting myself when I say that knowledge is a gift, because we all know a gift is free without having to do anything to get it. However, I'm telling you to pursue knowledge; this is not a contradiction. Yes, knowledge is a gift of God's Spirit and we can all have it through salvation, but the Bible also urges us to grow in this knowledge. The only way we can grow in it is to pursue it. Today's Scripture text says, "But grow in grace, and in the knowledge of our Lord and Savior Jesus Christ. To him be the glory both now and forever. Amen." Knowledge is a gift, but if you are ever going to use it you must increase it.

"The Scriptures will not deceive us. They will teach us truths that will stand for eternity."

A NEW DESIRE

Defining Faith

SCRIPTURE READING: Romans 10:17

Faith is the kindling needed to start the fire of our salvation. It is believing in a God we cannot see. Faith is the foundation of our Christian walk. Faith is God's gift to us through salvation.

Faith is a starter of our salvation and spiritual growth just as kindling is the starter for a fire. It only takes a little faith to increase our spiritual growth abundantly. Matthew 17:20 teaches us that with just a little faith we can move mountains. Just as the strength of a fire is based on how much kindling we use, the strength of our salvation is based on how much we exercise our faith.

Faith comes from within. It is not an object you can touch or feel. It is an invisible power, a source of strength. Faith comes from reading, studying and applying the word of God daily to our lives. Our Scripture for today teaches this principle clearly. Today's Scripture text says, "So then faith cometh by hearing, and hearing by the word of God." Faith only becomes visible when we are willing to trust it, try it and exercise it.

Romans 4:5 teaches us that through Christ we are justified as well as made righteous by Christ's imputed faith to us. It says, "But to him that worketh not, but believeth on him that justifieth the ungodly, his faith is counted for righteousness." We can't have righteousness without faith or vice versa. The two together form the foundation of our Christian life.

Faith is automatically imputed to us when we accept and believe that Christ took our place on the cross and died for our sins. This believing faith is counted for righteousness. On this foundation, we can build our Christian life for effective service and stability in Christ.

"Faith comes from within. It is not an object
you can touch or feel."

A Sure Foundation

SCRIPTURE READING: Colossians 2:7

When building our Christian lives, we must start with a sure foundation. We can simply convey the importance of this by comparing it to the building of a house. When building a house, the structure starts with a footer. A strong foundation relies on a footer filled with cement. If a foundation is laid without the cement footer, the building would eventually begin to lean or sag due to the weight of the structure and the softness of the ground. The purpose for the cement is to secure the footer and the foundation.

Faith is the key factor in building our Christian character, but outward faith (the footer) cannot be secured without the imputed or inner faith (the cement). Inner faith secures us and makes us stable in our Christian walk. Imputed faith is ours at the moment we believe; it is the cement of our salvation. Outward faith is the footer that can be washed away if we try to build cheaply by not securing the foundation with cement.

Colossians 1:23 urges us to build on a sure foundation. It says, "Continue in the faith grounded and settled, and be not moved away from the hope of the Gospel, which ye have heard, and which was preached to every creature which is under heaven." Our Scripture text for today urges us again to make our foundation sure: "Rooted and built up in him, and stablished in the faith, as ye have been taught, abounding therein with thanksgiving."

Once we have a sure foundation, it's time to demonstrate our faith by trusting it, trying it and exercising it.

> *"Faith is the key factor in building our Christian character."*

A Reliable Foundation

SCRIPTURE READING: Mark 5:36

Be not afraid, only believe. Those were the words of our Savior. Believing in God is trusting Him for all things. Sometimes its hard to trust and believe in what we can't see. Trusting in God requires us to study His Word, to pray daily and to seek a personal relationship with Him. The more we know our Lord, the closer we get to Him, and the closer we get to Him, the more we trust Him. Trust comes from loving someone, and we can't know the Lord enough to trust Him until we spend time with Him in prayer and study.

The key to trusting God is found in 2 Corinthians 5:7. Paul said, "For we walk by faith, not by sight." Jesus said to Thomas in John 20:29, "Because thou hast seen me, thou hast believed: blessed are they that have not seen, and yet have believed." We are rewarded by God when we trust in Him because we believe without seeing.

Faith's power does not fail. Jesus told Peter in Luke 22:32, "But I have prayed for thee, that thy faith fail not: and when thou art converted, strengthen thy brethren." Faith is increased and strengthened by God through the hearing of the Word. Faith not only gives us access to redemption, but through this invisible power we also have access to healing, freedom from evil power and the ability to receive whatsoever we ask according to God's will. The Bible says in John 1:12, "But as many as received him, to them gave he power to become the sons of God, even to them that believe on his name."

Faith comes by hearing, and hearing by the Word of God. Make your foundation stronger and more reliable by getting in His Word.

"Faith is increased and strengthened by God through the hearing of the Word."

The Power of Faith

SCRIPTURE READING: Matthew 9:22

Jesus demonstrated the power of God in great ways during His earthly ministry. Those who followed Him watched as He healed the sick and raised the dead, and they daily heard Him preach on faith. Jesus is the author and finisher of our faith (Hebrews 12:2). Those who were willing to follow Him, believe on Him and try the faith that He taught became very powerful in faith. Once they gave faith a try and felt its power, their faith grew even stronger. Their love for Christ became greater, and their relationship with Him became personal. Faith gives power to those who will try it.

Remember the story of the woman with the issue of blood? What did she have to lose if touching the hem of Jesus' garment didn't heal her? She had tried all of man's remedies, but none of them had worked for her. Naturally as she heard this Man preach on believing and watched Him speak healing to others, her willingness to try this faith became uncontrollable. Matthew 9:21 says, "For she said within herself, If I may but touch his garment, I shall be whole." In verse 22 we find that she was healed immediately upon touching His garment. Jesus said unto her, "Daughter, be of good comfort; thy faith hath made thee whole."

Oh, if we could learn to try this invisible power within us called faith! The Bible teaches us that faith can move mountains, and James 1:3–4 says, "Knowing this, that the trying of your faith worketh patience. But let patience have her perfect work, that ye may be perfect and entire, wanting nothing." If you have chosen Christ as your Savior, you have already seen faith at work. Faith is a holy, invisible power sent down from God that we may grow in knowledge and wisdom, but it will not grow if we don't try it.

> "Faith is a holy, invisible power sent down
> from God."

The Gift of Healing

SCRIPTURE READING: Romans 12:3–8

The gift of healing is mentioned only three times throughout the Bible. All three times it is mentioned in 1 Corinthians 12. In verse nine it is introduced as a gift given to us from the Holy Spirit. In verse 28 it is presented to the believer for the purpose of testimony and as a witness of the power of Jesus Christ and His Gospel. In verse 30, it is in question as to whether everyone is to have the gift of healing.

In addressing verse 30, I believe that everyone has access to the gift of healing, in the aspect that healing is a gift from God and that the gift of healing comes from God. Notice I am referring to the gift of healing for ourselves, personal healing, and not the power to heal others.

So many views of this gift are based on being able to heal others. If this were the case, then why wouldn't Paul have addressed this gift as a healer instead of healing? The word "healing" used here means a cure or to be made whole.

Romans 12:3–5 teaches that we're to use the gifts of healing in our service to God. It says, "For I say, through the grace given unto me, to every man that is among you, not to think of himself more highly than he ought to think; but to think soberly, according as God hath dealt to every man the measure of faith. For as we have many members in one body, and all members have not the same office: So we, being many, are one body in Christ, and every one members one of another." For example: I have been given the gift of healing in respect that God healed me of the seizures. Therefore, I now use this healing as part of my service to the Lord. I testify of my healing. It is part of my everyday witnessing program. I testify that if God will do it for me, He will do it for anyone. This is the gift of healing that we all have access to.

"If God will do it for me, He will do it for anyone."

Receiving Healing

SCRIPTURE READING: 1 Corinthians 2:5

When God healed me, He did it in an instant. There were no more symptoms or recurring problems. It was not a process; it was complete and finished at that moment. The building up of my faith was a long, drawn out process. However, the healing was instant and complete. There aren't, and never have been since February 17, 1991, any more seizure headaches or auras (signs of seizures coming on). There are no doubts that I was truly healed. There have been no more medications for the seizures and no more doctors visits. My friends, this is truly the gift of healing for us today.

I must admit that in the beginning of my illness I sought every man-made remedy. I tried the medical doctors, chiropractors, and neurologist, etc. I tried all of their prescribed medications, I tried being anointed with oil, and I allowed the elders to lay hands on me. None of these things worked.

In desperation I asked God why wasn't anything working for me? His reply was found in today's Scripture text: "Your faith should not stand in the wisdom of men, but in the power of God." All of those things I had been trying were man's wisdom and power instead of God's.

I started praying everyday in my secret place. I started searching for God's power and His gift of healing. I knew that only He could deliver me. God revealed Himself to me through His Holy Word. He taught me through His Scriptures how to receive healing. I was then held responsible to obey and apply it to my life.

If you want to receive the gift of healing, you must seek God for the remedy.

"To receive the gift of healing, you must seek God for the remedy."

The Working of Miracles

SCRIPTURE READING: 1 Corinthians 12:10

In today's Scripture text, we are taught that the working of miracles is one of the gifts of the Spirit. It says, "To another the working of miracles . . ." The word "working" here in this Scripture is the key word for correct interpretations of this passage of Scripture. This word means the effects or performance that a miracle has in our lives or the lives of others. The many miracles that we read of in the Scriptures are placed there for our example, as well as for non-believers, for proof that God is all mighty and all powerful. He can do anything in our lives.

Miracles are still being performed today by God and by God only. He can still raise the dead, heal the sick and save the lost. He can do it in the blink of an eye, or he can take as long as He feels necessary to perform. I often read of the miracles in the Bible, and it encourages me to never give up on God.

Miracles are never-ending in our lives because of God's love and mercy. It is truly a miracle that God allows us another breath. We are made worthy only through the death, burial and resurrection of Jesus Christ.

The working of miracles is a gift that we can all have. All you have to do is profess to the world the miracles that God has performed in your life. Remember the "working" is simply the effects of the miracle that God may have performed in your life.

"Miracles are never-ending in our lives because of God's love and mercy."

The Gift of Prophecy

SCRIPTURE READING: 1 Corinthians 14:3

The gift of prophecy is defined in today's Scripture text. It says, "But he that prophesieth speaketh unto men to edification, and exhortation, and comfort." This Scripture also gives us three forms of prophecy: edification, exhortation and comfort.

Edification means confirmation or building up. This is not a gift for just certain people. Anyone can build up someone's faith in God if they wish to. It is our responsibility as God's children to lift up our brothers and sisters in Christ. We can build up others by sharing God's Word with them as they need guidance or counsel in their walk with God.

Exhortation means to call near or to beseech. Simply put, it means "to urge strongly or call someone into the ways of the Lord". This is something else anyone can do.

Comfort means to console. All we need to do is put our arms around someone who's hurting or in need, and God will use us to prophesy God's love and comfort to that person. Anyone can prophesy in this way.

Prophecy is a gift for all who are willing to study, live by and share God's Word on a daily basis. Prophecy is simply a telling forth of God's Word in a way people can understand.

I can tell you that Jesus is coming soon. Some would say that makes me a prophet, but I wouldn't be telling you anything new. I would just be giving you God's Word. God's Word is the only truth we can stand on.

Don't close the door on God's gift. You, too, can demonstrate the gift of prophecy.

"Prophecy is a gift for all who are willing to study, live by and share God's Word on a daily basis."

A NEW DESIRE

The Power to Prophesy

SCRIPTURE READING: Luke 12:12

The old testament prophets had a different method for prophesying than we have today. We have the entire Word of God. It is the complete revelation of God's knowledge, wisdom and plan for our lives and this world. In addition to this, we have a power to prophesy that the old testament prophets did not have. Today's Scripture text says, "For the Holy Ghost shall teach you in the same hour what ye ought to say."

Old testament prophets didn't have the power of the Holy Spirit because Jesus had not yet died and risen again for the sins of the world. The Holy Spirit would come upon them and reveal the things God wanted them to know. They added to this their own knowledge to give God's Word to others. The gift of prophecy was not for everyone then. God used certain men, men who had spiritual and political respect, to carry His message in those days. Today, God chooses to spread His love and His message through all who are born again.

The gift of prophecy is not a confusing gift reserved for a chosen few. It is given to all who are chosen. God has given us His Holy Spirit in this age of grace to guide us in sharing His love.

Yield to the power of God's Spirit and share His love and His message with someone today!

"God has given us His Holy Spirit in this age of grace to guide us in sharing His love."

The Discernment of Spirits

SCRIPTURE READING: 1 John 4:1

The gift of discerning spirits is the ability to judge and separate the spirits of sincerity from the spirits of deception. Someone with this gift knows the voice of God from the voice of the enemy. This gift protects us from deception and false teachings. Today's Scripture text says, "Beloved, believe not every spirit, but try the spirits whether they are of God: because many false prophets are gone out into the world."

It is important that we understand and interpret this gift in the light of God's Word. Discerning the spirits means being spiritually mature and prepared to examine the spirits. If what we experience in the Christian life is not found in the Word of God as pleasing to Him, then we should be careful not to fall prey to a potentially false doctrine.

Satan, the flesh and the world can deceive us with thoughts, fleshly desires and wild imaginations about God and higher powers. These spirits can trick us into states of compromise and sin if we believe them. There are many spirits roaming around lying to us and trying to entice us to sin: fortune tellers, mediums and so on. Such spirits need to be tried because God doesn't honor those things people use to uplift themselves, control people's lives and deceive others about God and His power.

Discernment is also available to those who will listen to hear God's voice in every situation. Are you listening for God's voice?

"Discerning the spirits means being spiritually mature and prepared to examine the spirits."

The Tool for Discernment

SCRIPTURE READING: Hebrews 4:12

The Word of God is the first place to go to try the spirits to see if they are of God. If you want to find out the genuineness of what's going on around you, go to God's Word and let Him reveal it to you.

The gift of discerning of spirits is for all who will study God's Word. Learn the truth of God's principles and apply them to your situation. Too many people read just the parts of God's Word that justify their lifestyles and leave the rest out. God's Word will allow us to discern the spirits at work around and within our minds. Today's Scripture text says, "For the word of God is quick, and powerful, and sharper than any two-edged sword, piercing even to the dividing asunder of soul and spirit, and of the joints and marrow, and is a discerner of the thoughts and intents of the heart."

To be a discerner of spirits we must divide, examine, investigate and critique the words, actions and characteristics of those who profess godliness. Satan seeks to destroy and manipulate God through God's own people by deceiving us into a false hope. We can obtain the gift of discernment to overcome this deception by simply drawing closer to God. The more we learn about God and His Word, the easier it will be to discern what is truly of God and what is another one of Satan's deceptions.

Draw closer to God and learn of His Word. Learn to discern the spirits and overcome Satan's deceptions.

"The more we learn about God and His Word, the easier it will be to discern what is truly of God."

The Final Gifts

SCRIPTURE READING: 1 Corinthians 14:33

The final two gifts of the Spirit must be studied together to be fully understood. The gifts of divers kinds of tongues and the interpretation of tongues are great sources of confusion, especially among different denominations.

The most important thing to remember in studying these gifts is that God is not the author of confusion. Today's Scripture text says, "For God is not the author of confusion, but of peace, as in all churches of the saints." Paul said in 1 Corinthians 14:23, "If therefore the whole church be come together into one place, and all speak with tongues, and there come in those that are unlearned, or unbelievers, will they not say that ye are mad?" God doesn't give us gifts, including the gift of tongues, to make other people wonder what is going on.

The gifts are to be used in building up the body of believers and in growing in grace. I personally believe the ability to speak in tongues is the ability to speak in a language unknown to the person speaking it. Scripture teaches that this gift should be used along with the gift of interpretation in the presence of those who would be confused by it. The gift of interpretation is simply the ability to interpret what is being said in a foreign language (even if it is unknown to you).

To use these gifts properly, we must remember to use them without causing confusion and divisions, regardless of how we interpret them. Romans 16:17–18 says, "Now I beseech you, brethren, mark them which cause divisions and offences contrary to the doctrine which ye have learned; and avoid them. For they that are such serve not our Lord Jesus Christ, but their own belly; and by good words and fair speeches deceive the hearts of the simple."

However you interpret these gifts, use them only for the honor and glory of God. God will not honor them in any other form.

> *"The gifts are to be used in building up the body of believers and in growing in grace."*

Count Your Blessings

SCRIPTURE READING: Deuteronomy 28:2

Today's Scripture text is a reminder of the many blessings God provides to those who are faithful to Him. It says, "And all these blessings shall come on thee, and overtake thee, if thou shalt hearken unto the voice of the LORD thy God." How many blessings do we possess as children of God?

Through God's eternal security, we are free from all bondage of the flesh. We are eternally guarded from Satan's destroying power. We have been given the power of the Holy Spirit to protect and teach us and to deliver us from all evil. We possess towers and towers of blessings as children of God, and we have an untold number of promises to claim because Jesus is our Savior.

Thanksgiving should be continual rather than seasonal because we have more blessings than we can count. Thanksgiving and praise should be first and foremost in our daily walk with God. We should remember to praise Him each day for bringing us out of the filthy rags of our sin and making us heirs to the kingdom of God.

God deserves our undivided attention. He waits for our hands to be lifted in praise to Him and our hearts to burn with thankfulness. God is so good and merciful, so let's "enter into His gates with thanksgiving, and into his courts with praise: be thankful unto Him, and bless His name."

Can you count your blessings? I'm sure you'll find that there are too many to be numbered. God has truly bestowed mercy and grace beyond measure on all of His children. Today, thank the Lord for His goodness and for all that He has done in your life.

"Thanksgiving should be continual rather than seasonal because we have more blessings than we can count."

A Thankful Thanksgiving

SCRIPTURE READING: Colossians 3:12–15

In the age we live in, holidays are becoming more commercialized and less spiritual. God is being taken completely out of holidays; the world is erasing what the holidays are really all about. Holidays, especially Thanksgiving, are all about glorifying God and spending time together as families. It is also a time for sharing and caring and being with loved ones. Many families are not taking the time to love, share or even spend time with each other anymore. Most families are quarreling more than ever and refusing to make amends. Is this pleasing with God? No!

Colossians 3:12–15 says, "Put on therefore, as the elect of God, holy and beloved, bowels of mercies, kindness, humbleness of mind, meekness, longsuffering; Forbearing one another, and forgiving one another, if any man have a quarrel against any: even as Christ forgave you, so also do ye. And above all these things put on charity, which is the bond of perfectness. And let the peace of God rule in your hearts, to the which also ye are called in one body; and be ye thankful." These Scriptures reveal God's will for the holidays and every day.

Thanksgiving is a time we should cherish with friends and family. It is a time when all quarrels and hard feelings should be forgotten and forgiveness must be administered. The Lord forgave us of all our wrongs when He hung on the cross of Calvary, and we are commanded to forgive also. When we administer forgiveness toward others, we become pleasing to the Lord, and our lives will be much better. Thanksgiving will be more than a holiday; you will have thanksgiving in your heart year round.

When God is first in our lives, Thanksgiving is a joyous day in the Lord, and sharing Him with all of our loved ones on this special day is an exciting event. We can't wait to be together and share the experiences of our lives that we have faced throughout the year. In Jesus' name, I challenge you to examine your heart and give yourself a gift of this Thanksgiving Day. Lay aside all of your differences and let the peace of God rule in your hearts as you love one another on this day and every day hereafter.

"When God is first in our lives, Thanksgiving is a joyous day in the Lord."

A Handful of Quietness

SCRIPTURE READING: Ecclesiastes 4:6

Iniquities and oppressions can be overwhelming and devastating in our lives, but we, as women, have a tendency to be more devastated by travail and oppression than men or children. The day in and day out pressures of a woman's life keep us on alert. Women are more easily intimidated than men, and we are more insecure about our appearance, our education and our lifestyles. We wrestle daily with finding ourselves and releasing our excess baggage. With all of this noise in our lives, we long for a moment of inner silence.

This does not make us less or weaker in God's eyes, nor does it mean we're of no use to Him. God made every woman special. He made us just like He wanted us, and He made us in His image. He made us to be spiritual lights and strength in our homes, church and neighborhoods, to our companions, children and friends. God made us to be strong when everyone else is falling apart. He uses us the greatest when we feel like we're at our weakest.

All women are different in looks, personality and beliefs, but we are all the same in God's eyes. We can all have the same relationship with Him. God expects every woman to be saved and serving Him in all things. We must put Him first and trust Him with everything in our lives by using it for His honor and glory. This is the way to developing peace in our lives.

God is peace, and His peace rules our lives when we put Him first. We can be transformed from moody, complaining, nagging women into peaceful, quiet, controlled spiritual vessels. Today's Scripture text says, "Better is an handful with quietness, than both the hands full with travail and vexation of spirit."

Allow God's peace to rule your life with just a handful of quietness by putting Him first and foremost.

"God expects every woman to be saved and serving Him in all things."

Enter into His Gates with Thanksgiving

SCRIPTURE READING: Psalm 100:3–5

The focus of this entire week is thanksgiving to God for the mercy and grace that He has richly bestowed upon all of those who believe through Jesus Christ. Today's Scripture text, which will be the central theme for the entire study, says:

> Know ye that the LORD he is God: it is he that hath made us, and not we ourselves; we are his people, and the sheep of his pasture. Enter into his gates with thanksgiving, and into his courts with praise: be thankful unto him, and bless his name. For the LORD is good; his mercy is everlasting; and his truth endureth to all generations.

May we all recognize His authority and come before Him with thankfulness and praise for His ever present and all-knowing existence in our lives. He is our God; He made us and we are His. Oh, what a Shepherd we have. We should be thankful every day that He has allowed us to abide in His pasture, a pasture rich with blessing and love.

The greatest thanks of all, the thanks that should be rendered freely from the heart, is thanks for the gift of eternal life. God freely gave His Son, and He freely saves all those who choose to accept Jesus as their Savior. Through Christ's blood we are transformed from sinners to saints just for the asking. Through salvation we are given eternal security.

What more could we ask for? For salvation alone we should daily arise with newness of praise and thanksgiving in our hearts to God for His wonderful gift to all mankind. Don't wait for Thanksgiving day to let God know how thankful you are for the greatest of all gifts. Let's make every day a day of thanksgiving and praise.

"The greatest thanks of all, the thanks that should be rendered freely from the heart, is thanks for the gift of eternal life."

A NEW DESIRE

Finding Peace in Quietness

SCRIPTURE READING: Isaiah 32:17

A handful of quietness would be a haven of rest for many women today. In a world of sin and compromise, quietness is hard to be found in our hearts and minds. What we find instead is turmoil, misery and depression. We anxiously try to squeeze a 48-hour day into a 24-hour time period. This causes tensions to rise, tempers to flare, families to fall apart and children to be disobedient, rebellious or abused.

Few seem to find that happy medium. We long for more while hoping to find peace in the middle of toil and turmoil. Someone must be strong enough to take a stand and pull the others back together, retrieving the stability and unity of the home lost during the noise of life. That someone is the woman of God.

It may not seem fair or logical, but this is the reason God created us. He made us to be strong examples in a world we don't even feel at home in. He made us to be comforters, encouragers, teachers and friends. Even though we feel at times like we, too, are going to fall apart, this is God's plan for our lives. When do we get to be quiet and comforted for ourselves? Today's Scripture text says, "And the work of righteousness shall be peace; and the effect of righteousness quietness and assurance for ever." We will find our own quietness and comfort by allowing God to use us when we don't really feel like being the strong one.

The peace of God that passes all understanding comes when we refuse to fold under the pressures of life. Peace comes from living a life of righteousness as we become disciplined, sincere, Christian women. There are five elements to peace we'll study over the next several days:
Prayer
Endurance
Assurance
Control
Example

Are you a woman of peace? You can be.

"We will find our own quietness and comfort by allowing God to use us."

Prayer

Scripture Reading: 1 Timothy 2:1–2

Prayer is the first key to peace. Prayer is our open line of communication with God. Through prayer we make our request known to Him, and He makes His will for our lives known to us.

Prayer is the key factor for building a personal relationship with God. Through prayer we are able to lift others up and make intercession for them. Today's Scripture text says, "I exhort therefore, that, first of all, supplications, prayers, intercessions, and giving of thanks, be made for all men; For kings, and for all that are in authority; that we may lead a quiet and peaceable life in all godliness and honesty." This Scripture proves that we cannot have the peace of God without prayer.

The next few verses of this same passage of Scripture tell us prayer is good and acceptable in the sight of God. First Timothy 2:5–6 reveals the purpose for and the person behind our prayers: "For there is one God, and one mediator between God and men, the man Christ Jesus; Who gave himself a ransom for all, to be testified in due time." Without Jesus in our hearts, our prayers go unheard. The purpose of prayer is for God to reveal His will in our lives while we pray for His will in the lives of others.

When we pray, we aren't telling God anything He didn't already know about us. God uses prayer to show us things we didn't know about ourselves. Through prayer, God reveals the things that steal our peace and joy in Jesus and hinder us from living a victorious Christian life.

Get serious in prayer today and start working your way toward the peace of God that passes all understanding.

> *"Prayer is our open line of communication*
> *with God."*

A NEW DESIRE

Prayer Life Evaluation

SCRIPTURE READING: 1 Thessalonians 3:8–13

How is your prayer life? Are you wrapped up in a noisy life where you can't find any peace? Maybe you need to examine your heart to see if your communication with God is pleasing to Him. If your prayer life is up to par, perhaps God is trying to do another work in your life.

Prayer is the starting place for finding God's direction in your life. A praying hand is a righteous hand. God is faithful to hear all our prayers. We must endure in prayer.

Today's Scripture text says, "For now we live, if ye stand fast in the Lord. For what thanks can we render to God again for you, for all the joy wherewith we joy for your sakes before our God; Night and day praying exceedingly that we might see your face, and might perfect that which is lacking in your faith? Now God himself and our Father, and our Lord Jesus Christ, direct our way unto you. And the Lord make you to increase and abound in love one toward another, and toward all men, even as we do toward you: To the end he may stablish your hearts unblameable in holiness before God, even our Father, at the coming of our Lord Jesus Christ with all his saints."

God is able to give us strength to endure through prayer. This is the key to peace.

"Prayer is the starting place for finding God's direction in your life."

Endurance

SCRIPTURE READING: Ephesians 6:10

Prayer is the key to peace, but we must seek the Lord in other ways as well if we are going to stand strong in Him. After prayer, meditate on God's Word and let it strengthen you for the battle. We are too weak to endure in this flesh.

God's Word says we can do nothing without Him. We keep going by depending on His power. Today's Scripture text says, "Finally, my brethren, be strong in the Lord, and in the power of his might." We can't give up on God every time life gets a little tough. We must let the Spirit fight the battle by resting quietly under His wings of endurance.

In order to endure through the hard times, we must seek and heed to God's voice. God will direct us in every situation if we'll only listen for His voice. Usually, God's direction in our lives is directly opposite of what our flesh longs to do. Endurance is doing it God's way rather than our own. Then we can rest in the assurance of God's unfailing love.

God knows what's best for us. Depend on His power and direction for deliverance.

> *"Endurance is doing it God's way rather than our own."*

Assurance

SCRIPTURE READING: Isaiah 32:17

Assurance is knowing that God's gentle voice speaks even in the noisy rat race of life. He even speaks when we're too frantic to listen. He knows what it takes to regain our attention and turn our deaf ears back to Him.

Our assurance is in knowing that what is tragedy to us is triumph to Him. The afflictions of life are but lessons of love as we survive them through His leadership. As God's chosen ones, we are assured a place in Heaven. He gives us peace in our hearts that passes understanding. We can have His righteousness if we'll seek His ways. Today's Scripture text says, "And the work of righteousness shall be peace; and the effect of righteousness quietness and assurance for ever."

God is our only source of assurance in the things we face. We can go to Him in prayer and ask Him to confirm whatever we doubt. He will do it through the anointing of His Spirit and the reading of His Word. We can know all things about God's will for our lives and be stable and controlled in every way by doing these things.

Get in God's Word and let Him give you the assurance you need to face the battles of life.

> *"God is our only source of assurance in the things we face."*

Control

SCRIPTURE READING: Psalm 131

Control is the key to overcoming noisy and devastating situations. The best way to get control of these situations is to give control to God. We lose control when we try to fix things ourselves. Self stands in the way of God's sufficiency.

Pride destroys control because it takes control of our will. God wants us to humble ourselves and trust Him instead of reacting in pride. When we get angry, disappointed or frustrated and take things into our own hands, Satan uses the opportunity to cause turmoil. Satan works against us to distract us from God's sovereign love.

David tried to control his life by going after the desires of his flesh rather than following God's will for his life. The result was pain and devastation. After years of pain and heartache, David realized the consequences of self-indulgence. He turned back to the Lord in sincerity and humility. Today's Scripture text says, "LORD, my heart is not haughty, nor mine eyes lofty: neither do I exercise myself in great matters, or in things too high for me. Surely I have behaved and quieted myself, as a child that is weaned of his mother: my soul is even as a weaned child. Let Israel hope in the LORD from henceforth and for ever."

We must become like David. We must examine ourselves, find where we lost control and turn again to God. Pride must be stamped out, anger must be dealt with and disappointments must be overcome so we can move forward in God's perfect peace and rest.

Give all of your fears, frustrations and failures to God and trust Him to remove them from your life. Give God control and let Him give you peace.

> ## *"Control is the key to overcoming noisy and devastating situations."*

Examples

SCRIPTURE READING: 1 Thessalonians 4:1

G od created us to be examples. Our purpose in life is to live for Jesus regardless of the cost. Sometimes it's hard to set an example of Christianity, but God's Word says we must. First Thessalonians 4:3–4 says, "For this is the will of God, even your sanctification, that ye should abstain from fornication: That every one of you should know how to possess his vessel in sanctification and honour."

Sanctification means we are set apart and made holy for the work of the Lord. We are to separate ourselves from all distractions and let God use us for His work. We should be ready and willing to serve Him at all times in love and sincerity.

This is the example set by Christ. Jesus' example goes from Bethlehem to Calvary. We should strive to follow His example. Today's Scripture text says, "Furthermore then we beseech you, brethren, and exhort you by the Lord Jesus, that as ye have received of us how ye ought to walk and to please God, so ye would abound more and more."

We set examples of righteousness by living for Jesus and sharing Him with others regardless of our problems and fears. Peace is inevitable when we live this way.

Become an example to those around you today and live in God's peace.

> *"We set examples of righteousness*
> *by living for Jesus."*

Leisure or Labor?

Scripture Reading: Mark 3:15

In today's Scripture text, we find that Jesus had given His disciples power over unclean spirits. It says, "And to have power to heal sicknesses, and to cast out devils." He told them to go out and preach and teach repentance, to cast out devils and to heal the sick.

John the Baptist was beheaded for doing these things. The other disciples labored so greatly that they, too, had no time for leisure or rest. These are perfect examples of sold out Christians. These people were so in love with the Lord that they denied themselves of a leisurely life for a life of labor for the sake of the Gospel. The Scriptures verify their labors throughout the whole sixth chapter of Mark.

This should be our example and our encouragement to lay ourselves and our wants aside to be laborers of the good news of Jesus Christ. Too many times we will let ourselves be distracted from working for the Lord with something we can do to feed our flesh. We would rather lounge around, watch TV, listen to music or go somewhere of the world than to use our time to serve the Lord.

I challenge you to be a laborer for Jesus. Let God reward you for sacrificing your leisure time to labor for Him.

"These people were so in love with the Lord that they denied themselves of a leisurely life."

A NEW DESIRE

Of More Value

SCRIPTURE READING: Matthew 10:31

Many times, I have questioned my purpose, my value and my effectiveness as a Christian. Sometimes I wonder what good I am to anyone. At times I even feel like a failure. Does this sound familiar to you?

All of us are guilty of these feelings and thoughts of unworthiness. We allow the disappointments of life to make us feel degraded and less than others. The problem is that we base our worth on what others think, how others perceive us and what we hold materially.

God does not base our worth on what others think about us, how the world perceives us or how great our material possessions are. God bases our worth on who we are in Him. He tells us in Matthew 6:33 to seek Him first and all these things shall be added unto us. The only condition for being valuable is to put Him first. This makes us very valuable in God's eyes.

God looks on us, and He sees the blood of His Son upon our lives. That makes us of great price to Him. God uses the word "precious" to describe just how valuable we are to Him. In 1 Peter 2:4–5, He calls His Son and all who believe on Him precious. It says, "To whom coming, as unto a living stone, disallowed indeed of men, but chosen of God, and precious, Ye also, as lively stones, are built up a spiritual house, an holy priesthood, to offer up spiritual sacrifices, acceptable to God by Jesus Christ."

We must place some emphasis on four words in this passage of Scripture: "disallowed indeed of men". The Word tells us here that even Jesus could not escape man's requirements for fitting in and being accepted in this world. Jesus was rejected and degraded by His peers. Man did all they could to make Him feel of no value. This is why our Scripture text assures us that we are valuable to God. God knows how man rejects and degrades us. Therefore, He says, "Fear ye not therefore, ye are of more value than many sparrows."

"God knows how man rejects and degrades us."

A Genuine Diamond

SCRIPTURE READING: Jeremiah 17:1

Today's Scripture text tells us that a diamond is strong and enduring. It says, "The sin of Judah is written with a pen of iron, and with the point of a diamond: it is graven upon the table of their heart, and upon the horns of your altars."

A diamond is the hardest substance known. Therefore, it is virtually impossible to destroy. It's value is based on it's brilliance and fire.

Our lives are of great brilliance and sparkle to the Lord because of His finished work at Calvary. Jesus' blood made us diamonds. When we received Him, He cleansed us from all sin and impurities. He cut away all of our degradation, and He is the shine and strength of our diamonds. He is our strength to endure.

The Bible tells us in 1 Peter 1:7, "That the trial of your faith, being much more precious than of gold that perisheth, though it be tried with fire, might be found unto praise and honour and glory at the appearing of Jesus Christ." As God's chosen, we are diamonds in the rough. However, from this Scripture we know that the trial of our faith is of great value. We can rest assured that we are so valuable to God that He's still working the rough spots out of His gems. He's still chipping away our flaws and impurities. Our desire as God's diamonds should be to endure through the trials of life so His light shines through us.

The diamond represents strength, endurance and realness. Are you a genuine diamond?

"We are so valuable to God that He's still working the rough spots out of His gems."

Far Above Rubies

SCRIPTURE READING: Proverbs 31:10

Proverbs 31:10 says, "Who can find a virtuous woman? for her price is far above rubies." Have you ever really thought about this Scripture? It says that the value of a woman is far above rubies. That, my friend, is pretty valuable.

The ruby is the second hardest substance, and its value compares with that of the diamond. The ruby is also known for its strength and clarity. When held up to the light you can see straight though this highly prized gem. We, too, are highly prized gems. God sees us from the inside out. He has the power to see the intentions of our hearts. This is what makes us rubies in the heart of God. You see, God knows us better than we know ourselves. The transparency of the ruby represents the truth. Just like the ruby, we can hide nothing from God. He sees it all. God sees our pain, our past and our present, and He sees the finished product.

Proverbs 20:15 teaches us there is something even more valuable than rubies. It says, "There is gold, and a multitude of rubies: but the lips of knowledge are a precious jewel." Knowledge is the product of being a ruby.

As the diamond represents strength, endurance and realness, the ruby represents truth, righteousness and sincerity. These are the facets that will make us women far above rubies. Are you a woman of truth, righteousness and sincerity?

"Knowledge is the product of being a ruby."

The Pearl of Great Price

SCRIPTURE READING: Matthew 13:46

The pearl is quite different from the ruby and diamond, although it is also a very valuable gem. The Bible refers to the pearl as so valuable that in today's Scripture text it is referred to as being of great price. It says, "Who, when he had found one pearl of great price, went and sold all that he had, and bought it." This verse represents salvation. Jesus was the great price for the pearl. He bought us with His life. We must learn to see ourselves as He sees us.

In Matthew 7:6, we are urged not to cast our pearls before swine. This represents holiness. The Bible also says in 1 Peter 1:16, "Because it is written, Be ye holy; for I am holy." When we received Jesus as our Savior, we received holiness. Therefore, we can say that in the eyes of God we are pearls of great price.

Any woman who willingly serves the Lord will be shown her true value. God is faithful to make Himself known to His children. Regardless of our past, our failures or how invaluable we feel, God sees us as women of value and great price. He sees our excellence and what we are becoming. He is daily polishing His pearls so that we will shine with great brilliance for Him.

If life has made you feel worthless and useless, then reexamine your heart. Don't allow your feelings to steal your confidence in the Lord. Remember, because of your value you can approach God.

Just as the pearl represents salvation, holiness and authenticity, you represent Christ with these same characteristics. Does your life reflect a pearl of great price?

"If life has made you feel worthless and useless, then reexamine your heart."

Receiving and Accepting Christ

Scripture Reading: 1 Peter 4:1–2

When someone walks into our presence and hands us a gift, we receive it without hesitation. We excitedly open it with joy and accept its contents. We flash the gift around for everyone to see. We can't wait to show it off.

We must receive and accept many things in this life besides these gifts. Some of these things disturb our comfort zones, making them more difficult to receive and accept. Life always has unexpected and unwanted packages, but in spite of our rejection, they are delivered and left in our hands for proper handling. How we handle these gifts sets the standard of our response in accepting this gift.

Salvation is the perfect example to use in explaining the difference between receiving and accepting something. We, through faith in Jesus Christ, can receive salvation. All we have to do is ask for and believe it, and we automatically receive it. The next step is to accept it by applying its attributes to our lives for everyone to see. Accepting its attributes is very important and challenging.

As the old saying goes, "Everybody wants to go to Heaven, but nobody wants to die." For salvation the saying is, "Everybody wants to be saved, but nobody wants to change." The Bible teaches us that when the free gift of salvation is received into our hearts old things pass away and all things become new. I wonder why so many people profess to be saved, but we never see a change in their lifestyle or behavior. The answer is clear. They received Jesus as their Savior because they didn't want to go to hell, but they have never received Jesus as Lord of the life. Most saved people are still wanting to live their way instead of God's way. Therefore, they fail as Christians everyday.

Have you received and accepted Jesus, or have you simply received Him today? Accept Him as Lord of your life.

"Everybody wants to be saved, but nobody wants to change."

Life's Unwanted Packages

SCRIPTURE READING: 2 Corinthians 12:9

We receive unwanted packages all the time; defeat comes when we refuse to accept these packages as problems and hindrances. Instead, we think we can deal with them on our own rather than asking God to teach us how to handle them correctly. Running from problems never solves anything; it only provides time for the problem to grow bigger and to become more disastrous for us.

Sometimes God allows unpleasant things to come into our lives. He likes to challenge us to spiritual growth by putting us under pressure. He always knows the limit we are willing to go to for Him, but spiritual maturity comes from being willing to go beyond the limit by sacrificing and suffering as Christ did for us. First Peter 4:1–2 says, "Forasmuch then as Christ hath suffered for us in the flesh, arm yourselves likewise with the same mind: for he that hath suffered in the flesh hath ceased from sin; That he no longer should live the rest of his time in the flesh to the lusts of men, but to the will of God."

Paul received one of life's unwanted packages. Three times, he refused to accept it by asking the Lord to remove it from him. However, the Lord wanted Paul to accept this gift as a means of depending on Him. His response to Paul's request is found in today's Scripture text. It says, "And he said unto me, My grace is sufficient for thee: for my strength is made perfect in weakness. Most gladly therefore will I rather glory in my infirmities, that the power of Christ may rest upon me."

There is a blessing in accepting life's unwanted gifts. Accept yours today, and see what God has in store for you.

"There is a blessing in accepting life's unwanted gifts."

Think It Not Strange

SCRIPTURE READING: 1 Peter 4:12–13

My friend, unpleasant and trying circumstances in our lives can become gifts from God if we will accept them. The good parts of a bad situation never surface until we have come to grips with our circumstances. Once that takes place, we begin to see that it could have been worse. What we thought we couldn't deal with has already passed, and there is a brighter hope.

What in your life could you turn into a gift from God? I'm sure something is troubling you or controlling your thoughts to the point of discouragement or hopelessness. Turn it into a gift of God by accepting it! You no longer have to be under its stronghold. God is waiting for you to accept it and then give it back to Him for deliverance. He wants to make you free from the effects of this unwanted dilemma and show you the gift and lesson of it and the spiritual growth you received as you carried it.

You received this package the moment it came upon you. You had no choice in rejecting it. It was destined for your life and your life only. If you fought it, ran from it or pushed it out of your mind, then you did not accept it, and your life has been in constant turmoil. God has allowed this to enter into your life for a reason. He knows all about it. He has known all about it since before day one. He knows how you are reacting toward this, and He knows exactly how long you are going to fight this thing. The longer you reject it the greater your battle will be, but Jesus will carry it for you if you'll let Him.

Jesus wants the unwanted gift you're carrying for Himself, but He knows He can't force you to give it to Him. You must give it to Him of your own free will. Freely giving ourselves, our problems and our needs to Jesus reveals our love for and dependence upon Him and His power. First Peter 4:12–13 says, "Beloved, think it not strange concerning the fiery trial which is to try you, as though some strange thing happened unto you: But rejoice, inasmuch as ye are partakers of Christ's sufferings; that, when his glory shall be revealed, ye may be glad also with exceeding joy."

Give your unwanted gifts to Jesus today.

"Jesus wants the unwanted gift you're carrying."

The Power of Persecution

SCRIPTURE READING: 1 Peter 4:19

Can you imagine being so close to God and so full of his knowledge that people thrive on seeing you persecuted? When you sincerely live for the Lord, Satan will find a way to persecute you. We have to wonder how persecution produces righteousness when it seems so painful and uncomfortable. It's hard for some to grasp that God is love, yet to live for Him requires trials and tribulations.

When persecution comes, its power forces us into communication with God. We find ourselves calling upon him either in anger or desperation. God's love for us is so unlimited that He still hears our prayers of rage and self pity. How easily do you fall apart when persecutions come? Do you go to God for help or do you go to Him because you are angry with Him and you want to know why He let the persecution come your way?

The power of persecution produces an intimacy with Christ. He compassionately and mercifully reveals himself to us even when we are undeserving. Hebrews 4:15 says, "For we have not an high priest which cannot be touched with the feeling of our infirmities; but was in all points tempted like as we are, yet without sin."

Christ knows how you feel. He has experienced everything you have gone through or may be facing now. However, He never gave up; He remained dedicated to doing His Father's will. The power of His persecution produced His dedication. The power of persecution produces dedication in us also. This truth doesn't make it any easier for us to handle adversities, but we must persevere. First Peter 4:19 says, "Wherefore let them that suffer according to the will of God commit the keeping of their souls to him in well doing, as unto a faithful Creator."

Are you trusting Him through your trials?

"Persecution produces an intimacy with Christ."

A Mother's Prayer

SCRIPTURE READING: Proverbs 23:24–25

Several years ago when my children were younger and mischievous, I went through several months of fear for my boys. In this time of worry, I realized that I had to trust God for the safety and well-being of my children. On one particular day as I knelt to pray, I found myself writing my prayer on paper. I recently discovered that prayer among my prayer journals. As I reread it, my eyes filled with tears while my heart filled with joy to know that God has truly answered this mother's prayer. Today, I can truly identify with our Scripture text: "The father of the righteous shall greatly rejoice: and he that begetteth a wise child shall have joy of him. Thy father and thy mother shall be glad, and she that bare thee shall rejoice."

Perhaps, you are experiencing the same motherly fears. If you are, remember that God hears your prayers. He will protect your children. However, you must trust Him for their safety and well-being. I have reprinted below the prayer that I prayed for my children many years ago. I pray that it will comfort and strengthen your heart. It is titled "For My Children I Pray."

Each day I humbly pray Lord
That life won't be so hard
For the children that you have blessed us with.
May they always depend on you and always be on guard.
Dear Lord, there is no hope for children unless you lead each step they take.
Without you they will fall, rather than learn from their mistakes.
I pray their lives won't be so pressured in a world of compromise.
I pray they will stand on God's principles,
Willing to wear the scars that standing will require.
Lord, be the mender of their hearts when pain must stunt their growth.
I pray instead of drugs and alcohol that to you they'll make an oath.
I pray Lord, as their parents, in us they will see the light of Christ,
And will draw toward the light, when faced with turmoil and strife.
In Jesus Name I Pray. Amen.

"God hears your prayers.
He will protect your children."

Don't Be Deceived

Scripture Reading: Galatians 6:7–8

As we face each new day in life, we are faced with new temptations, lusts and evils. As Christians, we have predators stalking us every day with hopes of deceiving us with the unrighteous things of this world.

Our greatest predator is Satan. He seeks to deceive us with the things of this world by perverting our minds. He presents to us things that appeal to our flesh. These appealings range from drugs, sex and alcohol to social, material and financial diversions. Once Satan has diverted our attentions from righteousness to unrighteousness, he can then use the flesh and the world as additional predators. The flesh lusts for things that make it feel secure, successful and independent. The flesh likes to be in control of all things. It dominates our minds (Ephesians 2:3), conflicts with our Spirit (Romans 8:1–8) and reaps corruption (Galatians 6:8), and Satan knows just what our flesh longs for. Therefore, he puts the things before us he knows we will be tempted with. He wants us to be happy in the flesh so we will not depend on God's Spirit for anything.

You see, the devil knows your weaknesses, and he will use them against you by trying to make you feel secure in those areas. For example, if a teenager wants more friends or better grades in school, the devil will tempt them with things that can supply their wants in these areas. He will provide them with "friends" who will only stick around if the teen does sinful things. He will lure them to achieve better grades by cheating "just one test" or by using someone else's work, both of which are dishonest. These are Satan's deceptive tactics.

God warns us of such tactics in our Scripture text. It says, "Be not deceived; God is not mocked: for whatsoever a man soweth, that shall he also reap. For he that soweth to his flesh shall of the flesh reap corruption; but he that soweth to the Spirit shall of the Spirit reap life everlasting."

Where are you sowing your seeds?

*"The devil knows your weaknesses,
and he will use them against you."*

Great Deceptions

Scripture Reading: Psalm 139:23

Today's Scripture text says, "Search me, O God, and know my heart: try me, and know my thoughts." David prayed this prayer because he knew Satan's biggest deception is convincing us that we have done nothing wrong. He always points out others who seem to have slipped by God's chastisement when they did the same thing. My friend, I plead with you not to base the decisions in your life on what you see others get by with. I can assure you that God sees everything that a person does. All sin is found out and dealt with.

After Satan has fed your flesh, he seeks for ways to draw you into places where the next predator, the world, can devour you. Once you have wrapped yourself up in the lusts of your flesh, you begin to hunger for the things of the world. You begin to want what your neighbor has or to be more like your friends. You want to wear the clothes they wear, drive the cars they drive and make the money they make. You begin setting goals to have these things.

The world graciously accepts us as long as we conform to its ways. Education, popularity, talent and financial success are part of the requirements for being conformed to this world, and the world will provide for you a place to accomplish these requirements. Usually, it will be a place of sin.

Financial security is one of the greatest deceptions Satan has ever tickled our ears with. He wants us to believe that we can be rich and financially independent without any help from God. He shows us ways to make more money and have more things to buy until we become so deep in debt that we must bury ourselves in work just to carry the load. Satan has then successfully put God on the back burner of our lives.

Search your heart today. Are you greatly deceived?

"The world graciously accepts us
as long as we conform to its ways."

Diverted Attention

SCRIPTURE READING: Philippians 4:8

The world diverts our attention from the things of God to the things of the flesh. We are deceived into thinking we should use what we have to further ourselves in this world. This is a lie of the devil. He doesn't want you to use your talent, education, money or anything else for the glory of God, so he offers you an alternative by offering you the world. You will spend the rest of your life trying to convince the world that you are successful, secure and happy, but it will not work. The world does not care about your accomplishment; it thrives off of your failures. When you think you deserve a pat on the back for what you have done, the world will knock you for not having done it the way they thought you should have.

Being deceived by Satan, the flesh and the world leads only to spiritual barrenness. Deception allows us to be overtaken by these predators. When this happens, God is no longer important to us. We are on the road to sin, chastening and hardships.

There is a solution for your life of deception. It is never too late to bow yourself before God with a repenting heart. He is waiting for you to depend upon Him for deliverance and victory in your life. Today's Scripture text says, "Finally, brethren, whatsoever things are true, whatsoever things are honest, whatsoever things are just, whatsoever things are pure, whatsoever things are lovely, whatsoever things are of good report; if there be any virtue, and if there be any praise, think on these things." Give God control of your mind rather than letting the devil run wild in your head.

Confess to God your way of life, your sins and your desires, then surrender your life to His righteousness and His will for you. Be willing to change your life; seek God's will every day. Don't allow the devil room to separate you from full fellowship with God. Don't give into the lusts of your flesh or the ways of the world. Discipline your life to prayer, studying God's word and a Christian atmosphere of church family, Christian friends and Christian music and activities. The devil is subtle and tricky. He will tempt you with things that will look prosperous, pretty and pleasing to your life. Be prepared for his tactics and spiritually armed to stand against him.

"There is a solution for your life of deception."

Hearing God's Voice

SCRIPTURE READING: 1 Kings 19:11–12

Many times, in frustrating or trying situations, we begin to doubt and question God's presence and concern in our lives. We wonder where He is. Why hasn't He revealed Himself in the situation? We expect Him to creep out of the woodwork and make a grand appearance. We literally expect Him to slap us in the face to let us know He's there. When God doesn't appear to us in such a manner, we tend to think He has forgotten us.

God has not forsaken you. God is just as close by when we feel this way as He is when we can feel His presence. Consider how He revealed Himself to Elijah in today's Scripture text: "And he said, Go forth, and stand upon the mount before the LORD. And, behold, the LORD passed by, and a great and strong wind rent the mountains, and brake in pieces the rocks before the LORD; but the LORD was not in the wind: and after the wind an earthquake; but the LORD was not in the earthquake: And after the earthquake a fire; but the LORD was not in the fire: and after the fire a still small voice." Often times, God has to become less obvious in our lives in order to draw our attention to Him. He wants us to listen more closely to His still, small voice. God is not trying to point out a mistake or punish us; rather, He has a ray of light for us, and it will appear when we least expect it.

In these times, God's voice won't come in a mighty rushing wind, and His presence won't be seen in a lighting bolt of glory. God's voice, presence and will for your life will come in one word or a testimony. Maybe a song or a Scripture text will just jump out at you. Perhaps it will be a simple phrase spoken by a teacher, preacher, friend, family member or maybe even a stranger. These simple rays of light can change our lives if we'll look for Jesus in them.

God never fails to speak to us if we're faithful to listen for His voice. He will reveal His presence to us if we'll only look and listen in His direction. Just one word from God can be as sufficient as a miracle, sign or loud voice. We should never limit God's ability to reveal Himself to us. God is God, and one word from Him is all it takes if we will submit ourselves to obeying His voice.

"God has not forsaken you."

Rays of Light

SCRIPTURE READING: 1 John 1:7

God chooses to reveal Himself to us in many ways. Testimonies and personal experiences of how God has revealed himself in these ways abound. He may have revealed himself through a song, testimony or even a billboard. I'll never forget the day that God revealed Himself to me in such a way. I was driving down the road in despair when I called out to God, asking what He would have me do. I looked out the window to see a sign that read, "Troubled? Try Prayer." I knew God was speaking to me. I poured my heart out to God, and he comforted me on the spot. He gave me the peace and knowledge that He would speak to me if I would listen.

That billboard was a ray of light for me. My life seemed so dark and hopeless on that day, but God broke through the clouds of hopelessness to shine a ray of His presence into my life. Sometimes life appears dark and dreary, but God is always there to give us a glimpse of His will for our lives. We must stare into the darkness in search of one little ray of light, a glimpse of God's omnipresence. Once God appears in the midst of our darkness, we should take the ray of light and brighten it. We can increase the ray of light shining in our lives by verifying its purpose through God's Word.

Confirming God's presence and will in our lives keeps us out of the darkness and in His light. We will walk in a manner pleasing to Him because we will learn to depend on Him even in the trying times. We will learn to fulfill the truth of 1 John 1:7: "But if we walk in the light, as he is in the light, we have fellowship one with another, and the blood of Jesus Christ his Son cleanseth us from all sin."

Through Jesus Christ, we have the victory over darkness. He is the light of our lives if we've received Him as our personal Savior. The dark clouds that surround our lives are filled with rays of light, but we must be willing to wait for the rays of light to break through the darkness. When they break through, they give us the hope and peace that God is in control.

Let's always be on the alert for a ray of light. Let's open our hearts and minds to receiving the message God has for us. You never know what God has waiting for you. Watch for your ray of light.

"God is always there to give us a glimpse of His will."

A NEW DESIRE

Putting Forth an Effort

SCRIPTURE READING: Philippians 3:12–14

At the pool of Bethesda, there was a great multitude of sick people. An angel would go down into the waters of the pool and trouble them for the healing of disease. Whoever was first to enter the waters after they were troubled by the angel was healed of their infirmity. A certain man was there who had an infirmity of 38 years. Each time the angel stirred the waters, the man put forth the effort to step in, but someone always stepped in ahead of him. It seemed that his infirmity prevented him from moving quickly enough to be the first one in the pool.

Jesus saw this man lying there, and He knew the man had been there for a long time. Jesus knew this man had faithfully put forth an effort to step into that pool time and time again. In response to His efforts, Jesus asked him, "Wilt thou be made whole?" The man proceeded to tell Jesus that each time he made an effort to reach the water someone stepped before him. Jesus spoke to him and said, "Rise, take up thy bed, and walk." Immediately the man was healed. God honored this man's efforts.

Just as God honored this man's efforts, He also honors our efforts. We don't have to do everything perfectly or in order. If we'll do our best, God will do the rest. God is pleased when we put forth the effort to help ourselves. The man at the pool did all he could to get into the water. God honored it so much that He didn't even require this man to step into the pool. He simply spoke, and the man was healed.

Paul reminds us in Philippians 3:12–14, that we should be like him; we should strive to overcome our trials and press to be more for God. He says, "Not as though I had already attained, either were already perfect: but I follow after, if that I may apprehend that for which also I am apprehended of Christ Jesus. Brethren, I count not myself to have apprehended: but this one thing I do, forgetting those things which are behind, and reaching forth unto those things which are before, I press toward the mark for the prize of the high calling of God in Christ Jesus."

If we put forth the effort to seek God's will in every situation, we can move forward, overcome and please God all at the same time.

"If we'll do our best, God will do the rest."

Ye That Hope

SCRIPTURE READING: Psalm 31:23–24

It is easy to lose hope when life doesn't seem to respond to our efforts. Sometimes it seems that no matter how hard we try to overcome, things never work out for us. However, endurance is always the key to victory.

The man at the pool of Bethesda is a prime example of hope and endurance. Certainly he got aggravated and frustrated at his efforts to reach the water before someone else did. I'm sure that he asked "Why?" many times. After 38 years of trying, he probably even cried, got angry and often felt robbed and cheated. In spite of his emotions, he remained level headed. He was determined to make the best out of a bad situation.

We can make the best out of bad situations if we endure instead of giving up. Even when we feel like there is not a fight left in us, we must have hope. Jesus died to give us hope. Romans 8:24–25 says, "For we are saved by hope: but hope that is seen is not hope: for what a man seeth, why doth he yet hope for? But if we hope for that we see not, then do we with patience wait for it."

We must never make our decisions based on what we can see. Things are not always what they appear to be. Only God can reveal the true identity of things in our lives. If we choose to react to circumstances without consulting the Lord, we are reacting in our own power. When we rest in our own power, we react out of despair, and we have no courage. Today's Scripture text says, "O love the LORD, all ye his saints: for the LORD preserveth the faithful, and plentifully rewardeth the proud doer. Be of good courage, and he shall strengthen your heart, all ye that hope in the LORD." When we trust in the Lord, He will reveal to us the true appearance of our circumstances. He will even be the strength in us that provokes us to find a remedy. God is our hope and our strength. Without Him we can do nothing.

Once we receive Jesus, we should do whatever it takes to draw closer to Him. We are His children, and we should be anxious to manifest Him in our lives. We are the only lights some people see of Jesus. It is important to further our knowledge and wisdom of God. Don't let hindrances distract you from opportunities of spiritual growth and renewal.

"Jesus died to give us hope."

366 ~   A NEW DESIRE

Living Sincerely for the Lord

SCRIPTURE READING: Psalm 44:21

God knows the heart and mind of every person. He knows who is lost and who is saved. He knows who is sincere in serving Him. Today's Scripture text says, "Shall not God search this out? for he knoweth the secrets of the heart."

We need to realize the importance of God in our lives. He loves and protects us every day. We can't see the many things God protects us from. He is so worthy of our undivided attention. When opportunity arises for us to be with Him in service for worship, growth or renewal, we should do what we can to walk through this door of opportunity.

We can never be too close to or know too much about the Lord and His great love for us. We should never take our position with Him for granted. He died to give us the gift of eternal life. Therefore, we should live to give Him eternal praise, honor and glory in return on this Christmas day.

Putting forth an effort to be more for God requires us to discipline ourselves to studying, praying and pursuing righteousness. Just as we put forth an effort to have material possessions, jobs, homes and families, we must pursue a personal, intimate relationship with the Lord.

Whatever your infirmity may be today, you can rise above it. All you have to do is take the steps to get out of it. If the first step you take doesn't deliver you, then maybe you need to examine the system you chose for taking that step. See where you could have done better. For example, before you took the first step, did you go to the Lord for permission and instruction? Did you act on your knowledge and wisdom or the Lord's? We don't ever want to look at our mistakes as failures; rather they are lessons of life that should teach us more about Him.

Start living sincerely for the Lord.

"We can never be too close to or know too much about the Lord."

Call Upon the Lord

SCRIPTURE READING: 2 Samuel 22:7

Once you have examined the first step you took to get out of your situation, you must take the second step. Just keep trying until you find a way of deliverance. Personally, I would suggest that your first step should be to bow on your knees before God in prayer. Then, when you stand on your two feet, the next step will be led and honored by God Almighty. If you still don't succeed, remember that deliverance comes in God's way, not ours. He is faithful to see us through. In the meantime, we must endure. We must continue taking steps to the best of our ability. God will allow us to be tested and tried during this time, but if we keep putting forth the effort to survive and to live righteously, God will deliver.

Search your life; what is about to defeat you? What controls your every thought? What hinders you from serving the Lord? What prevents you from being more for God? Has something already provoked you to quitting on God and on life? It is never too late to have a change of heart. God is waiting to hear your voice in prayer. He really does hear when you pray, and He cares about you. In David's song of deliverance in 2 Samuel 22:7 he verifies this. It says, "In my distress I called upon the LORD, and cried to my God: and he did hear my voice out of his temple, and my cry did enter into his ears."

God hears every word you say. God cares about everything you face. He loves you with all His might, and He gets angry when His people are attacked. However, He can't deliver us if we don't call out to Him. He longs to bind the evil powers that stress us out. He doesn't want His people oppressed or depressed. He is the only one who can fight and win our battles. He fought David's battle, and He won. David walked away delivered. The man at the pool walked away delivered. You, too, can walk away delivered. I promise you that God will make a way of escape for you if you will not quit. Don't give up. Put forth an effort everyday to please the Lord and do the best you can. God, who is full of mercy, will make a way for you.

"It is never too late to have a change of heart."

Overcoming Exhaustion

SCRIPTURE READING: Matthew 6:33

At this time of year, we find ourselves physically, mentally and spiritually exhausted. Another year has drained us of our energy. Most of us feel like we need life to stand still for just a day so that our bodies can catch up with our minds and the fast paced life that outran us months ago.

When does all of this stop? It stops when we stop it! We must take the time to set our priorities. We need to set certain times in our life to reevaluate our activities and our schedules. It is so easy to get caught up in things that have no value or meaning to us. We easily allow ourselves to be volunteered for things we should have said "no" to.

If we feel more exhausted than in control, then we need to deal with our situation. God created us to be controlled, disciplined, holy people. The only way we can be that is to examine ourselves and make sure that our priorities are in order. God should be first in our life. Our family should come next in order. Our family will fall in place and be blessed if we put God first. Our spouses and children should always be able to see God as our Shepherd. He is the only place to go to for rest, relaxation and renewal. Today's Scripture text says, "But seek ye first the kingdom of God, and his righteousness; and all these things shall be added unto you."

If you find yourself exhausted, take the time to slow down and seek God. Weed out the unimportant and put first things first. God will honor your efforts, and exhaustion will turn to excitement.

> *"God created us to be controlled, disciplined, holy people."*

They Crucified Him

SCRIPTURE READING: Psalm 22:14

The word crucifixion is used to represent death on a cross. According to Merrill C. Tenney's Bible Dictionary, this was the most cruel and barbarous form of death known to man. It was so dreaded that even in the pre-Christian era, the cares and troubles of life were often compared to a cross. Many pass over the reality of the crucifixion by simply stating, "They crucified Him." This, my friend, was not all that the crucifixion consisted of. Before the actual ordeal itself, the prisoner was bent over, and tied to a post where the Roman lector applied blow upon blow to His bare back with a lash intertwined with pieces of bone or steel. This was frequently sufficient to cause death. Another factor of the agony was the painful but non-serious character of the wounds inflicted for crucifixion itself. There were two distinctive methods of affixing a living victim to a cross, tying or nailing. It is well established that Christ underwent the horror of the latter, or possibly both. The slightest movement would be accompanied with additional torture. Hanging for such a long period of time induced traumatic fever. Finally, death by crucifixion came from heart failure. David states in Psalm 22:14 the agony of it: "I am poured out like water, and all my bones are out of joint: my heart is like wax; it is melted in the midst of my bowels." Jesus' heart literally burst and emptied into His stomach.

Death by crucifixion was usually hastened by the breaking of the legs. With Jesus this was unnecessary. The Bible states in John 19:33, "But when they came to Jesus, and saw that he was dead already, they brake not his legs." Jesus wasn't killed by these people. He gave up His life; they just tortured Him until He died. Jesus confirms this fact in John 10:17–18. He says, "Therefore doth my Father love me, because I lay down my life, that I might take it again. No man taketh it from me, but I lay it down of myself. I have power to lay it down, and I have power to take it again. This commandment have I received of my Father." Jesus bore the cross, suffered the crucifixion and died for our sins of His own free will. He chose to willingly die, to take our place to spare us from the pits of hell. He gave His life for us; let's live for Him.

"Jesus died for our sins of His own free will."

The Reality of the Cross

SCRIPTURE READING: Mark 9:43–44

Jesus took our place in hell so we could go free. This is the reality of the cross. Without Jesus death, burial and resurrection the realness of hell's fire would already be manifested in our lives. Jesus describes the realness of hell for us, as He warns us of it in Mark 9:43–44. He said, "And if thy hand offend thee, cut it off: it is better for thee to enter into life maimed, than having two hands to go into hell, into the fire that never shall be quenched. Where their worm dieth not, and the fire is not quenched." The reason Jesus used the word "worm" in these Scriptures is because He knew that to the Jews, fire and worms always represented internal and external pain. He wanted to let us know that hell is a horrible place, filled with pain, agony and torture that never ends.

Jesus did not make hell for you and me. He made hell for Satan and his angels. Matthew 25:41 says, "Then shall he say also unto them on the left hand, Depart from me, ye cursed, into everlasting fire, prepared for the devil and his angels." If we reject Jesus Christ as our personal Savior then we have made the decision to go to hell; the cross and crucifixion is null and void in our lives. Disobedience in accepting Jesus as Savior will cast you into hell fire. The choice is yours alone.

Christ's death on the cross was a horrible one, but He did it just for you. How much more personal could anyone ever get in your life? Do you know of anyone else who would die for your wrong doings? Hell will be even more horrible for you than the cross was for Jesus. Christ gave up the ghost and died, but in hell the worm dieth not. You will live eternally in outer darkness in a lake of fire, destitute of God's love. Matthew 8:12 says, "But the children of the kingdom shall be cast out into outer darkness: there shall be weeping and gnashing of teeth."

Have you made a decision in your life about Jesus or Satan, Heaven or Hell? No one can make this decision for you; Christ has left it up to you. All you have to do is confess your sins to God; ask Him to forgive you and to save you. Believe by faith that because you asked Him, He came into your heart and He now lives within you through His Holy Spirit.

"Jesus took our place in hell so we could go free."

Willing or Wavering?

SCRIPTURE READING: James 1:6–8

When we chose to live the Christian life, we decided to break our fleshly will and give ourselves over to God's will. We come under His subjection, and we exercise our faith by putting our trust in Him. After this step of faith, we must decide just how much of our lives we completely turn over to God.

Everyone wants to be pleasing to God, but no one finds it easy to give up the things that separate us from a close, unhindered relationship with the Lord. This is where wavering overcomes our willingness because we try to compromise with God about the things we are not willing to sacrifice.

Wavering gets us into a spiritual slum. James 1:6–8 says, "But let him ask in faith, nothing wavering. For he that wavereth is like a wave of the sea driven with the wind and tossed. For let not that man think that he shall receive any thing of the Lord. A double minded man is unstable in all his ways."

When we waver, we show ourselves as unstable people. Let's examine our lives and give them willingly to God. Let's stop giving to ourselves and give to the work of the Lord. We must be willing to sacrifice our wants for God's best.

"Wavering gets us into a spiritual slum."

Conviction

SCRIPTURE READING: Revelation 3:15–16

Throughout the years of my Christian life, I have experienced many convicting moments. Countless times I have set under powerful convicting messages I thought were being preached just to me. The message seemed to fit my situation perfectly. I would sit there and wonder who told on me. On the other hand, I have been offended by messages that related to me. I have never really been angry at the one preaching, but I have been offended by the message in his sermon, especially if the sermon pinpointed my sins or invaded my comfort zone.

Conviction is placed upon us through the Holy Spirit's power. He makes our sins known to us. Our responsibility is to act on these convictions by confessing them to God, thanking Him for making our sins known and asking Him to turn us from them.

The majority of Christians today refuse to act upon the convicting power of the Holy Spirit. We push our convictions to the back of our minds and continue to live in our comfort zones. When we realize the issues in our lives that God is not pleased with, we must take steps to change them. We put ourselves in a greater state of sin and disobedience when we get offended. Taking our convictions out on others is never the answer. The Lord knows exactly where you need to be. He knows the message you need to hear to shake up your heart and mind. If God wants to speak to you through someone else, you should love Him enough to listen and to act on what He says.

God will not waste His time on people who refuse to turn from their disobedience and sin. Compromise stirs up the Lord's anger. Revelation 3:15–16 says, "I know thy works, that thou art neither cold nor hot: I would thou wert cold or hot. So then because thou art lukewarm, and neither cold nor hot, I will spue thee out of my mouth." It is better to feel conviction than to be spewed out of the mouth of God. God is a loving God. When we know what to do for Him and refuse to do it we must expect His chastening. What convictions have you been battling lately?

"Conviction is placed upon us through the Holy Spirit's power."

Other books written by
Brenda J. Robinson:

**A New Desire
Workbook**

It Is Finished

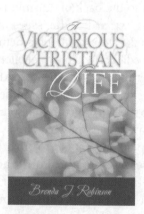

**A Victorious
Christian Life**

**Seized for His
Glory**

About the Author

Brenda J. Robinson, D.D. is the Executive Director of New Desire Christian Ministries, Inc. She is a Bible teacher, singer, songwriter and author of four books. She has taught thousands of women, and she speaks at many women's conferences throughout the United States sharing her testimony of healing from grand-mal epileptic seizures.

Brenda was diagnosed with epilepsy at the age of 24. Throughout the six years of seizures, she learned to depend on God in every situation. Her heart is to place a new desire in everyone by sharing what God has done for her in her life.

Brenda and her husband, Evangelist Dan Robinson founded New Desire Christian Ministries, Inc. in 1990. They have two children, Labron and Kevin. Brenda and her family have been serving in full-time ministry for 13 years. Their ministry started out with only two staff members and now has grown to a staff of 10.

For bookings, product or more information contact our ministry office at:

New Desire Christian Ministries, Inc.
PO Box 918
Aragon, Georgia 30104
(770) 684-8987
www.newdesire.org

To order additional copies of

A **NEW**

Desire

Have your credit card ready and call

Toll free: (877) 421-READ (7323)

or send $20.00 each plus $5.95 S&H* to

WinePress Publishing
PO Box 428
Enumclaw, WA 98022

www.winepresspub.com

*WA residents, add 8.4% sales tax

*add $1.00 S&H for each additional book ordered